# MODERN**SAUCES**

# MODERN SAUCES

## more than 150 recipes for every cook, every day

MARTHA HOLMBERG

photographs by ELLEN SILVERMAN

CHRONICLE BOOKS

SAN FRANCISCO

## ACKNOWLEDGEMENTS

I'd like to thank Anne Willan, for giving me so many splendid opportunities (including Paris). Thanks and affection also to chefs Fernand Chambrette and Claude Vauguet from La Varenne, who taught me how to think about cooking. And thanks to my collaborators on the project: Ellen Silverman, Sarah Billingsley, Alice Chau, Bill LeBlond, Denise Mickelsen, and Caroline Ford.

Text copyright © 2012 by Martha Holmberg.

Photographs copyright © 2012 by Ellen Silverman.

Library of Congress Cataloging-in-Publication Data available.

ISBN 978-0-8118-7838-8

Manufactured in China

Designed by **SARAH PULVER**
Prop styling by **PAIGE HICKS**
Food styling by **REBECCA JURGEVICH**

10 9 8 7 6 5 4 3 2 1

Chronicle Books LLC
680 Second Street
San Francisco, California 94107
www.chroniclebooks.com

# CONTENTS

# GETTING STARTED

A sauce is usually poured, ladled, dolloped, drizzled, or otherwise added to the more substantial ingredients in a dish. In other words, you could think of a sauce as just an add-on, an extra. For me, however, a sauce is the whole point. It's the main event, even though we might be talking about only two tablespoons of vinaigrette. Like an engine of deliciousness, a well-made sauce brings energy to a dish.

I wanted to write a book on sauces because I think sauce-making is such an important and gratifying part of cooking. Yet it's often seen as being too tricky, too time consuming, or not relevant to everyday eating. But none of that is true! There are hundreds of sauces that reward you with a hugely delicious payoff for very little trouble.

My goal with this book is to show that any cook in any kitchen can make fantastic sauces for any meal, every day. Honestly, you can incorporate a homemade sauce into breakfast, lunch, or dinner, and by doing so you'll elevate what might be a fine plate of food to a meal you're proud to have made and eager to eat.

## WHAT EXACTLY IS A SAUCE?

A sauce can be anything from a mustard vinaigrette that you spoon over roasted beets to a red pepper hollandaise that you nap over grilled halibut to a hot fudge sauce that you eat with a spoon right out of the pot. No matter what form your sauce takes, it will share the three traits that are the source of power for all good sauces: intense flavor, complex character, and the alchemical ability to pull all of the elements of a dish together into a delicious unity.

The way I learned to develop those traits in a sauce is the subject of this book. I want to share everything that I've discovered about sauces through my time at cooking school in Paris, my years as a food editor working with chefs and other amazing cooks, and my own cooking experiences as a private chef, caterer, and recipe developer as well as a home cook who needs to balance the pleasure of cooking with the constraints of a busy modern life.

I share recipes, of course, but, more important, I share my opinions, insights, and tricks, which I hope will have a big impact on your ability to understand and enjoy new sauces. In each chapter, I explain the essence of the sauce, I describe what you're trying to achieve, and I let you know what levers to push to get to your goal. Each time you cook anything, you arrive at moments when you need to make a decision that will nudge the dish in a certain direction. I call this process "getting to delicious," and that's where I hope we'll go together in this book.

## WHAT IS IN THIS BOOK?

The sauces I've included are the ones that I find myself cooking month after month, year after year. They're versatile, your family and friends will love them, and they're worth the time you put into them. You'll notice a bias toward French sauces. That's because I learned to cook in France and French cuisine has introduced so many important sauces to the culinary world. But you'll also find sauces inspired by Italy, Spain, Mexico, Morocco, Asia, the Middle East, and classic American comfort food—not to mention sauces that simply reflect the flavors I love. Of course, this book cannot capture the range of sauces in every cuisine. A big world of sauces exists out there, and this is just my tasty little corner of it. But I think you'll find that it's plenty big.

## HOW ARE THE RECIPES ORGANIZED?

Each chapter includes recipes that share a main ingredient, a key technique, or both. For example, all of the vinaigrettes in chapter two share the same method and most of the same ingredients, while the chocolate sauces in chapter fifteen use many different methods but all are made with chocolate or cocoa powder. My structure is loosely based on the French system of mother sauces, in which you have master sauces with lots of variations. Indeed, some of my sauce types are classic French mother sauces—hollandaise, mayonnaise, beurre blanc—and I include a béchamel and a velouté in the chapter on cream sauces. But I'm deliberately omitting one of the "big" French mother sauce categories, brown sauces, because I just don't think they're worth the effort and expense required of the home cook.

I've also included several dozen recipes for dishes that showcase the sauces, perhaps in ways that are new to you or that will inspire you to go beyond the obvious. Of course, a vinaigrette is delicious on salad greens, but it's also lovely on fish, meat, or fruit. I want cooks to be able to make their sauces and then to "deploy" them in inventive and satisfying ways.

## START HERE, IMPROVISE TO INFINITY

The one-hundred-plus sauces in this book are just the tip of a delicious iceberg. Each one can be riffed on to bring in new dimensions: use a different herb, add some red pepper flakes, try pistachios instead of almonds, splash in some Calvados. Once you understand the fundamentals of a sauce, you can improvise to suit your mood, pantry, or menu. You're equipped to create, delight, and nourish—all of the reasons cooks love to cook.

# SAUCE ESSENTIALS

**THREE KEYS TO RECIPE SUCCESS: ORGANIZING YOUR WORK, LEARNING TO SEASON, AND JUDGING DONENESS**

When I'm just cooking rather than recipe developing, I'm more an intuitive cook than a literal one. I make things up as I go along, using my technical training as a framework and then responding to the particular ingredients, equipment, weather, glasses of wine, appetites in the room, and mood that belong to me that day. So trying to write a recipe that distills all of those variables and locks them into numbers and words is hard. Every time you make a recipe, the world and its contents are a bit different, but here are three constants that will give you a good chance of success with the execution of any recipe.

## DO YOUR MISE EN PLACE. I can't

stress enough the importance of mise en place, which is a professional cooking term that means "prep work" (the translation from the French is more like "put in place"). Restaurants run on it and home kitchens should too. Mise en place is about breaking the work into small, manageable components, which is what I'm going to do with this explanation. Here is how to think about mise en place:

**READ THROUGH YOUR RECIPE.** You need to know where you're headed before you begin work so that you're not ambushed by a step you're not prepared for, such as "chill for 24 hours."

**GATHER YOUR EQUIPMENT AND HEAT THE OVEN OR GRILL.** Set up your battle stations, get your gear in gear. You don't want to be searching for a baking dish while you've got ingredients in the sauté pan. And you never want to put a dish in the oven before it's come to temperature. The immediate exposure to the correct oven temperature is part of what makes a dish work. For example, a soufflé batter, made from béchamel, needs to get very hot very quickly so that the air bubbles expand and give the soufflé

height before the protein in the batter has time to set and restrict any more rising. If the oven is too cool, that initial puff won't happen properly.

**GATHER YOUR INGREDIENTS.** Line up the food you'll be using; find substitutes for any ingredients you don't have.

**DO THE "DIRTY" PREP.** Before you proceed with cooking, do the prep work that involves washing, peeling, cutting meat— any tasks that are going to produce waste or require cleanup. I like to have two stainless-steel bowls handy to collect all the scraps, one for the trash and one for the compost.

**NOW, DO THE "FINE" PREP.** Here's where you chop, slice, grate, toast—anything you're instructed to do in the actual ingredients list. And, of course, here is where you measure. Please measure liquids using a vessel designed for that, such as a Pyrex measuring cup. And measure dry ingredients either with a dry measuring cup, which allows you to level off the contents with the back of a knife for accuracy, or with a scale.

You don't have to go as far as putting each prepped ingredient in its own little bowl, like cooks do on TV, but do arrange every ingredient so that it is within easy reach and in the right condition. And little bowls are actually handy—I have a ton of them.

Doing a thorough mise en place will sometimes feel frustrating because you're dying to jump into the recipe and get cooking. But doing the prep work *is* cooking. Having everything ready will allow you to have the control and concentration you need to manage the parts of the recipe where you need to watch, smell, taste, and react. Mise en place permits creativity.

## SEASON AS YOU GO. Whether a recipe

lists precise measurements for salt and other seasonings or it instructs you to "taste for seasoning" or "add salt and pepper if needed," you always want to taste and adjust the flavor until it's as delicious as you can make it. There is no way for a recipe to provide the perfect amount of seasoning because there are always variations in ingredients: one jalapeño is hotter than the next, one brand of vinegar has more kick, and these blackberries are sweeter than those. But how do you know you've got the seasoning just right, especially if it's the first time you're making the recipe? I recommend that you get in the habit of tasting at three points of each recipe:

**TASTE YOUR RAW INGREDIENTS.** As you're doing your mise en place, pop a berry in your mouth, take a tiny sip of the olive oil, chew on a parsley leaf, bite a bit of chile. Get a baseline sense of what things taste like before you start, even if you're not sure what you're supposed to do with that knowledge. It will function in your subconscious.

**NEXT, TASTE AS YOU GO.** I try to write my recipes so that you're seasoning at various points along the way, not just giving a final seasoning once everything is together. You want each component—the sautéed onions, the pork medallions, the whipped cream—to be nicely seasoned and balanced so that flavors are integrated throughout the dish and not just seasoned on the surface.

**LAST, DO A FINAL CRITIQUE OF THE SEASONING.** It can be a mad rush at the end of making a dish, especially when you're entertaining. You're focused on getting things plated and to the table, and perhaps you've had a glass of wine already. But you need to stop, clear your head, take a taste, and then tinker with the seasoning to be sure your dish is as good as it can be. This final check takes only a few seconds, but those are the seconds that ensure that all of your hard work up until now will pay off beautifully.

Sometimes it's obvious that your dish needs a squeeze of lemon juice or a sprinkling of salt, but other times you're not quite sure what it needs, especially if there are several key flavors contributing to the balance. I sometimes take out a spoonful of the sauce, add some seasoning to that portion, and then taste it to get a sense of what direction I need to go in. That way, I'm not jeopardizing the whole dish by adding too much sugar, for example.

**AND PLEASE DON'T UNDERSALT.** I rarely get home-cooked food that's too salty, but I often get food that's not salted enough. There's a reason that restaurant food is so good: chefs know how to salt. I think there's some free-floating anxiety about salt being bad for us, but unless you have a particular condition that calls for avoiding salt, there's no science that says it's bad. And just by living a life in which you eat food cooked from scratch rather than processed food, you've reduced your sodium intake.

## "DONE" IS WHEN IT LOOKS RIGHT, NOT WHEN THE TIMER RINGS.

One of the hardest aspects to quantify in cooking is how long to cook something. Will the broth be reduced in five minutes? Will the fruit be juicy in three minutes? The familiar vignette in any cooking-school student's memory is of asking the chef, "How long should I cook it?" and getting the terse reply "until it's done."

Ingredients have infinite variations: sugar, moisture, protein, temperature, capsaicin levels, and more. Different pans conduct heat and allow evaporation differently and cooktops and ovens deliver heat at their own rate, so assigning a number to an action is useful only as a guideline.

The best way to determine doneness is by describing what you're after. Brown just around the edges or all over? Cook until soft but still holding its shape or so soft that it's a purée? In every recipe, I try to give the clues that let you know it's time to do something, so please use these as your primary doneness tests, even if your timing is different than what is written in the recipe.

### MAKING THE SAUCES AHEAD

In each chapter, the recipes for dishes that use the sauces assume that you have your sauces made ahead, before you start work on the other components of the dish. Again, it's important to read through your recipe and do the mise en place. In some cases, however, it's better to make the sauce after you have completed other tasks. I've indicated that in those particular recipes.

**HOW LONG WILL SAUCES KEEP?** In each sauce recipe, I've indicated how long the sauce will keep in the fridge or freezer. These are minimal times. I played cautious, not knowing your fridge temperature, how often your kid reaches in for an Otter Pop, and the like. You'll find in some cases you can keep your sauces much longer than what I say, especially those containing lots of sugar, such as the caramel sauces.

Frozen sauces won't actually spoil after the two- or three-month limit I suggest, but they do lose their luster, and their flavor and texture deteriorate over time. This is true for all food, especially if your freezer is part of your fridge. Don't let stuff linger too long.

### HOW MUCH IS A PORTION?

You'll see that I've listed how much each sauce makes in volume rather than number of portions because the size of a portion depends on you and what you're doing with it. For example, ½ cup/120 milliliters vinaigrette could be enough to dress ten small side salads but only enough to dress six servings of potato salad.

## GOOD COOKS CHOOSE GOOD INGREDIENTS

A cook is only as good as his or her ingredients, so the first step of any good recipe really begins at the market. Choosing the freshest, ripest, highest quality you can is an overlooked but crucial step in "getting to delicious." There's no technique that can compensate for subpar ingredients. Here are my feelings about a few key items that I call for in this book.

**BUTTER.** I developed the recipes using unsalted butter, which lets you control the amount of salt you add to your recipe. You should always use good-quality, fresh ingredients, of course, but in recipes that rely on butter, like beurre blanc and hollandaise, it's worth making the effort to get excellent butter, such as one from a local dairy or imported from France.

**CREAM AND CRÈME FRAÎCHE.** I often list these as interchangeable in a recipe because for the most part they are. Cream has a sweeter flavor and crème fraîche is slightly tangy and nutty because it has been cultured. I prefer crème fraîche, but it's not always easy to find and it can be pricey. Bellwether Farms makes a version that tastes most like the French product. Crème fraîche will grow in volume if you whip it, but for true fluffy whipped cream, you need to use heavy cream or whipping cream.

**OLIVE OIL AND OTHER OILS.** I am often asked what type of oil is the best to use: any oil that's fresh. I am dismayed by how much rancid oil I encounter at people's houses, not that I'm riffling through their cabinets, of course! But even friends who cook often have opened bottles of olive oil that are six months old or older on their counter. I guarantee that the flavor is either very stale or downright rancid—not pleasant to eat and not healthful, either.

All oils get rancid the longer they are exposed to heat, light, and oxygen, even those you think of as shelf stable, such as canola or other vegetable oils. I keep most of my opened oils in the fridge, especially nut oils such as walnut. Extra-virgin olive oil will solidify in the cold, but will quickly melt back to normal as it sits at room temperature for a few minutes.

When you first open a new bottle of any oil, taste it so you have a benchmark of freshness; then taste it every few days or weeks to monitor the flavor. If it tastes funny or you feel a slight dryness on your tongue, the oil is probably rancid, so throw it out and start fresh.

For the sauces in this book that call for extra-virgin olive oil, I prefer one that is not too assertive. That type is better "naked," just for drizzling or dipping. The two mainstream brands I typically use are Unio, from Spain, and Lucini, from Italy. They have character but play well with others.

**NUTS.** Ditto re: freshness; nuts turn rancid easily. Store extra nuts tightly wrapped in the freezer, and always taste a couple of nuts before you use them in a recipe. You don't want to ruin your beautiful pesto with nasty pine nuts.

**PARMIGIANO-REGGIANO CHEESE.** I use a lot of Parmigiano in my life. I go through mounds every month. Adding a little Parmigiano to a dish to boost its savoriness is a frequent tactic in my kitchen (along with grated lemon zest; those two ingredients save many a dish!). Please invest in imported Parmigiano-Reggiano—not pregrated—even though prices can get quite steep. The cheese is intense so you won't use a lot, and the flavor and texture are superior to domestic Parmesans. I will sometimes use grana padano, a close cousin in flavor and texture that's an acceptable substitute if need be.

Be sure to wrap your Parmigiano well because it can dry out and get hard and slightly piquant. Some cooks abhor the notion of putting good cheese in plastic wrap because it doesn't allow the cheese to breathe, but I find cheese papers an inadequate protection, so I usually use plastic wrap and apologize to the cheese. The ideal would be to wrap the cheese in cheese paper and then pop that into a plastic bag or airtight container, and someday I will store my cheese that way.

**SALT.** All of the recipes in this book call for kosher salt. It's not the kosher part that matters. It's the structure of the grains of salt, which are larger than the grains of a typical table salt. I like Diamond Crystal brand, in the red box; it's sold in most grocery stores.

The large grains give you more control when you grab a pinch and sprinkle it on your food, and the Diamond Crystal is nicely crushable, so you can make it powdery as you pinch, for better blending.

You can use table salt or a fine sea salt as you like, but be aware that 1 teaspoon of table or fine sea salt will be roughly twice as "salty" as 1 teaspoon kosher salt, not because the sodium chloride is any different, but because the amount of salt per volume is different. Kosher salt is *fluffier*, for lack of a better term, and so less salt fills more space. Please adjust the recipes if you don't use kosher salt.

# VINAIGRETTES

**VINAIGRETTES GIVE YOU THE BIGGEST PAY-OFF FOR THE LEAST AMOUNT OF WORK OF ANY GROUP OF SAUCES.** A vinaigrette takes seconds to make, is incredibly versatile, and when the balance of flavors is right, is a catalyst that lifts simple ingredients to a new level.

Mastering vinaigrettes will also liberate you from a refrigerator full of bottled salad dressings. It's crazy to buy something from a factory when you can make your own easily, no? You will be able to create the perfect vinaigrette for the moment in just the amount you need, ensuring flavors are fresh and vibrant.

The vast world of mixed green salads is the most obvious destination for vinaigrettes. But many other foods benefit from a drizzle of one of these zingy dressings. Earthy, starchy vegetables, in particular, cry out for them, so dress potato, grain, and bean salads with a vinaigrette. (When you do, add the vinaigrette while the food is still warm so that instead of just sitting on top, it gets absorbed into the ingredients. This small step makes a huge difference!) A sharp vinaigrette will also bring out the sweetness in fruits and sweet vegetables, such as melon, peach, nectarine, mango, or strawberry. Sliced tomatoes, grilled vegetables, bread salads, sliced cold roast pork or beef, and grilled meats, poultry, and fish are all are good with a vinaigrette. Once you master this classic sauce, you'll see that the possibilities are actually endless.

I organize my vinaigrettes into three loose categories: (1) **simple,** where the pleasure and flavor balance come from the tension between the oil and the acid; (2) **creamy or thickened,** where cream or cheese or another ingredient enhances the role of the oil; and (3) **chunky,** which means that other ingredients—think nuts, bacon, olives—are stirred into the vinaigrette. The final character of the sauce is different for each, but the method for making them is essentially the same.

### WHAT'S GOING ON IN THIS SAUCE?

At its simplest, a vinaigrette is made of just two ingredients, oil and vinegar, plus salt and usually a few more items to make things interesting. Despite the expression oil and water don't mix, when making a vinaigrette, you convince them to mix by coaxing them into an emulsion. This means that the vinegar droplets are evenly dispersed throughout the oil, creating a blended, cohesive consistency. For a longer-lasting emulsion, you use other ingredients to bind the oil and vinegar (most often a small amount of mustard does the trick). The resulting consistency is smoother, thicker, and almost creamy.

Why do you care if a vinaigrette is emulsified? A blended texture means that the flavors of the vinaigrette will be distributed evenly over your salad or other food. This way, you won't have one bite that's too sharp and acidic and another that's too oily and bland. There is such a thing as a "broken" vinaigrette, in which the two components are not thoroughly mixed on purpose, so the colorful droplets of oil and vinegar add to the look of the dish. This is more for looks than flavor, however, and for me, flavor rules, so I like to blend my dressings.

### WHAT CAN GO WRONG AND HOW CAN I FIX IT?

The emulsion can break when you don't want it to, resulting in oil floating on top of the vinegar. The fix is simple: whisk it again. If it refuses to stay blended, you can whisk in a tiny bit of Dijon mustard, some egg yolk, or a touch of mayonnaise, all of which are good emulsifiers and won't change your original flavors too much.

Vinaigrettes stay blended much longer if you make them in a blender or food processor. For small quantities, I'll sometimes use my Aerolatte milk frother, a tiny immersion blender designed for foaming milk for cappuccinos. It's brilliant for vinaigrettes and a cinch to use and clean.

The flavor balance of a vinaigrette can be off, too. It's important to balance the acid and the oil. How many salads have you been served with a vinaigrette that is either flat and boring or wincingly sharp? Too many. Here's a useful ratio that will help you achieve the ideal balance: three parts oil to one part vinegar (or other acidic ingredient). Start with those proportions and then taste and adjust until the flavor is bright and balanced. I like to lean to the sharp side, so when I taste what I consider a properly balanced vinaigrette, the acidity makes me shudder just the tiniest bit. Remember, a small amount of vinaigrette is going to dress a large amount of blander food, so it needs to be bright and assertive.

### HOW MUCH SAUCE PER SERVING?

Typically, you won't need much more than 2 tablespoons per person, depending on what you're serving, of course.

### SPECIAL EQUIPMENT

A small bowl and a whisk are all you need. For larger batches, a blender or food processor comes in handy. Some people like to shake their vinaigrettes together in a jar, but I don't get a very long-lasting emulsion when I use the shake method. As I already mentioned, my favorite tool is actually a toy of sorts: a battery-powered milk foamer that you dip into your bowl of vinaigrette ingredients and turn on for a few seconds.

### STORAGE

Because vinaigrettes are so quick to make, I like to think of them as *à la minute* sauces, that is, you make them right before you serve them. But they'll keep perfectly well in an airtight container in the refrigerator for up to 1 week. Beyond that, the flavor flattens out. Also, dressings with anchovies taste "off" sooner; I like to use them within 2 days.

# CLASSIC SHERRY VINAIGRETTE

This is my go-to vinaigrette, perfect for dressing anything from a simple green salad to earthy French lentils to a platter of grilled vegetables. You can vary it by switching to a different oil or vinegar or by adding fresh herbs or other flavorings. I use sherry vinegar because I like its mellow, rounded flavor and I find it is less harsh and more complex than most red wine vinegars. My oil choice is usually a moderately priced extra-virgin olive oil with a fruity character. No cough-inducing bitterness typical of a big Tuscan oil, please. I like Unio and Lucini brands, the former from Spain and the latter from Italy.

2 tbsp sherry vinegar

½ tsp Dijon mustard

Kosher salt and freshly ground black pepper

6 tbsp/90 ml extra-virgin olive oil

In a small bowl, whisk together the vinegar, mustard, ¼ tsp salt, and ⅛ tsp pepper. Gradually whisk in the oil, a little at a time, until the sauce is creamy and blended. Taste and adjust the flavor balance and seasoning. Whisk again to blend just before using.

**MAKES ABOUT ½ CUP/120 ML**

**STORAGE** Refrigerate in an airtight container for up to 1 week.

**QUICK CHANGE**

Substitute an equal amount of red wine vinegar or white wine vinegar for the sherry vinegar.

Use half fresh lemon juice and half vinegar for the vinegar.

Add 1 tsp finely minced shallot with the vinegar and mustard.

Substitute walnut, hazelnut, or grapeseed oil for all or part of the olive oil.

Crumble in some blue or feta cheese after you've whisked in the oil.

# DOUBLE-MUSTARD VINAIGRETTE

A good mustard dressing is a must in every cook's repertoire. This one is nicely versatile, good on anything from a salad of bitter greens with blue cheese and bacon to grilled rib-eye steak or roasted potatoes. I like to use two kinds of mustard: whole-grain Dijon mustard adds an appealing texture and mellow note (mellow for mustard, that is), and smooth Dijon brings in more sinus-clearing heat and tang.

2 tbsp white wine vinegar

2 tsp whole-grain Dijon mustard (*moutarde à l'ancienne*)

½ tsp Dijon mustard

½ tsp honey

3 drops hot-pepper sauce such as Sriracha

Kosher salt and freshly ground black pepper

6 tbsp/90 ml extra-virgin olive oil

**MAKES ABOUT ½ CUP/120 ML**

**STORAGE** Refrigerate in an air-tight container for up to 1 week.

**QUICK CHANGE** Use walnut oil instead of olive oil.

In a small bowl, whisk together the vinegar, both mustards, honey, hot-pepper sauce, ¼ tsp salt, and ⅛ tsp pepper. Gradually whisk in the oil, a little at a time, until the sauce is creamy and blended. Taste and adjust the flavor balance and seasoning. Whisk again to blend just before using.

# CAESAR-STYLE VINAIGRETTE

This is my family's "house" dressing. In fact, I'd say that 75 percent of the salads we eat at home are dressed in some version of this lemon-Parmigiano vinaigrette. Yes, anchovies are part of the mix, but they create more of a savory background than a fishy note (for a stronger anchovy flavor, try the Creamy Anchovy-Caper Vinaigrette on page 27). Unlike a classic Caesar dressing, this recipe does not call for raw egg yolk.

I like this dressing to be fairly creamy, so I make it in a food processor. But you can easily make it with a bowl and a whisk as well, or with a mortar and pestle. If you do, your final texture may be slightly more nubby than creamy.

1 tbsp plus 1 tsp finely grated Parmigiano-Reggiano cheese

2 tbsp fresh lemon juice

1 tsp lightly packed finely grated lemon zest

1 tsp Dijon mustard

2 to 3 olive oil-packed anchovy fillets (see ingredient note, page 27)

1 to 2 cloves garlic

Kosher salt and freshly ground black pepper

6 tbsp/90 ml extra-virgin olive oil

**MAKES ABOUT ½ CUP/120 ML**

**STORAGE** Refrigerate in an air-tight container for up to 2 days.

**QUICK CHANGE** Add 1 tsp Worcestershire sauce before you add the oil and 1 tbsp thinly sliced fresh basil just before serving.

In a food processor, combine the cheese, lemon juice, lemon zest, mustard, anchovies, garlic, ½ tsp salt, and ⅛ tsp pepper and pulse until well blended. With the motor running, slowly pour in the oil and process until the vinaigrette is creamy and blended, stopping to scrape down the sides of the bowl with a rubber spatula as needed. Taste and adjust the flavor balance and seasoning. Whisk again to blend just before using.

# MELLOW GARLIC-BASIL VINAIGRETTE

I have a love-hate relationship with garlic: I love it when it's cooked and hate it when it's raw. I've solved the problem here by poaching the cloves in oil to capture their flavor without their raw harshness. You can save the tender poached cloves to spread onto bruschetta, blend into a soup, or whiz into homemade mayonnaise (see page 133).

6 tbsp/90 ml extra-virgin olive oil

3 small cloves garlic, lightly smashed

14 large fresh basil leaves

2 tbsp white wine vinegar

1 tsp lightly packed finely grated lemon zest

½ tsp Dijon mustard

Kosher salt and freshly ground black pepper

**MAKES ABOUT ½ CUP/120 ML**

**STORAGE** Refrigerate in an air-tight container for up to 5 days. The basil will darken but the flavor will be fine.

**QUICK CHANGE** Use balsamic vinegar instead of white wine vinegar and orange zest instead of lemon zest.

In a small saucepan, heat the oil and garlic over medium-low heat until the cloves are just barely sizzling but not browning, 4 to 6 minutes. Continue to poach at a low simmer for 10 minutes; do not allow the garlic to brown.

Remove the pan from the heat and add 10 of the basil leaves. Let the basil infuse the oil off the heat for 20 minutes, then remove the garlic and basil leaves, gently squeezing the oil from the leaves back into the pan. Discard the basil but save the garlic for another use.

In a small bowl, whisk together the vinegar, lemon zest, mustard, ¼ tsp salt, and ⅛ tsp pepper. Gradually whisk in the infused oil, a little at a time, until the dressing is creamy and blended. Stack the remaining 4 basil leaves, roll up the stack lengthwise into a tight cylinder, and slice crosswise to make thin shreds (this cut is called a chiffonade). Stir the sliced basil into the dressing. Taste and adjust the flavor balance and seasoning. Whisk again to blend just before using.

# SPICY GINGER-LIME-GARLIC VINAIGRETTE

The key to this dressing is to balance the tension between the sweet, salty, sour, and hot flavors. Once the dressing is made, let it sit for about 30 minutes, then taste and tinker a bit to dial in the right balance just before serving. Even though the flavors are zingy, this is still a delicate vinaigrette that is best served with delicate partners, such as grilled tofu, shrimp, steamed asparagus, or even chunks of honeydew.

2 tbsp plus 2 tsp fresh lime juice

1 tsp white wine vinegar

1 tsp peeled and minced fresh ginger

½ tsp lightly packed finely grated lime zest

½ tsp minced garlic

¼ tsp Dijon mustard

⅛ tsp granulated sugar

Kosher salt

6 to 10 drops hot-pepper sauce such as Sriracha

¼ cup/60 ml grapeseed, canola, or other neutral vegetable oil

**MAKES ABOUT ½ CUP/120 ML**

**STORAGE** Refrigerate in an airtight container for up to 1 week.

**QUICK CHANGE**

Add 1 tsp soy sauce with the lime juice.

Add 1 tbsp finely chopped fresh cilantro after adding the oil.

In a small bowl, whisk together the lime juice, lime zest, vinegar, ginger, garlic, mustard, sugar, ¼ tsp salt, and 6 drops hot-pepper sauce. Gradually whisk in the oil, a little at a time, until the sauce is creamy and blended. Let the dressing sit for 30 minutes to allow the flavors to blend, then taste and adjust the flavor balance and seasoning. Whisk again to blend just before using.

# TOMATO-GINGER VINAIGRETTE

This slightly sweet vinaigrette can be used to dress up much more than just salad. Spoon it over grilled white-fleshed fish, such as halibut, for a main course or over roasted red bell peppers for an antipasto. The tomato flavor in the vinaigrette comes from two sources, the sweet sun-dried tomato and the deeper tomato paste. The cider vinegar contributes a bright, acidic backbone.

2 tbsp cider vinegar

1 tbsp fresh orange juice

1 tsp lightly packed finely grated orange zest

1 tbsp minced oil-packed (or other soft) sun-dried tomato

1 tsp peeled and minced fresh ginger

½ tsp Dijon mustard

½ tsp tomato paste

½ tsp granulated sugar

Kosher salt and freshly ground black pepper

Few drops hot-pepper sauce such as Sriracha

6 tbsp/90 ml extra-virgin olive oil

**MAKES ABOUT ½ CUP/120 ML**

**STORAGE** Refrigerate in an airtight container for up to 1 week.

**QUICK CHANGE** Add 1 Calabrian chile in oil, finely minced, and 1 tbsp finely diced fresh tomato after adding the oil.

In a small bowl, whisk together the vinegar, orange juice, orange zest, sun-dried tomato, ginger, mustard, tomato paste, sugar, ½ tsp salt, ⅛ tsp pepper, and the hot-pepper sauce. Gradually whisk in the oil, a little at a time, until the sauce is creamy and blended. Taste and adjust the flavor balance and seasoning. Whisk again to blend just before using.

# RASPBERRY-THYME VINAIGRETTE

I started cooking in the late 1980s, around the time *The Silver Palate* cookbook was first published. I think of that era as The Age of the Raspberry Vinaigrette. The concoction was so overused that I couldn't go near the stuff for years. But a well-made raspberry vinaigrette is a beautiful thing, full of summery perfume and balanced fruit flavor, and I'm ready to embrace it again. I don't make mine with raspberry vinegar. I use real raspberries, either fresh or frozen, and I add fresh thyme to balance out the sweetness of the fruit.

2 tbsp white wine vinegar

1 tsp balsamic vinegar

½ tsp chopped fresh thyme

½ tsp Dijon mustard

¼ tsp granulated sugar

Kosher salt and freshly ground black pepper

6 to 8 fresh or frozen and thawed raspberries

6 tbsp/90 ml extra-virgin olive oil

In a small bowl, whisk together both vinegars, the thyme, mustard, sugar, ¼ tsp salt, and ⅛ tsp pepper. Add the raspberries and crush coarsely with a wooden spoon or the whisk. Gradually whisk in the oil, a little at a time, until the sauce is creamy and blended. Taste and adjust the flavor balance and seasoning, adding more sugar if needed. If time permits, let the vinaigrette sit at room temperature for up to 30 minutes before using so the berries release their juices. Whisk again to blend just before using.

**MAKES ABOUT ½ CUP/120 ML**

**STORAGE** Refrigerate in an air-tight container for up to 4 days.

**QUICK CHANGE**

Use ripe blackberries instead of raspberries, adding more sugar if the berries are tart.

Add 1 tsp chopped fresh tarragon after adding the oil.

Use fresh lime juice instead of white wine vinegar.

# FRESH ORANGE–SMOKED PAPRIKA VINAIGRETTE

I'm addicted to this flavor combination. It tastes like the exotic vacation that I never quite manage to take! Once you start cooking with smoked paprika, you'll find a million uses for it (see the box below), so don't hesitate to invest in a small can. It won't go to waste.

3 tbsp fresh orange juice

½ tsp lightly packed finely grated orange zest

2 tbsp sherry vinegar

1 tsp Spanish sweet smoked paprika (see ingredient note)

½ tsp granulated sugar

2 drops hot-pepper sauce such as Sriracha

Kosher salt

½ cup/120 ml extra-virgin olive oil

**MAKES ABOUT ¾ CUP/180 ML**

**STORAGE** Refrigerate in an air-tight container for up to 1 week.

**QUICK CHANGE** Add 2 tbsp finely diced roasted red bell pepper after adding the oil.

In a small bowl, whisk together the orange juice, orange zest, vinegar, paprika, sugar, hot-pepper sauce, and ¼ tsp salt until the sugar and salt are dissolved. Gradually whisk in the oil, a little at a time, until the dressing is creamy and blended. Taste and adjust the flavor balance and seasoning. Whisk again to blend just before using.

**INGREDIENT NOTE:** *Spanish smoked paprika, also known as* pimentón de la Vera, *comes in three types, sweet (dulce), medium-hot (agridulce) and hot (picante). Look for it in stores that specialize in Spanish foods or carry a wide selection of gourmet foods or online.*

---

### TEN DELICIOUS THINGS TO DO WITH SPANISH SMOKED PAPRIKA

1. Make a marinade for grilled shrimp with smoked paprika, finely grated lemon zest, minced garlic, and olive oil.
2. Add a few teaspoons to your favorite gazpacho recipe.
3. Mix into hummus.
4. Sprinkle on deviled eggs.
5. Make a steak rub with kosher salt, cracked black pepper, smoked paprika, ground cumin, and ground fennel.
6. Sprinkle onto chunks of juicy mango.
7. Add to a rice pilaf and serve with grilled sausages.
8. Gently sauté sliced red bell peppers until soft and compotelike, then season with smoked paprika and a few drops of sherry vinegar.
9. Use to season strips of chicken breast, then sauté for fajitas or burritos.
10. Sprinkle on fried potatoes and onions and serve with lemon wedges.

# TANGERINE–BROWN BUTTER VINAIGRETTE

Adding butter to vinaigrette might seem strange, but once you taste it, you'll wonder why you haven't done it before. The nutty, rich brown butter gives the dressing some extra flavor and richness, and the mild acidity of the tangerines is the perfect foil. This sauce is beautiful on delicate fish such as albacore tuna and richer fish such as salmon (see page 32), on steamed broccoli, or on roasted rings of butternut squash.

2 tangerines

2 tbsp sherry vinegar

1 tbsp finely chopped shallot

4 tbsp/55 g unsalted butter

½ tsp Dijon mustard

1 tbsp extra-virgin olive oil

Kosher salt

1 tbsp thinly sliced fresh chives

**MAKES ABOUT ½ CUP/120 ML**

**STORAGE** Refrigerate in an air-tight container for up to 4 days. The butter will solidify when cold, so take the vinaigrette out of the fridge 30 minutes before using it, or reheat it briefly in a microwave.

**QUICK CHANGE**

Add a few drops of hot-pepper sauce such as Sriracha.

Add ¼ tsp sweet Spanish smoked paprika to the reduced juice mixture.

Using a rasp-type grater, finely grate 1 tsp lightly packed zest from the tangerines and reserve. Squeeze the juice from the tangerines into a small saucepan, taking care not to let any seeds fall into the pan. You should have about ½ cup/ 120 ml. Add the zest, vinegar, and shallot; bring to a simmer over medium heat; and cook, stirring often, until reduced by about half (to ¼ cup/60 ml), about 4 minutes. Remove from the heat and reserve.

In another small saucepan, melt the butter over medium heat. Continue cooking the butter, swirling the pan every few seconds, until all of the water has sizzled off, the milk solids at the bottom of the pan have turned deep gold, and the butter smells nutty and fragrant, about 3 minutes. Immediately pour the butter into a small heatproof bowl so it stops cooking; keep warm.

Whisk the mustard into the reduced tangerine mixture in the saucepan. Then whisk in the brown butter (including the milk solids) and the olive oil. Season with a little salt, then taste and adjust the flavor balance and seasoning. Stir in the chives. Whisk again to blend just before using.

# TOASTED-ALMOND VINAIGRETTE

I first tasted a dressing like this at Clyde Common, one of my favorite restaurants in Portland, Oregon, and I've been tinkering with my own version ever since. Because I like the almonds very finely chopped, I use a food processor, but you could chop them by hand with a sharp chef's knife. (Some confusion exists over what are sliced almonds and what are slivered almonds, so here's how it goes: sliced are flat, waferlike slices and slivered are the tiny french-fry shapes.) One of my favorite ways to use this vinaigrette is to steam some green beans, line them up neatly on a plate, and pour a ribbon of the vinaigrette down the middle. It's a beautiful first course for a summer supper.

2 tbsp sliced almonds

2 tbsp fresh lime juice

¼ tsp Dijon mustard

¼ tsp granulated sugar

Kosher salt and freshly ground black pepper

¼ cup/60 ml extra-virgin olive oil or grapeseed oil

1 tsp minced shallot

**MAKES ABOUT ⅓ CUP/75 ML**

**STORAGE** Refrigerate in an airtight container for up to 5 days.

**QUICK CHANGE** Use hazelnuts instead of almonds and add ½ tsp chopped fresh tarragon with the nuts and shallot.

Heat the oven to 350°F/180°C/gas 4.

Spread the almonds on a baking sheet or pie pan and toast in the oven until lightly golden and fragrant, 3 to 4 minutes. Transfer to a plate to cool completely. Transfer the almonds to a food processor and pulse until very finely ground. Do not pulse until they become a paste, however. Or, chop the almonds by hand, if you like, but they must be very finely minced.

In a small bowl, whisk together the lime juice, mustard, sugar, and ¼ tsp salt. Gradually whisk in the oil, a little at a time, until the sauce is creamy and blended. Whisk in the almonds and shallot. Taste and adjust the flavor balance and seasoning. Let the dressing sit at room temperature for at least 15 minutes to allow the flavors to blend. Whisk again to blend just before using.

# CREAMY ANCHOVY-CAPER VINAIGRETTE

The flavor of this dressing is intense, but despite the number of anchovies, it's not fishy, I promise. The net effect of the anchovies is a deep savoriness, topped with some zing from the capers. I use a finishing touch of cream to blend all of the flavors together and give the dressing body.

Be sure to use high-quality anchovies packed in olive oil (see ingredient note). Making the dressing in a food processor will ensure the anchovies and capers are fully incorporated. A mortar and pestle will work too, with a bit more effort on your part. I love this vinaigrette over boiled new potatoes or as a dip for steamed artichokes or crusty bread.

10 olive oil–packed anchovy fillets, drained

2 tbsp white wine vinegar

1 tbsp drained capers

1 tbsp chopped fresh flat-leaf parsley

1 small clove garlic

3 tbsp extra-virgin olive oil

2 tbsp heavy cream or crème fraîche

Kosher salt and freshly ground black pepper

**MAKES ½ CUP/120 ML**

**STORAGE** Refrigerate in an airtight container for up to 2 days.

**QUICK CHANGE**

Use fresh lemon juice instead of white wine vinegar.

Use walnut oil instead of olive oil.

Add ½ tsp finely minced Calabrian chile in oil along with the capers.

In a food processor, combine the anchovies, vinegar, capers, parsley, and garlic and whiz until puréed, stopping to scrape down the sides of the bowl with a rubber spatula as needed. With the motor running, slowly add the oil and then the cream and process until well blended and slightly thickened, about 20 seconds. The dressing won't be completely smooth. Season with pepper. You probably won't need to add any salt because of the anchovies and capers, but taste the dressing and add some if you do; adjust the other flavors. Whisk again to blend just before using.

**INGREDIENT NOTE:** *It pays to buy good-quality olive oil–packed anchovy fillets. When I'm in the mood to splurge, I buy Spanish Ortiz brand fillets, which are always sweet and meaty. Roland, another Spanish brand, is less expensive but reliable. Scalia, from Sicily, is somewhere in the middle in both quality and price. Some cooks prefer salt-packed whole anchovies for their firmer texture and full flavor. I agree that they're delicious when well prepared, but they take work to get that way (soaking, filleting), so I usually opt for oil-packed fillets.*

# WARM MAPLE-BACON VINAIGRETTE

This rich and somewhat indulgent sauce calls for bacon fat, in addition to olive oil. That combination keeps the vinaigrette from seeming too greasy, especially once it cools a bit. Feel free to shift the balance toward even more olive oil, if you like.

The key to using a warm vinaigrette is to pair it with a sturdy partner. If it's a green salad, use frisée, escarole, radicchio, baby kale, or other hearty green that will wilt slightly from the heat but not turn into a slimy mess, which a tender lettuce, such as Bibb, would do. I also like warm vinaigrettes like this one on cooked lentils, roasted root vegetables, and especially on potatoes (see the warm potato salad on page 35).

4 slices bacon, cut crosswise into ½-in/12-mm pieces

2 tbsp extra-virgin olive oil, plus 1 tbsp for finishing (optional)

2 tbsp finely minced shallot

½ cup/120 ml sherry vinegar

¼ cup/60 ml pure maple syrup, preferably grade B

2 tbsp Dijon mustard

Kosher salt and freshly ground black pepper

Pinch of cayenne pepper, or dash of hot-pepper sauce such as Sriracha

**MAKES ABOUT ½ CUP/120 ML**

**STORAGE** Refrigerate in an air-tight container for up to 5 days. If you are making the vinaigrette in advance, store the bacon pieces and vinaigrette separately and add the bacon just before serving. Gently reheat until warm.

**QUICK CHANGE** Omit the maple syrup and use half balsamic and half sherry vinegar.

In a frying pan, combine the bacon and the 2 tbsp olive oil over medium heat and cook, turning the bacon occasionally, until it is browned and crisp and has rendered most of its fat, 6 to 8 minutes. Transfer the bacon to a paper towel–lined plate. Pour off all but 1 tsp of the fat from the pan into a small bowl and set the bowl aside.

Return the pan to medium heat, add the shallot, and cook, stirring constantly, until soft and fragrant, about 1 minute. Increase the heat to medium-high, add the vinegar (stand back, the fumes are pungent!), and stir with a wooden spoon to scrape up all the brown bits from the pan bottom. Let the vinegar reduce by about half, about 3 minutes. Add the maple syrup and mustard and cook, stirring, until well blended and heated through, another 30 seconds or so. (You can prepare the dressing up to this point up to 4 hours before serving. Just before serving, reheat gently.)

Whisk about 2 tbsp of the oil-bacon fat mixture, or 1 tbsp of the oil-bacon fat mixture and the remainig 1 tbsp olive oil, into the warm vinegar mixture, then taste. The flavor should be quite sharp, but if it's too sharp, whisk in more oil. Season generously with salt, black pepper, and cayenne, then taste and adjust the seasoning. Add the reserved bacon and dress your salad right away.

# APPLE and FENNEL SALAD with CANDIED WALNUTS and DOUBLE-MUSTARD VINAIGRETTE

Waldorf salad was my inspiration for this crunchy, sweet-tart salad. I've always liked the apple-celery-raisin Waldorf combo but never liked the cloak of mayonnaise. Here, the fruits and vegetables are paired with a tangy mustard vinaigrette, and I've swapped out the celery in favor of fennel.

This salad would also be lovely dressed with Classic Sherry Vinaigrette (page 17) or Mellow Garlic-Basil Vinaigrette (page 20). The candied walnut recipe makes more than you need for this salad, but once you taste them, you'll understand why I've included extras for munching.

**CANDIED WALNUTS**

1 egg white

1 tbsp water

¼ cup/50 g granulated sugar

1 tbsp lightly packed light or dark brown sugar

½ tsp kosher salt

¼ tsp ground cinnamon

¼ tsp ground coriander

¼ tsp chipotle chile powder or red pepper flakes

2 cups/250g walnut halves

**SALAD**

1 fennel bulb

½ cup/120 ml Double-Mustard Vinaigrette (page 18)

1 lb/455 g crisp apples such as Braeburn, Pink Lady, or Honeycrisp (about 2 medium), halved, cored, and sliced ⅛ in/3mm thick

¼ cup/40 g raisins

**SERVES 6**

**TO MAKE THE CANDIED WALNUTS,** heat the oven to 325°F/165°C/gas 3. Line a large rimmed baking sheet with parchment paper or aluminum foil.

In a bowl, whisk together the egg white and water until foamy. Whisk in both sugars, the salt, cinnamon, coriander, and chipotle chile powder. Add the walnuts and toss to coat evenly. Spread the nuts in a single layer on the prepared baking sheet, place in the oven, and toast the nuts for 15 minutes. Stir the nuts and continue to toast until fragrant and dry looking, 10 to 15 minutes more. Remove the nuts from the oven, let them cool until they can be handled, and then break up any clumps with your fingers and let cool completely. Coarsely chop enough nuts to measure 1 cup/125 g and set aside for the salad. Store the remainder in an airtight container at room temperature for snacking or other use.

**TO MAKE THE SALAD,** cut off the stalks and fronds from the fennel bulb so it doesn't look like a bagpipe anymore. Trim away the hard part at the base. If the outer layer of the bulb looks tough or fibrous, peel away the surface with a vegetable peeler. Cut the bulb into small dice, transfer to a bowl, drizzle with about 2 tbsp of the vinaigrette, and toss until thoroughly coated. Put the apples in another bowl, drizzle with about 3 tbsp of the vinaigrette, and toss until thoroughly coated. Refrigerate the apple and fennel separately for at least 30 minutes or up to 1 hour to crisp them.

Arrange the apple slices in a wide mound on a serving platter or in a large shallow bowl, and top with the fennel in a smaller mound so that the apples show underneath. Drizzle more of the vinaigrette over the top. You may not need all of the vinaigrette. Sprinkle the raisins over the fennel and then sprinkle the whole salad with the candied walnuts. Serve immediately.

# ORANGE SALAD with FRESH ORANGE–SMOKED PAPRIKA VINAIGRETTE, ICED ONIONS, and CILANTRO

Look for an interesting orange variety for this salad, such as Cara Cara (which has a lovely pink blush) or blood oranges (which are a deep magenta inside). If you're not a cilantro fan (I've heard that there are some of you out there), basil or parsley would work fine. Soaking the onion is a trick I learned at my one and only restaurant kitchen job, and a fine trick it is. It reduces the bite of raw onion and makes it crunchy and almost translucent.

This salad is good alongside anything from the grill, but it goes especially well with grilled steak. It also makes a nice last course if you don't want a sweet dessert.

⅛ small red onion, sliced paper-thin

3 juicy oranges such as blood or Cara Cara or other navel

½ cup/120 ml Fresh Orange–Smoked Paprika Vinaigrette (page 24)

2 tbsp coarsely chopped fresh cilantro, or whole cilantro leaves

In a small bowl, combine the onion slices with ice water to cover for at least 30 minutes or up to 2 hours.

Meanwhile, working with one orange at a time, cut a slice off each end to reveal the flesh. Stand the orange on a sliced flat end on a work surface. Using a sharp knife, slice away the peel, including all of the white pith, cutting from the top to the bottom and following the contour of the fruit. Take your time and work in wide strips. Turn the peeled orange on its side and cut crosswise into rounds ¼ in/6 mm thick. Repeat with the remaining two oranges.

Put the vinaigrette in a wide, shallow bowl, add the orange slices, and toss gently to coat. Arrange the oranges on a serving plate, overlapping them slightly. Pour any extra vinaigrette and juices from the bowl into a small pitcher for serving on the side.

Drain the onion slices and pat thoroughly dry with paper towels. Scatter the onion over the oranges, then sprinkle with the cilantro. You can prepare the salad as much as 4 hours ahead and refrigerate it, though don't add the cilantro until just before serving. The salad is not at its best when ice-cold, however, so take it out of the refrigerator at least 20 minutes before serving.

SERVES 6

# SALMON FILLETS on CREAMY MASHED POTATOES and TURNIPS with TANGERINE–BROWN BUTTER VINAIGRETTE

This is a great dish for late winter when spring is still just a concept but you're already hankering for something light and fresh. Halibut fillets work nicely here, too, but they're not as colorful as salmon on the plate. If you're preparing this for company, you can make the mashed potatoes and the base of the vinaigrette ahead, and have the fish ready to pop into the oven as you start to clear the dishes from the first course. Just reheat the potatoes, brown your butter, and assemble your plates.

2 lb/910 g medium Yukon Gold potatoes, peeled and quartered

1 lb/455 g turnips, peeled and quartered

Kosher salt and freshly ground black pepper

½ cup/120 ml heavy cream or crème fraîche

3 tbsp unsalted butter, at room temperature

Six 6- to 8-oz/170- to 225-g skinned wild salmon fillets

½ cup Tangerine–Brown Butter Vinaigrette (page 25)

2 tbsp chopped fresh chives or flat-leaf parsley

**SERVES 6**

In a large pot, combine the potatoes and turnips with generously salted water to cover, and bring to a boil over high heat. Reduce the heat to maintain a vigorous simmer and cook, uncovered, until tender when pierced with a fork, about 20 minutes. Scoop out and reserve about 1 cup/240 ml of the cooking water, and then drain the vegetables in a colander.

Return the potatoes and turnips to the pot, place over low heat, and heat, stirring constantly, to dry them out thoroughly, about 3 minutes. (You'll see a lot of steam rising from the vegetables at first, but as they dry, you should see less.) Transfer them to a stand mixer fitted with the paddle attachment, add the cream and 2 tbsp of the butter, and beat on low speed until very smooth. Or, remove the potatoes and turnips from the pot, put them through a ricer or a food mill held over the pot to keep warm, and then add the cream and 2 tbsp of the butter and mix with a wooden spoon until very smooth.

If the potatoes are a bit stiff, loosen them by incorporating a few spoonfuls of the reserved cooking liquid. Season generously with salt and pepper, then return them to the pot to keep warm if you have used a mixer. (You can make the potatoes up to 4 hours ahead and gently reheat them in a microwave or on the stove top with a little milk before serving.)

About 30 minutes before serving time, heat the oven to 425°F/220°C/gas 7.

Rub a 9-by-13-in/23-by-33-cm baking dish with ½ tbsp of the remaining butter.

Season the salmon fillets generously on both sides with salt and pepper and arrange in the prepared baking dish in a single layer (if your fillets are thick on one end, thin on the other, fold the thin end under to make neat fillets of even thickness). Dot with the remaining ½ tbsp butter and cover the dish tightly with aluminum foil. Bake until the fish is just barely opaque in the center, 10 to 12 minutes (a few minutes less for very thin fillets).

Put a mound of turnipy potatoes in the center of each warmed dinner plate and arrange a fillet on top or next to them. Spoon an equal amount of the vinaigrette over each fillet so that it drizzles down onto the potatoes, too. Sprinkle each plate with chives. Serve right away.

# CEASAR-STYLE HEARTS OF ROMAINE SALAD with GRILLED PARMIGIANO-REGGIANO CROUTONS and LEMON

Romaine lettuce is usually available two ways at the grocery store: the whole head, which can be found loose with other heads of lettuce, and the heart, which usually comes three to a bag. I don't normally buy bagged produce, but in this case I do. You get the tender, juicy, crunchy leaves of the romaine heart and not the raggedy outer leaves of a whole head, which I often end up composting anyway.

Grilling lemon slices is easy and is a delicious way to add a bright flavor to salads or grilled vegetable platters. Be sure to grill them until they start to brown and are quite soft and chewy. If you stop too soon, you end up with steamed lemon slices.

1 lemon, sliced crosswise ⅛ in/
3 mm thick and slices seeded

2 tbsp extra-virgin olive oil

Kosher salt

½ cup/55 g finely grated Parmigiano-Reggiano cheese

4 tbsp/55g unsalted butter,
at room temperature

1 clove garlic, finely minced or grated

½ tsp lightly packed finely grated lemon zest

3 large slices artisanal white bread,
1 in/2.5 cm thick

2 romaine lettuce hearts, cored and cut crosswise into strips 1 in/
2.5 cm wide

½ cup Caesar-Style Vinaigrette
(page 19)

¼ cup/10 g coarsely chopped fresh flat-leaf parsley

Prepare a medium fire in a charcoal or gas grill. The fire is ready when you can comfortably hold your hand, palm-side down, 2 to 3 in/5 to 7.5 cm above the grill rack for 4 seconds.

Brush the lemon slices with 1 tbsp of the olive oil and season generously with salt. Wrap the slices in a sheet of heavy-duty aluminum foil, sealing the edges so the oil doesn't leak out. Grill until soft and browned, about 15 minutes, flipping the packet once or twice. Transfer the lemons to a cutting board and chop finely.

While the lemons are grilling, in a bowl, stir together the cheese, butter, garlic, lemon zest, and ⅛ tsp salt. Brush one side of the bread slices with the remaining 1 tbsp olive oil. Grill, oiled-side up, until nicely browned, about 2 minutes. Flip the bread slices, spread the grilled side with the butter-cheese mixture, cover the grill, and grill until the bottom is browned and the cheese is melted and bubbly, 2 to 3 minutes. Transfer to a cutting board. When cool enough to handle, cut into 1-in/2.5-cm cubes.

In a large bowl, toss the romaine with the vinaigrette, coating evenly. Add the bread cubes, parsley, and chopped lemons. Toss to combine and serve right away.

**SERVES 4 TO 6**

# SMASHED NEW POTATO SALAD with WARM MAPLE-BACON VINAIGRETTE and SCALLIONS

In too many potato salads, the dressing slides around on the surface of the potatoes and never sinks in, so the experience is a disconnect between tangy and bland. I address that problem two different ways here: First, I smash the potatoes a bit to create lots of crevices to catch the dressing (who says potato salad equals diced potato?). Second, I use a warm dressing on warm potatoes, so the two get intimate quite quickly.

1½ lb/680 g small new potatoes or larger waxy potatoes, unpeeled, cut into 1-in/2.5-cm chunks

2 bay leaves (optional)

Kosher salt

½ cup Warm Maple-Bacon Vinaigrette (page 28)

Freshly ground black pepper

3 green onions (white and light green parts only), thinly sliced crosswise

In a large pot, combine the potatoes, bay leaves (if using), 2 tbsp salt, and water to cover by 1 to 2 in/2.5 to 5 cm and bring to a boil over high heat. Reduce the heat to maintain a vigorous simmer and cook, uncovered, until the potatoes are very tender when pierced with a fork, about 20 minutes. Scoop out about 1 cup/240 ml of the cooking water, and then drain the potatoes in a colander.

Return the potatoes to the pot off the heat and crush the potatoes lightly with a wooden spoon or potato masher. Pour about half of the vinaigrette over the potatoes, season generously with salt and pepper, and toss gently to coat. Let sit for a couple of minutes so the potatoes can absorb the dressing, and then pour over the remaining vinaigrette, and toss again. If the potatoes seem a touch dry, fold in a few spoonfuls of the cooking water to moisten them and make everything creamy.

Transfer to a serving bowl, garnish with the green onions, and serve warm or at room temperature.

**SERVES 4 TO 6**

# HERB SAUCES

IF FOR SOME KARMIC REASON I WAS REIN-CARNATED AS A SAUCE, I HOPE IT WOULD BE A PESTO. Pestos always smell like summer, fresh and alive. Their fresh herbs carry an intoxicating fragrance that begins to seduce you the moment you pick them from your garden or off the market shelf and continues as you chop them, make the sauce, and serve it. And the color, which ranges from vivacious grass green to deep jade (though they don't always stay green), is seductive too. Fragrance and color signal the flavors to come: bright and complex, perfect partners for mild starches and quiet vegetables (like green beans) that can use a personality boost.

Here, I'm grouping four Italian-style pestos with a trio of other fresh herb sauces inspired by the kitchens of France, Morocco, and Argentina. Although none of the latter shares a cultural heritage, they do share the vibrant color and perfume of fresh herbs. They are also united by an uncompromising need for pristine, flavorful herbs: fresh, supple, glorious, potent bunches of basil, cilantro, parsley, mint, or whatever you're using. No matter how good a recipe is or how superior your olive oil or cheese or pine nuts are, your herb-based sauce isn't worth making with a droopy clutch of herb sprigs trapped inside a plastic pack. So if the herbs at the store or market don't look, smell, and taste exceptional, skip making this kind of sauce and go for something else.

Herb sauces typically have a lot going on, so I like to match them with uncomplicated dishes that won't compete. The pestos, which are richer than the other herb sauces in the chapter because they contain cheese and/or nuts, are delicious on just about any pasta or plain starch, such as rice or potatoes. They are also wonderful spread on pizza, focaccia, sandwiches, or swirled into vegetable or bean soups.

The other herb sauces are more aggressive and include ingredients such as capers, cornichons, spices, and vinegars. I like these sauces with foods that can talk back a little, like grilled meat, fish, or chicken or sassy vegetables like roasted red peppers or roasted beets. These sauces also have a looser consistency, so they don't work as well as spreads or toppings.

### WHAT'S GOING ON IN THIS SAUCE?

There are two keys to a good herb sauce: releasing the flavor of the herbs without bruising or muddying them and balancing the herbs' flavors with the other ingredients. Techniquewise, you're either chopping herbs by hand or with a food processor. With both methods, you need to take care to avoid bruising the herbs, especially tender ones such as basil and tarragon. You want to slice cleanly through the leaves until you have the fineness you need. Don't enthusiastically chop-chop the way you might cut a clove of garlic or you'll end up crushing, rather than slicing, the tender herbs. Use a very sharp knife (you sharpen all your knives regularly, right?) or, if using a food processor, be judicious with your pulsing.

You also need to pay attention to how finely you want the herbs chopped and whether you want the final texture of the sauce to be blended and creamy, as with pesto, or loose and bitty, which is the case with the other sauces in this chapter.

### WHAT CAN GO WRONG AND HOW CAN I FIX IT?

As I mentioned, the main problem with fresh herb sauces comes from herbs that are past their prime or lack flavor. For slightly limp specimens, soak them in very cold water for about 20 minutes, then spin them until dry in a salad spinner. If the flavor is blah, add some fresh flat-leaf parsley to the mix to perk things up. Parsley is the unsung hero of the kitchen and is in almost every store. At a minimum, it usually has a decent flavor; at its best, it's sweet and grassy with just a touch of anise.

If the finished sauce tastes flat, a pinch of grated lemon zest and/or a few drops of lemon juice can add sprightliness. You'll find that my cure for everything in the kitchen is grated lemon zest. If you've overprocessed your pesto and it resembles the homogenous, murky stuff you find in store-bought jars, chop a few extra herbs by hand and stir them in to add texture.

### HOW MUCH SAUCE PER SERVING?

How much you need depends on how you're using the sauce, of course, but 3 to 4 tablespoons per person is average.

### SPECIAL EQUIPMENT

You need a sharp chef's knife and/or a food processor. A mortar and a pestle are fun for emotional reasons, though I don't recommend them. A rasp-type grater will make grating cheese and citrus zest a pleasure. Honestly.

### STORAGE

The pestos are at their peak the moment they are made and up to an hour or so after you make them. If you only know pesto from a jar, you'll taste the difference freshness makes. The other sauces benefit from at least 30 minutes of "marrying time," though it's okay to serve them straightaway. To avoid having to do everything at the last minute, you can measure and chop all of the ingredients other than the herbs and citrus zest up to several hours ahead, and then do the final chopping or processing when you assemble the sauce.

All of these sauces will keep in airtight containers in the refrigerator for up to 3 days. They freeze well, too: put a practical amount, such as ½ cup/120 milliliters (about right for two servings of angel hair pasta, for instance) into a small ziplock freezer bag, push out all of the air, zip closed, and mark with the contents and the date. Put the small bags in a larger freezer bag or container and freeze for up to 3 months. Whenever you need a taste of summer, just reach in and grab a bag. The sauce will thaw quickly at room temperature, or, and depending on the recipe, you can sometimes toss the pesto in frozen. The other sauces don't freeze as well, probably because the relatively high proportion of acid renders the herbs irredeemably flat after thawing.

# A GREAT BASIC PESTO

This is pretty much a regulation pesto, though I include a few more nuts for richness than some cooks do and some grated lemon zest for a bright note. Use a fruity extra-virgin olive oil, but not a powerhouse Tuscan type, which would be too bitter.

The classic destination for basil pesto is trenette or linguine, but I like it on angel hair pasta, too. Scoop out and reserve some of the pasta cooking water before you drain it, and then add a few spoonfuls to the pan as you toss the pasta with the pesto. The starchy cooking water will emulsify the sauce and make it creamy. And pesto has great potential beyond pasta: on grilled vegetables, in sandwiches, swirled into soups, or spooned on baked fish.

3 cups/70 g lightly packed fresh basil leaves

1 to 2 cloves garlic

¼ cup/35 g pine nuts

Kosher salt

½ tsp lightly packed finely grated lemon zest

½ cup/120 ml fruity extra-virgin olive oil

½ cup/55 g grated Parmigiano-Reggiano cheese

In a food processor, combine the basil, garlic, pine nuts, 1 tsp salt, and the lemon zest and pulse a few times to make a coarse purée. With the motor running, slowly pour the oil through the feed tube. Stop processing as soon as all of the oil is blended with the other ingredients. If you want a finer, smoother consistency, continue processing until the pesto looks good to you.

Add the cheese and pulse for another second or two. Taste and add more salt, if you like.

Transfer the pesto to a small bowl, press a piece of plastic wrap directly onto its surface, and refrigerate until you're ready to use it.

**MAKES ABOUT 1 CUP/240 ML**

**STORAGE** This sauce is best if served within the hour, but it can be refrigerated in an airtight container with plastic wrap pressed directly onto its surface for up to 3 days. Or, freeze in one or more ziplock freezer bags for up to 3 months.

**QUICK CHANGE**

Use parsley instead of the basil.

Use almonds, walnuts, or pecans, or a mixture of nuts, instead of the pine nuts.

Use a mix of aged pecorino and Parmigiano-Reggiano.

Omit the cheese for a leaner, grassier pesto.

# A VERY FRENCH PESTO

This pesto includes the traditional *fines herbes* combination of tarragon, parsley, chives, and dill, which gives it a decidedly French feel. It may seem like an unusual addition, but I add butter to this sauce, because it helps to transfer the delicate herbal flavors to whatever I am serving it with.

I like to rub this pesto under the skin of a chicken, slip a lemon half into the bird's cavity, and then roast the chicken. It emerges from the oven tasting like Paris. The pesto also provides a quick and easy way to dress up side dishes: spoon it over steamed new potatoes, fold a few spoonfuls into steamed rice, or drizzle it over broiled or grilled tomato halves.

2 cups/55 g lightly packed fresh flat-leaf parsley leaves

¼ cup/7 g lightly packed fresh tarragon leaves

¼ cup/7 g lightly packed fresh chive lengths (1-in/2.5-cm pieces)

¼ cup/7 g lightly packed fresh dill fronds

¼ cup/35 g pine nuts

Kosher salt

½ tsp lightly packed finely grated lemon zest

½ cup/120 ml fruity extra-virgin olive oil

2 tbsp unsalted butter, at room temperature

¼ cup/30 g grated Parmigiano-Reggiano cheese

**MAKES ABOUT 1 CUP/240 ML**

**STORAGE** This sauce is best if served within the hour, but it can be refrigerated in an airtight container with plastic wrap pressed directly onto its surface for up to 3 days. Or, freeze in one or more ziplock freezer bags for up to 3 months.

**QUICK CHANGE**

Replace ¼ cup/7 g of the parsley leaves with ¼ cup/7 g fresh chervil leaves.

Use almonds or hazelnuts instead of pine nuts.

Omit the cheese for a leaner, grassier pesto.

In a food processor, combine the parsley, tarragon, chives, dill, pine nuts, ¾ tsp salt, and the lemon zest and pulse a few times to make a coarse purée. With the motor running, slowly pour the oil through the feed tube. Stop processing as soon as all of the oil is blended with the other ingredients. If you want a finer, smoother consistency, continue processing until the pesto looks good to you.

Add the butter and cheese and pulse for another second or two. Taste and add more salt, if you like. Transfer the pesto to a small bowl, press a piece of plastic wrap directly onto its surface, and refrigerate until you're ready to use it.

# SPICY CILANTRO–MARCONA ALMOND PESTO

You can find salted, fried Marcona almonds, the flattish almonds from Spain, in many stores these days, but they're not all great quality. Avoid overtoasted Marconas, which will be fairly dark, almost the color of a brown-paper bag, and oily, and choose nuts that are lightly tanned and just faintly glistening with oil.

The Marconas add enough richness and body to this sauce that I leave out the cheese. The flavor of the almonds comes through better and the sauce tastes fresher and greener—an exciting accent to a bean soup (see page 49) or an omelet.

3 cups/60 g lightly packed fresh cilantro leaves and tender stems

1 small jalapeño chile, about 1 oz/30 g, stemmed and seeded

¼ cup/35 g salted, fried Marcona almonds or lightly toasted slivered almonds

1 to 2 small cloves garlic

½ tsp kosher salt

½ tsp lightly packed finely grated lemon zest

½ cup/120 ml fruity extra-virgin olive oil

In a food processor, combine the cilantro, chile, almonds, garlic to taste, salt, and lemon zest and pulse a few times to make a coarse purée. With the motor running, slowly pour the oil through the feed tube. Stop processing as soon as all of the oil is blended with the other ingredients. If you want a finer, smoother consistency, continue processing until the pesto looks good to you.

Transfer the pesto to a small bowl, press a piece of plastic wrap directly onto its surface, and refrigerate until you're ready to use it.

**MAKES ABOUT ¾ CUP/180 ML**

**STORAGE** This sauce is best if served within the hour, but it can be refrigerated in an airtight container with plastic wrap pressed directly onto its surface for up to 3 days. Or, freeze in one or more ziplock freezer bags for up to 3 months.

**QUICK CHANGE**

Use basil instead of cilantro, or use a mix of cilantro and basil.

Omit the chile.

Pulse in ½ cup/55 g grated aged Manchego cheese after adding the oil.

Use toasted pine nuts instead of Marcona almonds.

# PARSLEY-MINT PESTO WITH WALNUTS AND FETA

This pesto has a slightly husky personality from the bold walnuts and assertive fresh mint. I like the way walnuts and feta taste together, but if you're not sure about the combination, hold back and use the feta as a garnish for the sauce.

Walnuts turn rancid easily, so taste them before using them (preferably taste them right in the store—hooray for bulk bins!). Walnut oil isn't cheap, but it is so delicious that you'll find lots of other uses for it (including drizzling it on lentils, on potato and leek soup, on green salads, on steamed green beans). Imported French brands are usually good, and I also like La Tourangelle, a French company that makes a good walnut oil stateside, in California.

This sauce suits sturdy pasta shapes such as penne or orecchiette, but it has great potential for dishes beyond pasta, too. Try it as a dip for pita that has been brushed with olive oil and toasted or grilled; as a finishing sauce for grilled sardines with chunks of ripe tomato and black olives; or stirred into orzo, which is then turned into a bed for grilled lamb chops or kebabs.

2 cups/55 g lightly packed fresh flat-leaf parsley leaves, or 1 cup/30 g each lightly packed parsley and fresh basil leaves if parsley tastes too strong

1 cup/20 g lightly packed fresh mint leaves

½ cup/55 g chopped walnuts

1 small clove garlic

1 tsp lightly packed finely grated lemon zest

Kosher salt

½ cup/120 ml walnut oil

¼ tsp hot-pepper sauce such as Sriracha

¼ cup/30 g crumbled feta cheese (optional)

**MAKES ABOUT 1 CUP/240 ML**

**STORAGE** This sauce is best if served within the hour, but it can be refrigerated in an airtight container with plastic wrap pressed directly onto its surface for up to 3 days. Or, freeze in one or more ziplock freezer bags for up to 3 months.

**QUICK CHANGE**

Add a few fresh dill sprigs with the other herbs to give the pesto a Greek or Turkish flavor.

Use Parmigiano-Reggiano or Manchego cheese instead of feta.

Use extra-virgin olive oil instead of walnut oil.

In a food processor, combine the parsley, mint, walnuts, garlic, lemon zest, and ¾ tsp salt and pulse a few times to make a coarse purée. With the motor running, slowly pour the oil through the feed tube. Stop processing as soon as all of the oil is blended with the other ingredients. If you want a finer, smoother consistency, continue processing until the pesto looks good to you. Add the hot-pepper sauce and pulse two or three times to mix.

If you want to keep things simple, it's okay to omit the feta; the pesto is delicious at this stage. If using the feta, add it and pulse for another second or two. You want the cheese to be in little bits, not completely blended. Taste and add more salt, if you like. Transfer the pesto to a small bowl, press a piece of plastic wrap directly onto its surface, and refrigerate until you're ready to use it.

# SAUCE VIERGE

This herb-based sauce, which you'll see in many permutations, is looser and more tangy and briny than a pesto and doesn't call for cheese. In France, you'll see it called both sauce vierge and sauce verte: *vierge* (virgin) because there's no heat applied to it . . . hmmm . . . and *verte* (green) because it is green, *bien sûr*.

Other cuisines have a similar sauce, so this version is just my mash-up that incorporates a bit of everything. The idea is to go for zing. If you enjoy using a knife (and I hope you do—it's meditative!), you'll love this sauce because you chop everything by hand for the best texture.

⅓ cup/14 g finely chopped fresh flat-leaf parsley

⅓ cup/14 g finely chopped fresh basil

¼ cup/30 g finely chopped pitted buttery green olives such as Cerignola or Castelvetrano

2 tbsp finely chopped cornichon

1 tbsp minced shallot or onion

1 tbsp drained capers, coarsely chopped

2 tsp minced fresh hot chile such as jalapeño

1 tsp lightly packed finely grated lemon zest

6 olive oil–packed anchovy fillets (see ingredient note, page 27), drained and minced

1 small clove garlic, minced

¾ cup/180 ml extra-virgin olive oil

1 tbsp fresh lemon juice, or more if needed

1 tbsp fresh lime juice, or more if needed

Kosher salt and freshly ground black pepper

**MAKES ABOUT 1⅓ CUPS/315 ML**

**STORAGE** This sauce is best if served within the hour, but it can be refrigerated in an airtight container for up to 2 days. This sauce doesn't freeze well.

**QUICK CHANGE**

Fold in ½ cup/85 g peeled, seeded, and finely diced tomato.

Add some fresh mint and/or tarragon with the other herbs.

Add some finely chopped hard-cooked egg just before serving.

Swap out the fresh chile for a pickled pepperoncino.

In a bowl, toss together the parsley, basil, olives, cornichon, shallot, capers, chile, lemon zest, anchovies, and garlic. Stir in the olive oil, and then stir in the lemon and lime juices.

Taste and add enough salt to make the sauce highly savory (the amount added will depend on the saltiness of your other ingredients) and season with several grinds of pepper. Let the sauce rest at room temperature for 30 minutes to allow the flavors to develop, then taste and adjust the seasoning again with salt, pepper, and the citrus juices if needed. Refrigerate until you're ready to use it.

# FRAGRANT CHARMOULA

This aromatic fresh herb sauce has roots in North African cooking, but I've added some sweetness and smoke with a little honey and smoked paprika—nontraditional but delicious additions. I have also used Aleppo chile, which adds moderate heat and a pleasant fruitiness.

2 to 3 cloves garlic

1 tbsp Spanish sweet smoked paprika (see ingredient note, page 24) or Hungarian sweet paprika

1½ tsp ground cumin

Kosher salt

¼ tsp coarsely ground Aleppo chile (see ingredient note), or a few dashes of hot-pepper sauce such as Sriracha

2 cups/55 g lightly packed fresh flat-leaf parsley leaves

2 cups/40 g lightly packed fresh cilantro leaves

½ cup/120 ml extra-virgin olive oil

⅓ cup/75 ml fresh lemon juice

1 tsp lightly packed finely grated lemon zest

1 tbsp honey

**MAKES 1 CUP/240 ML**

**STORAGE** Refrigerate in an air-tight container for up to 4 days. This sauce doesn't freeze well.

**QUICK CHANGE**

Include a few fresh mint leaves in the mix.

Add 1 tsp sherry vinegar along with the lemon juice.

Use fresh orange juice and zest instead of lemon.

Add 2 tsp minced preserved lemon after adding the oil.

In a food processor, combine the garlic to taste, paprika, cumin, 1 tsp salt, and Aleppo chile and pulse to mince the seasonings. Add the parsley and cilantro and pulse until roughly chopped. Do not purée the ingredients. Add the olive oil, lemon juice, lemon zest, and honey and pulse to blend. Taste and adjust the seasoning with salt if needed. Let the sauce sit for about 15 minutes so the flavors can marry.

**INGREDIENT NOTE:** *The Aleppo chile is a fruity, fragrant, moderately hot pepper that originated in Syria and is now grown in Syria and Turkey. It is dried and sold coarsely ground. I like this chile because its heat level doesn't overpower its other flavors.*

# CHIMICHURRI, IN SPIRIT

Traditional *salsa chimichurri* comes from Argentina. The base is parsley, and oregano or mint is added to amp up the herbal flavors. Instead of using nuts or cheese for richness, as with a pesto, *chimichurri* usually has some husky-hot spice notes from cumin, hot-pepper sauce, or red pepper flakes, and a ton of tanginess from red wine vinegar. It's a fairly assertive sauce, so I like serving it with meat or grilled chicken. It's a classic partner for grilled steak, but it's delightful on a grilled hamburger, too.

1 cup/30 g lightly packed fresh flat-leaf parsley leaves

1 cup/20 g lightly packed fresh cilantro leaves and tender stems

1-in/2.5-cm chunk of shallot (¾ oz/20 g)

¼ cup/60 ml sherry vinegar, or more if needed

2 small cloves garlic

½ tsp dried oregano

½ tsp cumin seeds, lightly toasted in a dry skillet until fragrant, or ¼ tsp ground cumin

Kosher salt

½ cup/120 ml extra-virgin olive oil

**MAKES 1 CUP/240 ML**

**STORAGE** Refrigerate in an airtight container for up to 5 days. The sauce does not freeze well.

**QUICK CHANGE**

Omit the cilantro and use all parsley leaves.

Add 1 small jalapeño chile, stemmed and seeded, with the herbs.

Stir in finely diced red bell pepper at the end.

In a food processor, combine the parsley, cilantro, shallot, vinegar, garlic, oregano, cumin, and 1 tsp salt and pulse a few times to make a coarse purée. With the motor running, slowly pour the oil through the feed tube. Stop processing as soon as all of the oil is blended with the other ingredients. Taste and adjust with salt, if needed, and with vinegar to bring the sauce up to the edge of pungency. If time permits, let the flavors marry for at least 30 minutes at room temperature before serving.

# CRESPELLE with PESTO, RICOTTA, and ARUGULA SALAD

A tender crepe spread with fragrant pesto and milky ricotta, topped with a tangle of spicy arugula salad, and rolled up is a beautiful way to start off a summer dinner party. And if you serve each guest two crepes (called *crespelle* in Italian), you have a light main course. Any fresh salad green will do as long as it's supple enough to be rolled up inside the crepe.

You can make the crepes up to 4 hours ahead, stack them on a plate, cover with plastic wrap, and keep at room temperature. Or, you can make the crepes a day ahead, stack and wrap them on the plate, and refrigerate overnight. Reheat the crepes in a 350°F/180°C/gas 4 oven for 10 minutes or for a few seconds in the microwave on medium power before filling.

## CREPES

¾ cup/180 ml whole milk, plus more if needed

2 large eggs

¼ tsp kosher salt

¾ cup/90 g all-purpose flour

2½ tbsp unsalted butter, melted, plus more for the pan

1 bunch arugula (about 5 oz/140 g), thick stems trimmed

Extra-virgin olive oil and fresh lemon juice for dressing salad

Kosher salt and freshly ground black pepper

1 cup/240 ml pesto of choice (see pages 39–42)

½ cup/115 g fresh whole-milk ricotta cheese

**SERVES 8 AS A FIRST COURSE OR 4 AS A MAIN COURSE**

**TO MAKE THE CREPES,** in a blender, combine the milk, eggs, and salt and whiz for a few seconds to blend everything together. Add the flour and whiz until very smooth, about 20 seconds. Pour in the butter and whiz until combined, about 10 seconds more.

Transfer the batter to a large glass measuring cup or a bowl with a spout (or a bowl into which you can easily dip a ¼-cup/60-ml measuring cup or ladle). Let the batter rest for at least 30 minutes, or cover and refrigerate for up to 24 hours. When you are ready to make the crepes, test its consistency: the batter should be as thick as heavy cream, not as thick as pancake batter. If it is too thick, whisk in more milk.

Heat a crepe pan, nonstick frying pan, or well-seasoned frying pan with an 8-in/20-cm base over medium-high heat until a drop of water flicked onto the surface sizzles on contact. Using a folded paper towel, spread about ½ tsp butter around the interior of the pan. The butter should sizzle on contact, but you don't want the pan so hot that the butter burns.

Pour about ¼ cup/60 ml of the batter into the center of the pan. As you pour, lift the pan from the heat and tilt and turn it in all directions so the batter spreads evenly across the bottom of the pan in a thin circle. If the crepe has any holes in it, quickly add a few drops of batter to fill them in. Or, if you have too much batter and the crepe looks too thick, immediately pour the excess back into the measuring cup or bowl. You can always trim off the "tail" that's left behind.

Cook the crepe until the edges begin to dry and lift from the edge of the pan and the bottom is nicely browned, about 1 minute. To check for color, use a table knife, thin offset spatula, or your fingers to lift up an edge of the crepe and look underneath. When the first side is ready, use the knife, spatula, or your fingers to lift the crepe and quickly flip it over. Smooth out any folded edges or pleats, then cook until the center is firm and the second side is browned, about 20 seconds more.

*continued . . .*

Slide the crepe from the pan onto a large plate or cooling rack. Repeat with the remaining batter, adjusting the heat and spreading the pan with more butter as you cook. As each crepe is finished, stack it on top of the previous one. You should end up with 8 crepes. The crepes will soften as they cool.

In a large bowl, toss the arugula with a little olive oil, lemon juice, salt, and pepper, dressing the greens lightly.

Spread a generous layer of pesto onto the center of each crepe, top with a few small dollops of the ricotta, and then with a little of the arugula. Roll up loosely and place seam-side down on a plate. Or, roll the crepe with the pesto and ricotta and dress with a handful of the salad on top. When all of the crepes are assembled, serve right away.

# BEAN SOUP with SPICY CILANTRO–MARCONA ALMOND PESTO

This is my all-purpose bean soup recipe. It's wonderfully versatile and loves to be adapted to whatever you have on hand. I like the sweet earthiness of pinto beans paired with the bright-flavored cilantro pesto, but white or black beans would be nice, too, or try one of the many interesting heirloom varieties.

The cooking time for beans can range dramatically depending on age and variety, so give yourself plenty of time and cook them just until you're happy with their tenderness. And don't worry that I call for salt to be added early in the cooking process. I know that many cooks believe that salt prevents the beans from softening, but in fact, it's acidic ingredients, not salt, that have that effect, which is why the tomatoes go into the pot near the end of cooking.

1 lb/455 g dried pinto beans, picked over for debris

3 tbsp extra-virgin olive oil

1 small yellow onion, peeled and cut into ¼-in/6-mm dice

2 leeks (white and tender green parts only), chopped

2 celery stalks, cut into ¼-in/6-mm dice

1 large carrot, peeled and cut into ¼-in/6-mm dice

2 small cloves garlic, finely chopped

4 cups/960 ml homemade turkey broth (see page 165), chicken broth, or canned reduced-sodium chicken broth

2 bay leaves

3 large fresh thyme sprigs

Kosher salt

1 cup/240 ml water

One 14-oz/400-g can crushed tomatoes

Hot-pepper sauce such as Sriracha

½ to ¾ cup/120 to 180 ml Spicy Cilantro–Marcona Almond Pesto (page 41)

In a large pot, combine the beans with water to cover by at least 2 in/5 cm. Bring to a boil over high heat, remove from the heat, cover, and let sit for at least 1 hour. When it's time to cook the soup, drain and rinse the beans.

In a large, heavy pot or Dutch oven, heat the oil over medium-high heat. Add the onion, leeks, celery, and carrot and cook, stirring occasionally, until the vegetables are soft, about 10 minutes. Do not allow them to brown.

Add the drained beans, garlic, broth, bay leaves, thyme, 1 tsp salt, and the water and bring to a boil. Reduce the heat to maintain an active simmer, cover, and cook until the beans are very tender, 2 to 3 hours, depending on the age of the beans. Add more water as needed to keep them nicely covered.

Remove and discard the bay leaves, then add the tomatoes and continue to simmer uncovered, stirring occasionally, for 15 to 20 minutes longer to blend the flavors.

Transfer about half of the soup to a blender and purée until smooth. (If you have an immersion blender, you can half-purée the soup in the pot.) Return the purée to the pot and add water as needed to adjust the consistency of the soup to your liking. Season with the hot-pepper sauce, then taste and adjust the seasoning with salt if needed. Heat until piping hot.

Ladle the soup into warmed soup bowls. Top each bowl with about 2 tbsp of the pesto, and then run the tip of a paring knife through the pesto to swirl it a bit. Serve right away.

SERVES 4 TO 6

# ROASTED CAULIFLOWER with SAUCE VIERGE

Talk about a transformation. Starting point: pale, crumbly, bland raw cauliflower (my apologies to any grocery-store salad bar designers). Process: toss with olive oil and roast for 20 minutes. End result: golden, moist-chewy, sweet cauliflower that you never dreamed was possible. Roasting is the best method for this vegetable, and drizzling with a sprightly green sauce just makes things better.

2 heads cauliflower (1¼ lb/570 g each), cored and cut into 1½-in/4-cm florets

⅓ cup/75 ml extra-virgin olive oil

1 tbsp chopped fresh thyme or lemon thyme

Kosher salt and freshly ground black pepper

⅓ to ½ cup/75 to 120 ml Sauce Vierge (page 43)

Heat the oven to 425°F/220°C/gas 7.

Don't worry if when you cut the cauliflower into florets, you end up with a few smaller ones. They will create delicious crispy bits. In a large bowl, toss the cauliflower with the olive oil and thyme and season generously with salt and pepper. Spread the cauliflower on one or two large rimmed baking sheets.

Roast until the florets are tender, collapsed, and golden brown on their cut faces and around the edges, at least 20 minutes and possibly longer. The darker the cauliflower the better it will taste (short of burnt, of course).

Pile the cauliflower into a warmed serving bowl and drizzle generously with the sauce. Serve warm or at room temperature.

**SERVES 4 TO 6 AS A SIDE DISH**

# COUSCOUS with BRAISED VEGETABLES in CHARMOULA

On a night when you discover you don't have much in the fridge other than odds and ends, this recipe will make you happy. I like making it with the mix of vegetables given here, but you can use just about anything you have on hand. I always keep couscous and canned chickpeas in the pantry, and the charmoula sauce is also mostly pantry ingredients, plus, of course, the fresh herbs. If you want to add some protein, grilled tofu, sausages, or skewers of chicken-thigh chunks would be lovely.

4 tbsp/60 ml extra-virgin olive oil

8 oz/225 g Yukon Gold or red waxy potatoes, peeled and cut into 1-in/2.5-cm chunks

1 small sweet potato, peeled and cut into 1-in/2.5-cm chunks

Kosher salt and freshly ground black pepper

1 red bell pepper, stemmed, seeded, and cut lengthwise into strips ½ in/12 mm wide

1 Anaheim or other large, mild green chile, stemmed, seeded, and cut into ½-in/12-mm dice

8 oz/225 g cauliflower florets (about ½ small cauliflower)

2 small tomatoes, cored and cut into ½-in/12-mm dice

One 14-oz/400-g can chickpeas, rinsed and drained

1½ cups/360 ml water

¾ cup/180 ml Fragrant Charmoula (page 44)

1 cup/170 g couscous

Plain yogurt for serving

In a large frying pan, heat 1 tbsp of the olive oil over medium-high heat. Add the potatoes and sweet potato, sprinkle with salt and pepper, reduce the heat to medium, and cook, undisturbed, until well browned on the first side, about 2 minutes (they'll stick if you try to turn them too soon). Flip the potatoes to another side and cook again, undisturbed. Continue to flip and cook undisturbed until nicely browned on all sides, 8 to 10 minutes longer. Transfer to a bowl.

Add 2 tbsp of the oil to the pan and return to medium-high heat. Add the bell pepper and chile. Sprinkle lightly with salt and pepper and cook, stirring often, until lightly browned and starting to soften, 3 to 4 minutes.

Return the potatoes and sweet potato to the pan, add the cauliflower, tomatoes, and chickpeas, and sprinkle lightly with salt and pepper. Stir to combine the vegetables and then add ½ cup/120 ml of the water. Cover, adjust the heat to maintain a nice simmer, and cook, stirring occasionally, until all of the vegetables are tender, 12 to 15 minutes. If a lot of liquid remains in the pan once the vegetables are tender, uncover the pan, increase the heat to medium-high, and let the liquid boil off for a minute, taking care not to burn the vegetables.

Turn off the heat and gently fold in the sauce. Season with salt and pepper and keep warm while you make the couscous.

In a saucepan, bring the remaining 1 cup/240 ml water to a boil over high heat. Stir in the couscous and ½ tsp salt, then remove the pan from the heat. Cover and let sit undisturbed until the couscous has absorbed the water and is tender, about 5 minutes. Fluff the couscous with a fork, drizzle it with the remaining 1 tbsp oil, and fluff again.

Pile a mound of couscous in the center of each dinner plate (or wide, shallow bowl), ladle the vegetables on top, and serve with a dollop of yogurt.

SERVES 4 TO 6

# TOMATO SAUCES

TOMATOES MIGHT POSSIBLY BE THE MOST PERFECT INGREDIENT—beautiful and shapely, with a flavor that's both bright and deep, savory and sweet, clean and rich, subtle and sassy. And most important (especially for this book), tomatoes make brilliant sauces.

You can emphasize different aspects of a tomato's character with different cooking methods, so that's how I have structured the recipes in this chapter. Three kinds of tomato sauces are here: fresh, canned, and roasted.

For fresh tomato sauce, I cook the tomatoes quickly over high heat, without a lot of other ingredients, to keep their vivacious flavor intact. This method depends on good tomatoes with lots of flavor and acid, so I use cherry tomatoes, which I feel are reliably tasty and bright.

Canned tomatoes are not an inferior second choice to fresh tomatoes. On the contrary, canned tomatoes have lots of virtues, an obvious one being that they are always available. And they're already peeled! Most of the tomato sauces in this chapter are made with canned tomatoes.

Roasting tomatoes concentrates their flavors and caramelizes their flesh. That translates to sauces with a deep flavor and lush texture and a big hit of umami. When tomatoes are roasted, they cook down a lot, which means that you need a lot of tomatoes to produce a small amount of sauce, so I only roast tomatoes for sauces at the height of tomato season when there are plenty to be had at a good price or in my garden.

### WHAT'S GOING ON IN THIS SAUCE?

It's important to know that the amount of sugar, acid, moisture, and other flavor compounds is different in every tomato, and that will make a difference in every tomato sauce you make. You'll find dramatic variation among fresh tomato varieties, seasons, and sources. Even canned Italian tomatoes that carry the San Marzano DOP label, indicating they're grown within a designated region in southern Italy, can be quite different from can to can. Sometimes they're fat, red, and meaty, and other times they're stringy, pale, and have a hard, white stem end. Although finding a canned brand you like and trust can mitigate the mood swings, it's most important to learn to deal with these differences once you're in the kitchen.

Another key to tomato sauce, be it fresh, canned, or roasted, is knowing when to stop cooking it. Two important things are happening when you simmer any tomato sauce: One, the tomato flesh is softening and breaking down so the sauce is becoming smoother. Two, the water in the tomatoes is evaporating so the flavors are concentrating, taking the sauce from where it just tastes like tomato to where it tastes like essence of tomato, or the beau ideal of tomato. The only way you'll know when to stop cooking is by tasting as you go.

The third challenge with these sauces is finding a good balance among sweet, acid, and savory. You'll notice that all of my recipes call for a final tinkering with lemon juice, sugar, salt, and sometimes Worcestershire sauce to dial in the perfect tension among these flavors.

### WHAT CAN GO WRONG AND HOW CAN I FIX IT?

The biggest problem you'll run into with tomato sauces is a lack of flavor in the tomatoes themselves. Generally, a little more cooking, whether in the saucepan or in the oven (for roasted tomatoes), can concentrate whatever flavor you do have into a delicious sauce. Adjusting the flavor of the finished sauce with lemon and/or sugar, as mentioned previously, is also helpful. But in some cases, you may need to add a tablespoon or two of tomato paste; having a tube of imported tomato paste in the refrigerator means you're armed for the situation. Sometimes I even add a little orange juice and orange zest, which brings both lively acidity and a sweet fruitiness that harmonizes well with the tomatoes. And finally, as with many things, a generous glug of good-quality extra-virgin olive oil can fix a lot of problems.

### HOW MUCH SAUCE PER SERVING?

The amount you use depends on how you're using the sauce, of course, but you will probably use about ½ cup/ 120 milliliters per person.

### SPECIAL EQUIPMENT

Although the image in the movies is of grandma stirring a tall pot of red sauce, I like to make these sauces in a shorter pan with a wide surface area, which encourages evaporation and speeds up cooking. I use a deep, 12-inch/ 30.5-centimeter sauté pan, but a wide Dutch oven, large saucepan, or a rondeau (a wide, shallow pot with straight 4-inch/10-centimeter sides) would work as well. No matter what you use, aim for a pan with a heavy base to avoid hot spots where the sauce might stick and burn. For the roasted-tomato sauces, you need a rimmed baking sheet, a blender or food processor, and a fine-mesh sieve.

### STORAGE

Sauces made from fresh tomatoes are best when eaten just after you have made them. But you can refrigerate the canned and roasted-tomato sauces for a good week or freeze them for up to 3 months. I like to make a huge batch and divvy it up into 3-cup/720-milliliter portions in freezer bags (that's a good amount for a meal for my family of three, with leftovers).

# FLASH-SAUTÉED FRESH CHERRY TOMATO SAUCE

I'm a big fan of cherry tomatoes because you can find reliably flavorful ones even in wintertime. I think the best selection for this sauce is a mix of fruity and sweet orange Sun Golds (my favorite tomato; I plant about a dozen bushes every year) and a basic red cherry. You could make this sauce with chunks of larger tomatoes, too, but only if they're brightly acidic, the way even ho-hum cherry tomatoes tend to be. This sauce is a pleasure simply tossed with penne and a handful of grated Parmigiano-Reggiano. But it's also delicious on grilled polenta or grilled fish. My favorite destination for this sauce is the angel hair dish on page 64.

3 tbsp extra-virgin olive oil

2 tbsp minced, seeded jalapeño, serrano, or other fresh hot chile or *pepperoncino*

Kosher salt

5 cups/800 g ripe cherry tomatoes, stemmed and halved if large

1 clove garlic, minced

1 tsp lightly packed finely grated lemon zest

1 tsp fresh lemon juice, plus more if needed

3 tbsp chopped fresh flat-leaf parsley, basil, mint, or a mixture

1 tsp unsalted butter

**MAKES ABOUT 2½ CUPS/600 ML**

**STORAGE** This sauce loses its vibrancy after a few hours, so use it as soon as possible after making it.

**QUICK CHANGE** Add 1 tbsp drained capers or chopped, pitted green olives with the garlic.

In a large sauté pan, heat the oil over medium-high heat. Add the chile and ½ tsp salt and cook, stirring often, until soft and fragrant, 2 to 3 minutes. Add the tomatoes and cook, stirring often, until they begin to burst and release their juice, 4 to 6 minutes. Add the garlic and cook for another 30 seconds or so, then stir in the lemon zest and juice. Remove the pan from the heat, add the parsley and butter, and swirl the pan to blend them into the sauce. Taste and balance the seasoning with salt and lemon juice if needed. Serve right away.

# GOOD AND VERSATILE MARINARA SAUCE

I love this sauce on its own merits, but I love it doubly because it's a great base for lots of other sauces, which is why I usually make a double or triple batch and freeze the excess. That way, I can defrost a bag and be more than halfway to a rich meat sauce, savory mushroom sauce, or vivacious sauce laced with olives, capers, and anchovies. (I share these recipes on the following pages.) Plus, I'm well on my way to assembling a lasagna or other sauce-rich dish. A freezer loaded with a stack of tightly sealed bags of this sauce makes me feel equipped to handle anything life may throw at me.

½ cup/120 ml extra-virgin olive oil

1½ cups/225 g finely chopped yellow onions

½ cup/85 g coarsely grated or finely chopped, peeled carrot

¼ cup/40 g coarsely grated or finely chopped celery

Kosher salt

1 large clove garlic, minced

Two 28-oz/800-g cans crushed tomatoes

¼ cup/10 g thinly sliced fresh basil leaves, chopped fresh flat-leaf parsley, or a mixture

¼ tsp hot-pepper sauce such as Sriracha

Pinch of granulated sugar, if needed

Fresh lemon juice, if needed

**MAKES ABOUT 6 CUPS/1.4 L**

**STORAGE** Refrigerate in an airtight container for up to 1 week or freeze in one or more ziplock freezer bags for up to 3 months.

**QUICK CHANGE**

Add 1 cup/160 g finely chopped fennel with the onion, carrot, and celery.

Stir in ¼ cup/30 g grated Parmigiano-Reggiano cheese and 2 tbsp unsalted butter at the end of cooking.

In a large, wide, heavy saucepan or large, deep sauté pan, heat the oil over medium heat. Add the onions, carrot, celery, and ½ tsp salt and cook, stirring occasionally, until soft, fragrant, and lightly golden, 10 to 15 minutes. Add the garlic and cook for another 30 seconds or so (don't let it brown). Add the tomatoes and herbs and bring the tomatoes to a simmer. Reduce the heat to maintain a low simmer and cook uncovered, stirring every once in a while, until the sauce is reduced, glistening with oil, and concentrated in flavor. Taste as you go. It should take between 30 and 40 minutes. Add the hot-pepper sauce, then taste and adjust the flavor balance, if needed, with sugar and with more salt and lemon juice.

# BOLD AND SPICY TOMATO SAUCE

This recipe is inspired by puttanesca sauce, which, according to many sources, was a dish that Neapolitan prostitutes in the mid-twentieth century served to their customers. Is that true or just legend? I have no idea, but I know it's not that backstory that would tempt me to make the sauce. I prefer to emphasize all of its zesty, bold, and briny elements. Serve the sauce with pasta; spoon some sauce into a baking dish, nestle cod or halibut fillets in it, and bake; or grill pita or other flat bread and top it with the sauce.

You can customize the sauce as you like. I can't handle more than a modicum of chile heat, so I've been cautious here. But if you can stand the fire, add more chile than the recipe calls for. If you like tangy flavors, add more olives, and for more salt and umami, increase the amount of anchovies. About those anchovies: Please don't skip them unless you're a vegetarian. They add so much to this—and any—dish.

2 tbsp extra-virgin olive oil

10 olive oil–packed anchovy fillets (see ingredient note, page 27), drained

1 tsp lightly packed finely minced Calabrian or other hot chile in oil

6 cups/1.4 L Good and Versatile Marinara Sauce (facing page)

1½ cups/170 g chopped, pitted Kalamata olives

¼ cup/50 g coarsely chopped, drained capers

½ cup /20 g coarsely chopped fresh flat-leaf parsley

½ tsp lightly packed finely grated lemon zest

Kosher salt and freshly ground black pepper

**MAKES ABOUT 7 CUPS/1.6 L**

**STORAGE** Refrigerate in an airtight container for up to 1 week or freeze in one or more ziplock freezer bags for up to 3 months.

**QUICK CHANGE**

Use basil instead of parsley.

Add a few chopped leaves of mint and/or oregano with the parsley.

Add chopped, cooked guanciale or pancetta with the marinara sauce.

Use pepperoncino instead of, or in addition to, the hot chile in oil.

Add one or two 6-oz/170-g cans good-quality olive oil–packed tuna, drained and flaked, with the marinara sauce.

In a large, wide, heavy saucepan or a Dutch oven, heat the oil over medium heat. Add the anchovies and chiles and cook, stirring once or twice, until slightly sizzling, about 30 seconds. Add the marinara sauce, olives, and capers and cook, stirring often, until heated through and the flavors have blended, about 10 minutes. Stir in the parsley and lemon zest. Taste and adjust the seasoning with salt and/or pepper (you probably won't need either).

# VERY MUSHROOMY PORCINI TOMATO SAUCE

The term *umami* describes the so-called fifth flavor, a deep meatiness that we all crave whether we eat meat or not (sweet, sour, salty, and bitter are the other four flavors), and I've developed this sauce to highlight that character. Tomatoes are naturally rich in umami (due to the presence of glutamic acid), dried porcini are like little engines of umami, and Worcestershire sauce is like liquid umami. In other words, this sauce is savory.

If you want to make it vegetarian, skip the Worcestershire sauce (most brands contain anchovies). It's excellent with lighter, sweeter partners, such as butternut squash–filled ravioli, or layered with lasagna noodles and ricotta mixed with lemon zest and lots of fresh parsley, dill, and chives. It is also good spooned over creamy polenta made with a generous measure of Parmigiano-Reggiano and Cheddar (yes, I know, Cheddar isn't Italian, but it's so good in polenta).

1½ cups/360 ml red wine (nothing too oaky or tannic)

1 oz/30 g dried porcini mushrooms, rinsed if dusty

2 tbsp extra-virgin olive oil

2 tbsp unsalted butter

1 lb/455 g white or cremini mushrooms, trimmed and finely chopped

Kosher salt

About 12 turns freshly ground black pepper

6 cups/1.4 L Good and Versatile Marinara Sauce (page 56)

1 tsp fresh thyme leaves

1 tsp fresh lemon juice, plus more if needed

1 tsp Worcestershire sauce, plus more if needed (omit to make this vegetarian)

Hot-pepper sauce such as Sriracha

Pinch of granulated sugar, if needed

**MAKES ABOUT 7 CUPS/1.6 L**

**STORAGE** Refrigerate in an airtight container for up to 1 week or freeze in one or more ziplock freezer bags for up to 3 months.

**QUICK CHANGE** Use fresh chanterelle, oyster, maitake, or shiitake mushrooms instead of the cremini; if using shiitakes, reduce the amount to 8 oz/225 g, as they have a strong flavor.

In a small saucepan, combine the wine and porcini and bring to a simmer over medium-high heat. Remove from the heat and let sit until the mushrooms are soft, at least 30 minutes. Scoop out the mushrooms, squeeze out as much wine as you can, chop the mushrooms fine, and set aside. Return the wine to medium-high heat and simmer until reduced to 2 to 3 tbsp, 10 to 15 minutes. Set aside.

In a large, heavy saucepan or Dutch oven, heat the oil and butter over medium-high heat. When the butter melts, add the fresh mushrooms, ½ tsp salt, and the pepper and cook, stirring often, until the mushroom liquid has been released and has evaporated and the mushrooms are fragrant and starting to brown, 12 to 15 minutes.

Add the marinara sauce, the reserved porcini, the reduced wine, the thyme, lemon juice, and Worcestershire sauce and stir well. Adjust the heat to maintain a simmer and cook, stirring occasionally, until the sauce is slightly reduced and the flavor is deep and savory, 25 to 35 minutes. Season with hot-pepper sauce, then taste and adjust the flavor balance, if needed, with sugar and with more salt, lemon juice, and Worcestershire sauce.

# VERY MEATY TOMATO SAUCE

I envy Italian families who spend Sundays around the table eating pasta dressed with long-simmered meaty ragu. It's not the family part I envy—I like my own (though we'd more likely have been eating ham sandwiches on white bread . . . ), but I long for the deep savoriness of hunks of meat simmered in tomato sauce. In this recipe, I think I get to that same savory place, but in less time and with no Italian heritage required. The key is three types of meat: pancetta for salty-fattiness, Italian sausage for more pork and fennel notes, and ground beef for sweetness and texture. A final dose of Worcestershire pulls it together.

4 oz/115 g sliced pancetta, cut into 1-in/2.5-cm pieces

1 tbsp extra-virgin olive oil

8 oz/225 g sweet Italian sausage, casings removed if using link sausage

8 oz/225 g ground beef

6 cups/1.4 L Good and Versatile Marinara Sauce (page 56)

1¾ cups/420 ml homemade turkey broth (see page 165), chicken broth, or canned reduced-sodium chicken broth

1 fresh rosemary sprig, 4 in/10 cm long

1 bay leaf

1 tsp Worcestershire sauce, plus more if needed

1 tsp granulated sugar, plus more if needed

Hot-pepper sauce such as Sriracha

Kosher salt

MAKES ABOUT 8 CUPS/2 L

**STORAGE** Refrigerate in an airtight container for up to 1 week or freeze in one or more ziplock freezer bags for up to 3 months.

**QUICK CHANGE**

Add a few red pepper flakes with the sausage and beef.

Add 2 tbsp each chopped fresh basil and flat-leaf parsley when you add the marinara sauce.

Omit the pancetta, use ground turkey and turkey sausage instead of ground beef and Italian sausage, and increase the olive oil to 3 tbsp.

Freeze the pancetta until mostly solid, then pulse in a food processor until ground.

In a large, wide, heavy saucepan or a Dutch oven, heat the oil over medium-high heat. Add the ground pancetta and cook, stirring occasionally, until the fat is rendered and the pancetta is golden but not browned, 4 to 5 minutes. Add the sausage and beef and cook, breaking up the meat with a wooden spoon or spatula, until the pink is gone (don't let the meat brown or get crusty), 3 to 4 minutes. If there is a lot of fat, pour some off, but leave a nice amount (2 to 3 tbsp), which will make the sauce more flavorful.

Stir in the marinara sauce, broth, rosemary, bay leaf, and Worcestershire sauce. Cover, reduce the heat to maintain a simmer, and cook, stirring and scraping the pan fairly frequently, for about 45 minutes.

Uncover and continue to simmer until the sauce is slightly reduced, very concentrated, and glistening with oil, another few minutes. Stir in the sugar and a few drops of hot-pepper sauce. Taste and adjust the flavor balance, if needed, with salt, sugar, Worcestershire sauce, and hot-pepper sauce.

# LAMB AND FRAGRANT SPICES SAUCE

The bright acidity of tomato sauce is a perfect foil for the rich sweetness of lamb. I keep the sweet-tangy balance finely tuned with lemon juice, vinegar, and sugar. This sauce is wonderful on grilled eggplant, penne topped with chunks of feta, or on top of brown rice.

4 tbsp/60 ml extra-virgin olive oil

1½ lb/680 g ground lamb

Kosher salt

½ yellow onion, very thinly sliced

3 to 4 cloves garlic, finely chopped

1 tsp Spanish sweet smoked paprika (see ingredient note, page 24)

1 tsp ground cumin

½ tsp ground cinnamon

½ tsp ground allspice

6 cups/1.4 L Good and Versatile Marinara Sauce (page 56)

1¾ cups/420 ml homemade turkey broth (see page 165) or chicken broth

1 tsp fresh lemon juice, plus more if needed

1 tsp balsamic vinegar, plus more if needed

1 tsp granulated sugar, plus more if needed

Hot-pepper sauce such as Sriracha

¼ cup/10 g coarsely chopped fresh flat-leaf parsley

¼ cup/7 g coarsely chopped fresh mint

**MAKES 8 CUPS/2 L**

**STORAGE** Refrigerate in an airtight container for up to 1 week or freeze in one or more ziplock bags for up to 3 months.

**QUICK CHANGE**

Add 8 oz/225 g merguez sausage, crumbled, along with the lamb.

Add ½ cup/55 g chopped, pitted black olives with the marinara sauce.

Add 1 cup/225 g diced roasted red bell pepper with the marinara sauce.

In a large, wide, heavy pan, heat 1 tbsp of the oil over medium-high heat. Add the lamb and ½ tsp salt, and cook, breaking up the meat with a spatula, until the pink is gone (don't let the meat brown), 3 to 4 minutes. Transfer the lamb to a fine-mesh sieve to drain off excess fat.

Return the pan to medium-high heat and heat the remaining 3 tbsp oil. Add the onion and cook, stirring often, until beginning to soften, 3 to 4 minutes. Reduce the heat to medium and continue cooking, stirring and scraping frequently, until the onion starts to turn golden, 5 to 7 minutes. Add the garlic, paprika, cumin, cinnamon, and allspice and cook, stirring, until fragrant, another 30 seconds.

Stir in the marinara sauce, broth, and cooked lamb. Cover, reduce the heat to maintain a simmer, and cook, stirring and scraping the pan fairly frequently, for about 45 minutes. Uncover and simmer until the sauce is slightly reduced, very concentrated, and glistening with oil, another few minutes. Stir in the lemon juice, vinegar, sugar, and a few drops of hot-pepper sauce. Taste and adjust the flavor balance, if needed. Stir in the parsley and mint.

# RICH ROASTED-TOMATO SAUCE

It takes a lot of tomatoes to make a moderate amount of roasted-tomato sauce, so make this sauce during the summer when tomatoes are at their peak and less costly. Don't use picture-perfect tomatoes, however. Save those for caprese salads, BLTs, and the like. I ask one of the farmers at my local market to sell me his seconds (the less-than-perfect specimens), and he does so at a great price, so every few weeks in early September I roast a half bushel for sauce. Then I congratulate myself all winter long as I use this intensely flavored sauce on polenta and pasta, with shrimp or crab, or even as the base for tomato soup.

5 lb/2.3 kg fresh ripe tomatoes, cored and halved

6 tbsp/90 ml extra-virgin olive oil

Kosher salt

2 tsp coarsely chopped fresh rosemary, thyme, or a mixture (optional)

2 cloves garlic, minced

⅛ tsp red pepper flakes

1 cup/240 ml homemade turkey broth (see page 165), chicken or vegetable broth, or canned reduced-sodium chicken or vegetable broth

1 tsp fresh lemon juice, plus more if needed

½ tsp granulated sugar, plus more if needed

Hot-pepper sauce such as Sriracha

**MAKES ABOUT 3½ CUPS/840 ML**

**STORAGE** Refrigerate in an air-tight container for up to 1 week or freeze in one or more ziplock freezer bags for up to 3 months.

**QUICK CHANGE** Add ¼ to ⅓ cup/60 to 75 ml crème fraîche or heavy cream and 2 tbsp vodka to the sauce near the end of cooking.

Heat the oven to 350°F/180°C/gas 4.

Arrange the tomatoes, cut-side up, on a large rimmed baking sheet. Don't use a rimless sheet pan (a cookie sheet), because the tomatoes will release a lot of juice. A glass baking dish or metal baking pan works well, too. You should be able to fit all of the tomatoes in a single layer on a half sheet pan (13 by 18 in/ 33 by 46 cm). If you need to use two pans, that's fine. But if there is too much space between the tomatoes, their juices will burn, so aim for a cozy fit. The tomatoes will shrink as they cook.

Drizzle about ¼ cup/60 ml of the oil over the tomatoes, then sprinkle on some salt and the herbs (if using). Roast the tomatoes until collapsed, shrunken, concentrated, and just beginning to brown on their undersides and around the edges. The pulp of the tomato should still be very soft and the skin should be slightly chewy. You don't want the consistency to be as leathery as a sun-dried tomato. The cooking time will vary greatly—crazily, in fact—depending on the character of the tomatoes, so count on at least 1½ hours but allow up to another hour or more. After about 1 hour of cooking, check the amount of juice in the pan. If there is a lot, carefully pour or spoon it off into a small saucepan. You'll add it back to the sauce later, but removing it helps the tomatoes roast instead of simmer. (Don't worry if you don't have any juices in the pan; sometimes that's the case.)

While the tomatoes are roasting, heat the remaining 2 tbsp oil in a large sauté pan or medium Dutch oven over medium heat. Add the garlic and pepper flakes and cook, stirring, until fragrant but not browned, about 30 seconds. Remove from the heat and set aside.

When the tomatoes are done, transfer them and any juice in the pan to a blender or food processor. Add the mixture of oil, garlic, and pepper flakes and process until very smooth.

Return the sauté pan to the stove top over medium-high heat and carefully add the tomato purée. Add the broth and any reserved tomato juices, stir a few times, and then simmer until slightly reduced, about 10 minutes. The sauce can be sort of lavalike, forming big, splattery bubbles, so watch out, and cover the pan partially if this happens.

Because the sauce will probably have too many seeds and bits of skin in it to have a good texture, pour it through a fine-mesh sieve, pushing it through with a rubber spatula or the back of a spoon. Drizzle a few spoonfuls of water or broth over the tomato skins and push again to be sure you get all of the sauce.

Add the lemon juice and sugar and a few drops of hot-pepper sauce, then taste and adjust the flavor balance, if needed, with salt, lemon juice, sugar, and hot-pepper sauce.

# ANGEL HAIR PASTA with FLASH-SAUTÉED FRESH CHERRY TOMATO SAUCE, TUNA, and GREEN OLIVES

Don't have a clue what to fix for dinner tonight? This dish is always a great solution to that problem. The tomatoes and parsley are the only fresh ingredients you need; everything else is probably in your fridge or pantry. For a splurge, use Spanish tuna in olive oil; for a bargain, try Genova brand, also in olive oil but half the price.

Kosher salt

1 lb/455 g angel hair pasta

2½ cups/600 ml Flash-Sautéed Fresh Cherry Tomato Sauce (page 55), heated

Two 6-oz/170-g cans good-quality tuna packed in oil, drained and flaked

½ cup/55 g pitted green olives such as Lucques or Castelvetrano

1 tbsp rinsed capers

¼ cup/10 g chopped fresh flat-leaf parsley, or other fresh herbs as you like

Bring a large pot of generously salted water to a boil over high heat. Add the pasta, stir, and cook until just shy of al dente (about 1 minute less than the package instructions). Just before the pasta is ready, scoop out about ½ cup/120 ml of the cooking water and set aside. Drain the pasta.

Return the pasta to the pot over medium heat. Add the tomato sauce and toss to coat evenly. Fold in the tuna, olives, and capers, and then fold in a few spoonfuls of reserved pasta water to create a nice saucy consistency.

Divide the pasta among warmed pasta bowls and sprinkle with the parsley. Serve right away.

SERVES 4

# EGGS POACHED in BOLD and SPICY TOMATO SAUCE with GARLICKY TOASTS and PECORINO

Americans tend to think of eggs as breakfast food, but fortunately other cuisines remind us of their value on the dinner table. This simple Italian-inspired dish is both comforting and exciting—eggs and toast for comfort, spicy sauce and assertive cheese for dramatic flavor. Although I call for my Bold and Spicy Tomato Sauce here, any of the marinara-based sauces in this chapter will work.

About 4 cups/960 ml Bold and Spicy Tomato Sauce (page 57)

4 large eggs

4 large slices artisanal white bread such as ciabatta or sourdough

2 tbsp extra-virgin olive oil

1 clove garlic, halved

½ cup/55 g grated pecorino romano or other good-quality salty aged cheese

Position an oven rack about 6 in/15 cm from the broiler element and heat the broiler.

In a 10-in/25-cm broiler-safe frying pan, bring the sauce to a simmer over medium-high heat. Cook, stirring frequently, until slightly thickened and very hot, about 10 minutes.

Crack one of the eggs into a small bowl. With a spoon or spatula, make a little well in one quadrant of the tomato sauce and slip the egg into the well. Repeat with the remaining eggs, spacing them evenly in the pan. Reduce the heat to low, cover, and cook until the whites of the eggs are just starting to set but the yolks are still soft, 9 to 12 minutes.

Meanwhile, brush both sides of each bread slice with the olive oil. Arrange the bread on a rimmed baking sheet in a single layer. Broil the bread, flipping once, until golden brown, about 1 minute on each side, depending on your broiler. Rub the garlic halves on one side of each piece of toast.

When the eggs are starting to set, sprinkle the sauce and eggs with the cheese and transfer the pan to the broiler. Broil until the cheese is lightly browned and the eggs are set (I like to keep the yolks runny), about 30 seconds. If you want your eggs cooked through a bit more, keep them under the broiler for another 30 seconds.

Put a piece of toast in the bottom of each individual wide, shallow bowl. Spoon an egg and an equal amount of the sauce over each toast. Serve right away.

SERVES 4

# CHICKEN and PEPPERS BRAISED in
# VERY MUSHROOMY PORCINI TOMATO SAUCE

This easy and savory stew was inspired by chicken cacciatore, that is, "hunter's style" stew. The idea is that a hunter bags a bird, then forages some lovely mushrooms in the forest on the way home. I'm not sure where the peppers come from, perhaps a neighbor's garden? In any case, the flavors are deep and bold and satisfying, particularly during the colder months.

You can use any cut of chicken you like. I'm a true believer in the skin-on, bone-in chicken thigh. I think it's the only part of modern chickens that has any flavor, and the texture stays moist no matter how long you cook it. I also like the bites of chicken close to the bone, which are particularly tender and flavorful. But if you prefer boneless and skinless, that's fine too. The stew is especially delicious with good-quality egg noodles or homemade spaetzle.

2¼ lb/1 kg chicken thighs (about 8)

Kosher salt and freshly ground black pepper

2 tbsp extra-virgin olive oil

2 or 3 mild peppers such as red bell pepper, Italian frying pepper, or Anaheim chile, stemmed, seeded, and cut lengthwise into slices ¼ in/ 6 mm wide

3 cups/720 ml Very Mushroomy Porcini Tomato Sauce (page 58)

½ cup/120 ml water, if needed

½ cup/20 g coarsely chopped fresh flat-leaf parsley

10 oz/280 g dried egg noodles, freshly cooked, tossed with 1 to 2 tbsp unsalted butter, and kept hot

Generously season the chicken all over with salt and pepper. In a large frying pan (12 in/30.5 cm is a good size), heat the oil over medium-high heat. Add the peppers, season lightly with salt, and cook, stirring frequently, until lightly browned and starting to soften, 4 to 5 minutes. Transfer to a plate.

Return the frying pan to medium-high heat; you shouldn't need to add any more oil. Arrange the chicken pieces, skin-side down, in the pan in a single layer. (If they don't all fit comfortably in a single layer, you'll need to use a second pan and a little more oil.) Reduce the heat to medium and cook, turning once, until nicely browned on both sides, about 7 minutes per side.

Pour off any visible chicken fat (save the fat and use it for cooking potatoes another time; it is delicious), return the peppers to the pan, and add the tomato sauce. If the sauce doesn't cover the chicken by about halfway, stir in up to ½ cup/120 ml water. Adjust the heat to maintain a nice simmer, cover, and cook, turning the pieces once halfway through cooking, until the chicken is cooked through and is very tender when you poke it with a knife, about 30 minutes more.

Transfer the chicken to a platter or warmed dinner plates. Add the parsley to the sauce and season with salt and pepper. Pour the sauce over the chicken and serve right away with the noodles.

**SERVES 4 TO 6**

# COMFORTING RISOTTO with VERY MEATY TOMATO SAUCE

I generally like to keep my risotto as a fairly light dish so the rice really shines, but it can also be delicious in a more robust form, as in this recipe. It's sort of the difference between sliding a cashmere cardigan around my shoulders and bundling up in a chunky Irish fisherman sweater.

Look for Arborio rice in well-stocked grocery stores. Be sure to buy an Italian brand, as I have found the domestic brands are not as good. Carnaroli rice, which has a particularly high starch content and firm texture, is also a good choice for making risotto. Fior di Riso is my favorite brand, as much for the charming mistranslations on the packaging as for the excellent quality of the rice.

2 cups/480 ml Very Meaty Tomato Sauce (page 60)

2 tbsp unsalted butter or extra-virgin olive oil

¾ cup/100 g finely chopped yellow onion or shallot

1 cup/215 g Arborio or Carnaroli rice

½ cup/120 ml dry white wine

3 to 4 cups/720 to 960 ml homemade turkey broth (see page 165), chicken broth, or canned reduced-sodium chicken broth, heated

Kosher salt and freshly ground black pepper

½ cup/55 g grated Parmigiano-Reggiano cheese

In a small saucepan, bring the tomato sauce to a simmer over medium-high heat. Cook, stirring often, until very concentrated and thick, about 20 minutes.

Meanwhile, in a medium, heavy saucepan, melt the butter over medium-high heat until foamy. Add the onion and cook, stirring often, until very soft and fragrant but not browned, 4 to 5 minutes. Add the rice and cook, stirring constantly, until coated with the fat and glistening, 1 to 2 minutes more.

Stir in the wine and simmer, stirring, until evaporated, 1 to 2 minutes. Stir in about ½ cup/120 ml of the hot broth. Adjust the heat so the liquid bubbles merrily and cook, scraping the bottom of the pan frequently, until the broth is almost entirely evaporated. Continue adding broth about ½ cup/120 ml at a time, stirring frequently and cooking until the broth is almost entirely evaporated before adding more, until the rice is tender but still slightly firm at the center and it is in a creamy matrix of starchy broth, about 20 minutes more. When the rice is almost done, add the broth in smaller amounts and taste as you go so you don't overcook the rice.

When the risotto is tender, season with salt and pepper. Divide evenly among warmed wide, shallow bowls and make a well in the center of each serving. Ladle some of the hot tomato sauce into each well and sprinkle with the cheese. Serve right away.

SERVES 4

# VEGETABLE, CHILE, AND NUT SAUCES

THE RECIPES IN THIS CHAPTER ARE UNITED BY A MARRIAGE OF CONVENIENCE RATHER THAN A DEEP AFFINITY OF TECHNIQUE OR INGREDIENT. The sauces are similar in that they are purées (for the most part) of vegetables, chiles (which are vegetables), and nuts, and some of the sauces use vegetables, chiles, and nuts together, so it made sense to corral them all here, even though they have distinct and varied personalities. Many of these sauces have roots in cuisines from around the world, though they are not meant to be authentic versions of anything other than authentic to the way I cook at home. And they only scratch the surface of the countless sauces that cooks in other parts of the world make every day.

## WHAT'S GOING ON IN THIS SAUCE?

Most of these sauces are made by simply cooking the main ingredient until soft, pureeing it, and then seasoning it (you'll see that not all are cooked, or puréed, but most are). The question the cook needs to ask when making these sauces is how to capture enough depth of flavor so they become sauces and not simply purées. One answer comes with a little help from our usual friends: flavorful oils, vinegars, spices, and aromatics such as garlic and herbs. Each of the sauces in this chapter benefits from another ingredient that is an accent, counterpoint, or underpinning for the flavor of the primary ingredient in the sauce: fruity extra-virgin olive oil blended with nuts in the walnut sauce (see page 77) or the reduced balsamic vinegar that gives nerve to the butternut squash sauce (see page 80).

Another key is cooking the main ingredient enough so that its flavor and texture are more concentrated than they were in the ingredient's original state, ensuring the sauce delivers the necessary flavor punch. Finally, it's critical to control the texture of these sauces. The primary ingredients have seeds and skins and fibers and chunks and other textural elements that you need to wrangle.

## WHAT CAN GO WRONG AND HOW CAN I FIX IT?

These sauces are dependent on texture, whether fluid and flowing or thicker and "dollopy," and that ideal texture can be elusive, given the variation in the consistency of your main ingredients. The methods for most of these sauces are straightforward: puréeing and straining. Although these techniques are seemingly simple, how you execute them can make or break your sauce.

You can purée your sauce ingredients in a blender or food processor, pass them through a food mill, or, if very soft, push them through a sieve. The French use a sieve designed specifically for this purpose called a *tamis* (pronounced tah MEE), which is also known as a drum sieve. (I bought one during cooking school, but after a few years, I realized that I was only using it as a steamer basket, so I sold it at a yard sale.)

THE BLENDER will give you the best consistency. But, as I've noted elsewhere, I think a blender can be a pain to use and clean, so I use it only with large quantities. The trick, however, is to begin by puréeing only the solids, adding any liquid ingredients once you have a thick purée.

That way, the blades are more efficient and you don't end up with solid bits floating in liquid that sometimes just bounce around and never become thoroughly pulverized. Do stop the blender as needed and scrape down the sides with a rubber spatula, being careful not to push so far down that the spatula snags on the blades (one of the reasons I hate blenders).

A FOOD PROCESSOR is a good choice if the main ingredient you are puréeing is quite soft. If the vegetables or chile is undercooked, the processor doesn't always do the best job of eliminating the graininess. You also need to scrape down the sides of a food processor midwhirl, but that's simple enough to do. A mixture with a lot of liquid can be trouble, however, because of the hole in the center of the processor bowl.

A FOOD MILL is a good old-fashioned piece of equipment that is fantastic for puréeing potatoes, celery root, and other fall-apart starchy vegetables and is also brilliant at separating out skins and seeds. So while the bell pepper skins in the Smoky Red Pepper Coulis (page 75) are puréed along with the flesh of the peppers if you use a blender or food processor, most of the skins will be strained out if you use a food mill. This results in a silkier sauce, though some volume is lost.

This leads me to the issue of straining. I'm all for leaving things natural if the flavor is satisfactory. But with a sauce, straining is often worth the extra effort. Not only does it remove distracting bits of cellulose, but it also aerates the sauce, adding just a hint more creaminess to the feeling on your tongue.

To strain, I use a fine-mesh sieve that is 7 inches/17 centimeters in diameter and has a long handle on one side and a small loop on the other, which allows me to secure the sieve over a bowl or saucepan as I work the contents through the mesh. The best way to do that is with a rubber spatula, though a wide wooden spoon is good, too. One of my prize kitchen tools is an unassuming white plastic card that I bought in Paris, curved on one side and straight on the opposite side. It's called a *racle-tout*, or "scrape-all," and it's excellent for scraping out the last bit of batter from a bowl and for forcing a mixture through a sieve and scraping off the purée that clings to the underside. You'll find a few different versions of this handy tool at cookware stores. The one I like is made by Matfer.

## HOW MUCH SAUCE PER SERVING?

The sauces are so diverse in this chapter that the serving sizes vary from a couple of tablespoons for something like the Butternut Squash and Apple Cider Sauce to ½ cup/ 120 milliliters for the red chile sauce when used in the Simple and Delicious Enchiladas.

## SPECIAL EQUIPMENT

Almost all of these sauces are puréed, which is best accomplished by using a food processor or blender. I prefer the processor unless the sauce is very liquidy, in which case the blender is best. A fine-mesh sieve lets you give your sauces a satiny texture.

## STORAGE

Most of these sauces need to be eaten within a few days, so it's good to have a plan in mind when you make them. The Roasted Green Chile and Tomatillo Sauce with Avocado is an exception—no need to plan, because it's so good that you can put it on everything.

# CARAMELIZED ONION COULIS

Onions are a beautiful vegetable to transform into a sauce because their flavor is sweet and their texture is silky and melting. They won't get that way, however, if you don't give them enough time to caramelize slowly, so don't rush the cooking and be sure they don't brown too quickly.

2 tbsp unsalted butter

1½ lb/680 g onions, thinly sliced

½ tsp kosher salt

1 fresh rosemary sprig, 4 in/10 cm long

¼ cup/60 ml crème fraîche, plus more if needed

½ cup/120 ml homemade turkey broth (see page 165), chicken or vegetable broth, or canned reduced-sodium chicken or vegetable broth

1 tsp fresh lemon juice, plus more if needed

Freshly ground black pepper

**MAKES 1½ CUPS/360 ML**

**STORAGE** Refrigerate in an air-tight container for up to 4 days. The sauce does not freeze well.

**QUICK CHANGE** Use olive oil instead of butter and vegetable broth instead of crème fraîche to make the sauce vegan.

In a large, heavy frying pan, melt the butter over medium-high heat. Add the onions and salt and stir to mix. Once the onions start to steam and sizzle a bit, cover the pan, reduce the heat to medium, and cook until the onions are starting to get juicy and soft, about 10 minutes.

Uncover, turn the heat to low, and cook slowly, stirring and scraping frequently, until the onions have collapsed and are starting to turn golden. After about 30 minutes, toss in the rosemary and keep cooking, taking care to scrape the bottom of the pan so nothing burns, until the onions are sweet and deeply golden, 1 to 1¼ hours total.

Scrape the onions into a blender and return the pan to medium heat. Add the crème fraîche and broth, bring to a simmer, and deglaze the pan, scraping up all of the good brown bits on the pan bottom. Add the contents of the pan to the blender along with the lemon juice and process until you have a smooth purée. Taste and season with a few twists of pepper, then adjust with more salt, pepper, or lemon if needed. If the purée is too thick, add a bit more crème fraîche.

# SMOKY RED PEPPER COULIS

This is a slight "upgrade" on a basic roasted red pepper sauce. I like to use a mix of peppers (bell and pimiento are great together) when I can find interesting sweet varieties at the farmers' market, and I like the way the smoked paprika extends that sweet pepper flavor. Vinegar keeps the sweetness balanced. I love this sauce drizzled over fat grilled shrimp or slices of rare grilled flank steak.

3 tbsp olive oil

2 lb/910 g mixed sweet red peppers, stemmed, seeded, and cut lengthwise into strips ½ in/12 mm wide

Kosher salt

1 large clove garlic, smashed

1 fresh rosemary sprig, 4 in/10 cm long

1½ tsp Spanish sweet smoked paprika (see ingredient note, page 24)

1 tsp sherry vinegar, plus more if needed

MAKES 1 CUP/240 ML

**STORAGE** Refrigerate in an airtight container for up to 5 days or freeze in a ziplock freezer bag for up to 3 months.

**QUICK CHANGE** Add 1 fresh hot red chile, stemmed, seeded, and chopped, with the sweet peppers.

In a heavy, medium frying pan, heat the oil over medium heat. Add the peppers, 1 tsp salt, garlic, and rosemary. Cover, and cook the peppers until they start to release some steam, about 3 minutes. Reduce the heat to medium-low and cook the peppers slowly until they become very soft and sweet and have released some juices, about 30 minutes more. Uncover, add the paprika, and cook until the juices are reduced to a thick glaze, 8 to 10 minutes. Stir in the vinegar, remove from the heat, and let cool slightly.

Transfer the pepper mixture to a blender or food processor and purée; add a little water or broth if the sauce is too thick. Taste and adjust the salt and vinegar, if needed, for a sweet-tangy balance. Push the sauce through a sieve for a perfectly smooth texture. (You can use it unstrained, too. You just detect tiny bits of skin in the sauce.)

# ROMESCO SAUCE

My friend and fellow food writer Matthew Card makes a mean romesco, so I asked him to contribute his recipe to the book. If he hadn't, I would have been trying to duplicate his version of the classic Spanish sauce anyway, so he spared me the espionage. His sauce gets most of its body from fleshy roasted red peppers—from a jar is fine—but gets layers of can't-stop-eating-this flavor from fried bread, two kinds of nuts, and a bit of sherry vinegar.

1 cup/55 g lightly packed ½-in/12-mm rustic artisanal bread or baguette cubes

3 cloves garlic, halved

6 tbsp/90 ml extra-virgin olive oil

1 ripe plum tomato, cored and halved

½ cup/75 g almonds, toasted

½ cup/75 g hazelnuts, toasted and skinned (see box)

2 tsp packed minced fresh thyme

2 tsp Hungarian sweet paprika or Spanish sweet smoked paprika (see ingredient note, page 24)

Small pinch of cayenne pepper, plus more if needed

8 oz/225 g jarred roasted red peppers, rinsed, dried, and coarsely chopped (about 1⅓ cups)

1 tbsp sherry vinegar

Kosher salt

**MAKES 2 CUPS/480 ML**

**STORAGE** Refrigerate in an air-tight container for up to 3 days. The sauce does not freeze well.

**QUICK CHANGE** Use all almonds, or even salted, fried Marcona almonds for an extra-rich touch.

In a small frying pan, combine the bread cubes, garlic, and 4 tbsp/60 ml of the oil over medium heat. Cook, stirring frequently, until the bread is lightly browned, about 5 minutes. Using a heat-resistant rubber spatula, transfer the bread to a food processor, scraping out as much oil as possible.

Return the pan to medium-high heat. Add the tomato, cut-side down, and cook without moving it until browned, 3 to 5 minutes. Flip and lightly brown the skin side, about 3 minutes. Remove from the heat and chop coarsely when cool enough to handle.

Add the nuts, thyme, paprika, and cayenne to the processor and process with the bread until ground and evenly combined, about 30 seconds, stopping as needed to scrape down the sides of the work bowl. Add the peppers, tomato, and vinegar and process until thoroughly blended, about 30 seconds. Taste and adjust the seasoning with salt and cayenne if needed. Finally, add the remaining 2 tbsp olive oil and pulse briefly just until combined.

### TOASTING AND SKINNING HAZELNUTS

To toast the nuts evenly without the risk of burning, heat the oven to 350°F/180°C/gas 4, spread the nuts in a pie pan, rimmed baking sheet, or shallow baking pan, and toast until fragrant and lightly browned, 10 to 15 minutes. To skin the hazelnuts, allow them to cool until they can be comfortably handled, then rub them back and forth between your palms. Alternatively, place them in a sieve and rub them back and forth with your hand; the mesh will act like sandpaper and help scrape off the skins.

# CREAMY WALNUT SAUCE

Walnuts play a bigger role in many cuisines, such as those of the Middle East and eastern Europe, than they do in what we call American cuisine. This sauce is a marriage of a traditional Turkish *tarator* sauce and an Italian sauce called *agliata*, with some meddling around of my own, of course. It's amazing how smooth and creamy the walnuts become, and their slight nip of tannins gives a pleasing edge to the sauce.

This sauce is particularly good on grilled vegetables, especially asparagus and thick eggplant slices (see page 82). It also complements grilled fish, or it can be tossed with pasta and then the pasta topped with grilled vegetables.

1 cup/115 g walnut halves

1 slice good white bread (artisanal with crusts removed or sandwich loaf is fine)

¼ cup/60 ml homemade turkey broth (see page 165), chicken broth, canned reduced-sodium chicken broth, or water

1 tbsp sherry vinegar or fresh lemon juice, plus more if needed

1 clove garlic

½ cup/120 ml extra-virgin olive oil

Kosher salt and freshly ground black pepper

MAKES 1½ CUPS/360 ML

**STORAGE** Refrigerate in an airtight container for up to 2 days. The sauce does not freeze well.

**QUICK CHANGE** Add ½ cup/55 g sliced yellow onion to the processor with the nuts and bread.

Heat the oven to 325°F/165°C/gas 3. Spread the walnuts in a pie pan or rimmed baking sheet, place in the oven, and toast lightly, 6 to 8 minutes. They should be just fragrant and beginning to take on color but not turning deep brown. Pour onto a plate and let cool.

Meanwhile, rip the bread into pieces, put it in a small bowl, add the broth and vinegar, and toss to moisten evenly. Leave to soak for about 15 minutes.

In a food processor, combine the cooled nuts, the bread and any remaining liquid, and the garlic and process until a thick purée forms, stopping as needed to scrap down the sides of the work bowl. With the motor running, drizzle in the oil to form a creamy emulsion. If the mixture seems a bit thick and gloppy, pulse in a few tablespoons of water. Season generously with salt and pepper and taste and adjust with more vinegar if needed. Serve at room temperature.

# ASIAN PEANUT SAUCE

We all know that skewers of grilled satay are just an excuse to eat the peanut sauce that usually comes with them, so make a lot of this sauce and use it during the week on grilled meats and vegetables, on noodle dishes, or spring rolls.

There are many approaches to making this sauce, and usually, I take a multicultural and easy approach—I use mass-market peanut butter, which is simpler than whole nuts, plus it gives the sauce a lovely consistency that stays emulsified with the other ingredients better. If you can't find the small can of coconut milk I call for, buy the larger size, measure out ½ cup plus 3 tbsp/165 ml, and freeze the rest.

Be sure to tinker with the final seasoning until until the sauce has a bright tension from tart lime juice, sweet coconut milk, spicy hot-pepper sauce, and salty fish sauce.

1 tbsp canola or other neutral vegetable oil

2 tbsp minced shallot

1 tbsp minced, seeded fresh hot chile such as jalapeño

1 clove garlic, chopped

1 tbsp peeled and finely chopped fresh ginger

One 5½-oz/165-ml can coconut milk
(stir together the thick cream and thinner milk before measuring)

¾ cup/210 g creamy peanut butter

3 tbsp soy sauce

3 tbsp fresh lime juice

2 tbsp water

1 tbsp lightly packed palm or light brown sugar

2 tsp Asian fish sauce

¼ tsp hot-pepper sauce such as Sriracha

**MAKES 1¾ CUPS/420 ML**

**STORAGE** Refrigerate in an airtight container for up to 5 days. The sauce does not freeze well.

**QUICK CHANGE** Add 1 tbsp Thai red curry paste with the coconut milk.

In a medium saucepan, heat the oil over medium heat. Add the shallot, chile, garlic, and ginger and cook, stirring frequently, until the aromatics are very soft and fragrant, 2 to 3 minutes. Do not allow them to brown.

Add the coconut milk and simmer for 1 to 2 minutes, then remove the pan from the heat and stir in the peanut butter. As it begins to melt, switch to a whisk and whisk until a smooth emulsion forms. Return the pan to low heat, whisk in the soy sauce, lime juice, water, sugar, fish sauce, and hot-pepper sauce and simmer for 4 to 5 minutes to blend everything nicely. Taste and adjust all of the flavorings so the sauce is creamy but bright and exciting. Serve slightly warm or at room temperature.

# GARLICKY POTATO SAUCE

Potato may seem an unlikely main ingredient for a sauce, but when puréed and emulsified with olive oil, lemon juice, and a bit of water, this Greek-inspired sauce is luscious and a great dip for vegetables. Use a good-quality olive oil, something fruity and fragrant but not biting, and add the garlic cloves to your taste.

8 oz/225 g starchy potatoes such as russets, peeled and cut into chunks

Kosher salt and freshly ground black pepper

1 to 2 cloves garlic

½ cup/120 ml extra-virgin olive oil

2 to 3 tbsp fresh lemon juice

½ tsp lightly packed finely grated lemon zest

**MAKES ABOUT 1½ CUPS/360 ML**

**STORAGE** Refrigerate in an air-tight container for up to 3 days. The sauce does not freeze well.

**QUICK CHANGE** Add 1 tbsp fresh dill with the lemon juice.

In a medium saucepan, combine the potatoes, 2 tsp salt, and water to cover by 1 to 2 in/2.5 to 5 cm and bring to a boil over high heat. Reduce the heat to maintain a vigorous simmer and cook, uncovered, until very tender when pierced with a fork, 20 to 25 minutes. Scoop out about 1 cup/240 ml of the cooking water and reserve and then drain the potatoes in a colander.

Transfer the potatoes to a food processor, add the garlic, and pulse a few times. Then, with the motor running, drizzle in the oil. (The sauce may look slightly curdled at this point, but it will smooth out as you add cooking water later.) Pulse as you add the lemon juice and lemon zest and then add enough of the cooking water to give the sauce the consistency of thin sour cream. Season generously with salt and pepper.

# BUTTERNUT SQUASH AND APPLE CIDER SAUCE

Butternut is the winter squash in which flavor and a smooth texture intersect deliciously, so it's not surprising that it makes a lovely sauce. It's a natural for pasta and gnocchi, but it is also wonderful with a simple pork cutlet.

One 1-lb/455-g butternut squash

1 tbsp olive oil

1 small shallot, diced

Kosher salt

1 cup/240 ml unfiltered apple cider

1 fresh thyme sprig

1 small dried hot chile such as árbol

¼ cup/60 ml water

½ tsp balsamic vinegar, plus more if needed

2 tbsp unsalted butter

**MAKES 1½ CUPS/360 ML**

**STORAGE** Refrigerate in an airtight container for up to 3 days or freeze in one or more ziplock freezer bags for up to 2 months.

**QUICK CHANGE** Use rosemary instead of thyme.

Using a large chef's knife, cut a thick slice off the top and bottom of the squash, then cut the squash in half crosswise. Place half of the squash cut-side down on the cutting board and, using a sharp paring knife, cut away the peel. The peel is tough and can resist you, so work carefully. Repeat with the second half of the squash. You'll see that one of the halves is solid flesh and the other has the seeds in it. Cut the seeded half open lengthwise, scoop out the seeds with a spoon, and discard them. Cut the flesh of both halves into 1-in/2.5-cm cubes and set aside.

In a large saucepan, heat the oil over medium-high heat. Add the shallot and a pinch of salt and cook, stirring, until soft and fragrant but not brown, about 1 minute. Add the squash and sauté until lightly golden, another 3 to 4 minutes. Add the cider, thyme, and chile and simmer until the cider is reduced to about ¼ cup/60 ml. Add the water and continue to simmer until the squash is very tender when pierced with a fork, 4 to 6 minutes longer. Remove from the heat, remove and discard the thyme and chile, and let cool slightly.

Transfer the squash mixture to a food processor or blender and process until a smooth purée forms. If the purée is at all fibrous, push it through a fine-mesh sieve. Return the purée to the pan over medium heat, add the vinegar, and season with salt. If the sauce is too thick, thin it with a little more water. Heat to serving temperature and whisk in the butter. Taste and adjust the seasoning again before serving.

# FRUITY AND SPICY DRIED RED CHILE SAUCE

The day I realized that I could make my own sauce for enchiladas was a day when life's lovely possibilities glowed a few degrees brighter. The sauce turns ordinary corn tortillas and a few drizzles of sour cream into a feast (see page 88).

12 dried New Mexico chiles

2 ancho chiles

2 tbsp olive oil, lard, or rendered chicken fat

½ yellow onion, sliced

Kosher salt

3 large cloves garlic, smashed

½ tsp ground cumin

1 tsp sugar, plus more if needed

½ cup/120 ml homemade turkey broth (see page 165), chicken or vegetable broth, or canned reduced-sodium chicken or vegetable broth

MAKES ABOUT 2 CUPS/480 ML

STORAGE Refrigerate in an air-tight container for up to 1 week or freeze in one or more ziplock freezer bags for up to 2 months.

QUICK CHANGE Add ½ cup/120 ml sour cream with the broth to make the sauce richer and even less authentic!

Break open the dried chiles, discard the stems, and shake out the seeds. Depending on how brittle the chiles are, you can use your hands or use kitchen scissors. The chiles contain a natural chemical that can irritate your skin or eyes, so be careful. If your skin is particularly sensitive, wear rubber gloves. Be sure to wash your hands thoroughly with soap and water when you have finished.

Place a large frying pan over medium-high heat, add the chiles, and toast them by pressing them flat onto the hot surface with a metal spatula. Once they change color and you can start to smell them, they are ready. Don't toast them too long or they'll scorch. Transfer the chiles to a medium bowl, add hot water to cover, and let soak until quite soft, at least 30 minutes.

While the chiles are soaking, in a medium frying pan, heat the oil over medium-high heat. Add the onion, season with ¼ tsp salt, and cook, stirring frequently, until the onion starts to sizzle. Then reduce the heat to low and continue to cook until the onion is very soft and sweet and is starting to caramelize, about 15 minutes. Add the garlic, cumin, and sugar and cook for another 30 seconds or so. Remove from the heat and set aside until the chiles are ready.

Drain the chiles, reserving the soaking water. In a blender, combine the chiles and the onion mixture and process until puréed, adding enough of the broth to create a smooth purée and stopping to scrape down the sides of the blender. Now add the remaining broth and process, adding a little of the soaking water if needed to get a nice pouring consistency reminiscent of very thick canned tomato juice. Taste and adjust the seasoning with more salt or sugar if needed.

# ROASTED GREEN CHILE AND TOMATILLO SAUCE WITH AVOCADO

My friend and great cook Gilberto Martin del Campo showed me how to make this brightly flavored, pretty green sauce. It's so easy to whip up and so much better than any commercial salsa verde. Use it on melty-cheesy nachos, on scrambled eggs with feta cheese, and as a base for a pork and green chile stew (though save the avocado to use as a garnish, not in the sauce).

3 to 4 jalapeño chiles, stemmed and seeded

1 poblano chile, stemmed and seeded

1 lb/455 g tomatillos, papery husks removed, rinsed, and halved

1 yellow onion, thickly sliced

3 cloves garlic, smashed

2 tbsp olive oil

Kosher salt

1 small ripe avocado, halved, pitted, peeled, and finely diced

2 tbsp fresh lime juice, plus more if needed

½ cup/20 g chopped fresh cilantro

**MAKES 4 CUPS/960 ML**

**STORAGE** Refrigerate in an airtight container for up to 5 days or freeze in one or more ziplock freezer bags for up to 2 months.

**QUICK CHANGE** Omit the avocado and add 2 small plum tomatoes, chopped, with the lime juice and cilantro.

Heat the oven to 425°F/220°C/gas 7. In a large bowl, combine the chiles, tomatillos, onion, garlic, and oil; season with salt; and toss to coat. Spread the vegetables on a rimmed baking sheet.

Roast the vegetables, turning them a couple of times about midway through cooking, until they have collapsed and started to brown, 15 to 25 minutes. Remove from the oven and let cool.

Scrape the cooled vegetables into a food processor or blender and pulse to create a chunky purée. Transfer to a medium bowl and taste and adjust the seasoning with salt. Gently fold in the avocado, lime juice, and cilantro. Let the sauce sit for 20 minutes or so to allow the flavors to marry, then taste and adjust the seasoning with salt and with more lime juice, if needed. Serve at room temperature or chill before serving.

# FRESH CHILE AND SUMMER TOMATO SALSA

This is a regulation fresh salsa, nothing groundbreaking but delicious nonetheless. It's also a template for improvisation. You can play with the mix of chiles, try different types of tomatoes, add extra spices, use different herbs, and even include diced fruit, black beans, or diced radish or jicama. I'm taking the unusual step of soaking the onion in cold water to leech out some of the harsher compounds. I love the flavor of raw onion but it can feel like an assault on my system sometimes. You can opt to skip this step. I salt the tomato ahead of time to draw off some of the juice and concentrate the tomato flavor. This prevents the salsa from being watery. And many salsa recipes don't call for oil, but I find that the oil helps unlock and distribute flavors better.

The salsa itself is immensely versatile: pair it with chips, of course, but also with everything from fresh fish, eggs, sliced steak, beans, and corn bread to grilled cheese.

½ cup/70 g finely diced yellow onion

2 cups/340 g finely diced fresh ripe tomato

Kosher salt

¼ cup/30 g finely diced jalapeño chile

½ cup/55 g finely diced fresh Anaheim or other mild fresh chile

1 to 2 tbsp lime juice

1 to 3 cloves garlic, minced

¼ tsp ground cumin

2 tbsp olive oil

½ cup/20 g chopped fresh cilantro

MAKES ABOUT 3 CUPS/720 ML

**STORAGE** Refrigerate in an airtight container for up to 2 days. The sauce does not freeze well.

**QUICK CHANGE** Roast the onion and chiles in a 450°F/230°C/gas 8 oven until softened and slightly charred, about 20 minutes, before dicing.

Put the onion in a bowl of very cold water to cover and soak for 20 minutes. Drain and blot dry on paper towels.

Toss the tomato with 1 tsp salt and let sit while the onion soaks. After draining the onion, drain off the accumulated juices from the tomato.

In a medium bowl, toss together the onion, tomato, jalapeño, Anaheim, 1 tbsp of the lime juice, garlic, cumin, and olive oil. Let sit for 20 minutes to allow the flavors to blend. Taste and adjust the seasoning with salt and more lime juice, if needed. Just before serving, add the cilantro and toss to mix.

# GRILLED EGGPLANT ANTIPASTO with CREAMY WALNUT SAUCE, TOMATO, and FETA

I often serve this dish as part of a spread of salads and vegetable dishes, all laid out on pretty platters, which is my favorite formula for summer entertaining. Sometimes I include a meat dish, such as sliced grilled pork tenderloin, but usually the meal feels festive and complete without it, as long as there is a good variety of vegetables and a grain or bean dish or two. I find that eggplant is "meaty" tasting, so it's a key part of the balance.

You can use smaller Japanese eggplants and split them lengthwise, but I like the nice round medallions that you get from an Italian or globe eggplant. I avoid super-bulbous ones, however, because they usually conceal lots of seeds.  If you want to salt your slices, do so, though I don't see a huge benefit to that extra step. Most fresh eggplants are not that bitter. Use any good-quality feta cheese; I like Valbreso brand, which is made from sheep's milk in France.

1 lb/455 g eggplant, stem cut off

Olive oil for brushing

Kosher salt

3 medium, ripe tomatoes such as Early Girl, or 1 pt/480 ml cherry tomatoes

1½ cups/360 ml Creamy Walnut Sauce (page 77)

4 oz/115 g feta cheese, crumbled

¼ cup/10 g chopped fresh flat-leaf parsley (optional)

**SERVES 8 TO 10 AS PART OF AN ANTIPASTO SPREAD**

Prepare a medium fire in a charcoal or gas grill. The fire is ready when you can comfortably hold your hand, palm-side down, 2 to 3 in/5 to 7.5 cm above the grill rack for 4 seconds. Brush the grill rack so that it is perfectly clean.

Using a vegetable peeler or a sharp paring knife, peel strips of skin lengthwise off the eggplant to cover it completely in vertical stripes. This eliminates much of the can-be-tough skin but leaves enough to keep your slices intact. Now cut the eggplant crosswise into rounds ½ in/12 mm thick.

Brush both sides of each slice with the oil and season with salt.

Place the eggplant slices on the grill rack and grill, turning once, until nicely grill marked on both sides and tender, 3 to 4 minutes per side. Pile the slices on a plate, cover with aluminum foil, and leave to steam and finish cooking for another 15 minutes. This will create the creamy texture you want.

If using the medium tomatoes, core them and then cut into very thin slices. Spread them out on a plate, season lightly with salt, and let some of the juices drain off so they won't make the eggplant slices soggy, about 10 minutes. If using cherry tomatoes, remove the stems and quarter the tomatoes lengthwise. Put them in a colander or sieve, salt them lightly, and let them drain for about 10 minutes.

Arrange the eggplant slices on a platter, overlapping them slightly. Spread some of the sauce on each slice, lay a thin tomato slice or a big pinch of tomato pieces on top, then finish with crumbled feta and with a little parsley (if using). Serve cool or at room temperature. The dish can also be assembled up to 1 hour in advance and refrigerated. Let it sit at room temperature to warm up a bit before serving.

# GOAT CHEESE and LEEK TART
## with BUTTERNUT SQUASH SAUCE

This is a simple-to-assemble appetizer pastry that is made special by pouring a ribbon of autumn-colored sauce around it. Pepperidge Farm puff pastry is easy to find in most grocery stores, but it isn't made with butter so the flavor is not the best. Look for Dufour brand if you want an all-butter pastry or make your own (I teach you how in my cookbook *Puff*).

3 leeks, about 8 oz/225 g each before trimming

2 tbsp unsalted butter

2 tbsp olive oil

Kosher salt and freshly ground black pepper

1 fresh thyme sprig

1 clove garlic, minced

8 oz/225 g puff pastry dough, thawed if frozen (1 sheet Pepperidge Farm, ½ sheet Dufour, or homemade)

2 tbsp Dijon mustard

4 oz/115 g fresh goat cheese

1 cup/240 ml Butternut Squash and Apple Cider Sauce (page 80), heated

2 tbsp chopped fresh flat-leaf parsley

**SERVES 10 AS
A FIRST COURSE**

Trim off the roots and dark green tops of the leeks. Split the leeks in half lengthwise and rinse very well, separating the leaves to wash away the grit hiding between them. Cut the leeks crosswise into slices ¼ in/6 mm thick.

In a large frying pan, melt the butter with the oil over medium heat. Add the leeks and season lightly with salt and pepper. Add the thyme sprig, cover, and cook, stirring and scraping the bottom of the pan often so the juices don't burn, until the leeks are just tender, about 10 minutes. Uncover, stir in the garlic, and continue cooking until the leeks are very tender and the juices are just barely browning on the bottom of the pan, 3 to 5 minutes more. If the leeks look like they are at risk of burning or sticking, add a few spoonfuls of water to loosen them. Remove from the heat, remove and discard the thyme sprig, and let the leek mixture cool completely.

Heat the oven to 400°F/200°C/gas 6. On a lightly floured work surface, roll out the pastry into an 11-by-15-in/28-by-38-cm rectangle. Cut the rectangle in half lengthwise so you have two 5½-by-15-in/14-by-38-cm rectangles. Slide one rectangle onto a large rimless baking sheet and prick it all over with a fork. Moisten the long edges with some water and fold them over to create a ½-in/12-mm border. Press firmly to secure the border.

Spread the pastry with half of the mustard, and then spread half of the cooled leeks evenly on top. Crumble half of the goat cheese evenly over the leeks. Repeat with the remaining pastry rectangle, mustard, leeks, and goat cheese and transfer to the baking sheet.

Bake until the pastry is puffed around the edges and deep golden brown (lift up the edge to check the bottom), 22 to 25 minutes. Slide the tarts onto racks and let cool until just barely warm.

Slide the tarts from the racks onto a cutting board. Cut each tart crosswise into five slices. Transfer to individual plates and spoon a generous ribbon of sauce around each piece. Sprinkle with the parsley and serve warm. (You can bake and cool the tarts up to 8 hours ahead and reheat in a 350°F/180°C/gas 4 oven for about 15 minutes.)

# POTATO OMELET with ROASTED GREEN CHILE and TOMATILLO SAUCE with AVOCADO

This is definitely a weeknight, make-dinner-from-what's-in-the-fridge dish, but one that rewards you highly for modest effort. You need to have the chile sauce already made, but if for some reason you don't, it's okay to use a good *salsa verde* from a jar and add some avocado. I like Desert Pepper Trading Company and Frontera brands, but many other good ones are on the market.

1 small potato, peeled and cut into small chunks

Kosher salt and freshly ground black pepper

4 or 5 large eggs

2 tbsp unsalted butter, or 1 tbsp each unsalted butter and olive oil

½ cup/120 ml Roasted Green Chile and Tomatillo Sauce with Avocado (page 82)

¼ cup/30 g shredded cheese such as Monterey Jack, Havarti, or Gruyère

In a small saucepan, combine the potato, 1 tsp salt, and water to cover by 1 in/ 2.5 cm and bring to a boil over high heat. Reduce the heat to maintain a vigorous simmer and cook, uncovered, until very tender when pierced with a fork, about 15 minutes. Drain well in a sieve, transfer to a small bowl, and crush lightly with a fork. Season with salt and pepper and cover to keep warm.

In a medium bowl, whisk the eggs until well blended. Add ½ tsp salt and several good twists of pepper and whisk again.

In a 9-in/23-cm nonstick or well-seasoned frying pan, melt the butter over medium-high heat. After it foams and the bubbles start to subside, pour in the eggs. Reduce the heat to medium and let the eggs sit undisturbed until the edges start to lighten up as they set, about 30 seconds. With a heat-resistant rubber spatula, lift up an edge and let some of the liquid egg run underneath. Work your way around the pan, lifting the edge and allowing the egg to run underneath. (This creates nice layers of omelet beneath the top layer.) Take care that the eggs are not browning. If they threaten to brown, turn down the heat or work faster.

When the surface of the omelet is almost set, distribute the potato in a line down the center, fold one side over, and then fold the other side. Slide the omelet onto a cutting board and let it sit for a few seconds to settle.

Cut the omelet in half crosswise and transfer to individual plates. Spoon the green chile sauce over half of the omelet on each plate, covering the cut end. Top with the cheese, dividing it evenly, and serve right away.

SERVES 2

# SIMPLE and DELICIOUS ENCHILADAS

My Mexican-born friend Gilberto Martin del Campo, who taught me how to make the green chile sauce on page 82, also showed me how to make these enchiladas, which is how a lot of people in Mexico prepare them and is very unlike the gloppy "cheese enchiladas" of the typical Tex-Mex place on this side of the border. Sometimes Gilberto will put some queso fresco into the center of the tortilla before he folds it, which is a lovely variation. Make a platter of these enchiladas and serve them with fresh fruit for a perfect light supper or lunch. Of course, it will be difficult to fill the platter because the cook usually wants to eat them right from the frying pan.

This method of frying a sauce-coated tortilla probably seems unusual, but you're not frying the tortillas to get them crisp and golden. The idea is to make them supple, tasty, and hot. La Tortilla Factory packages "hand made style corn tortillas," which are a blend of corn and wheat and have a lovely springy-tender texture. They're a good choice for this dish. Or, if possible, buy locally produced real handmade corn tortillas. Cotija cheese, named after a town in the Mexican state of Michoacán, is a slightly dry and crumbly cow's milk cheese with a nice tang. It's available in many grocery stores, but if you can't find it, use a dryish feta cheese instead.

2 cups/480 ml Fruity and Spicy
Dried Red Chile Sauce (page 81)

4 tbsp/60 ml olive oil

Twelve 6-in/15-cm corn tortillas

½ cup/55g crumbled Cotija cheese

½ cup/120 ml sour cream

1 tsp fresh lime juice

**SERVES 4**

Heat the oven to 250°F/120°C/gas ½ to keep the enchiladas warm.

To keep things from getting messy, set up your workstation like this: Pour the chile sauce into a shallow dish, such as a pie plate. If you're right-handed, set this to the left of the stove and put the stack of tortillas within easy reach. Put a large baking dish—a 9-by-13-in/23-by-33-cm dish is a good size—to the right of the stove.

In a frying pan, heat 1 tbsp of the oil over medium-high heat. Dip a tortilla into the chile sauce, coating on both sides and letting a little bit drip off, and then lay the tortilla in the hot oil. Watch out, as it will spit and sizzle. If there is room in the pan, coat a second tortilla and add it. Cook for 30 seconds, turn, and cook on the second side for a few more seconds until the tortilla is floppy and hot. Slip tongs or a long, thin metal spatula carefully under the middle of the tortilla, lift it carefully, and let any oil drip back into the pan. Transfer the tortilla to the baking dish, fold it in half, and then in half again to make a loose triangle.

Repeat with the rest of the tortillas, adding more oil to the pan as needed, and snugging the tortillas together in a neat single layer in the baking dish. Crumble the cheese evenly over the folded tortillas and pop them into the oven to warm back up, 5 to 7 minutes.

In a small bowl, stir together the sour cream and lime juice and drizzle over the surface of the enchiladas. Serve right away.

# BUTTER SAUCES

It has a reputation for being tricky to make, finicky to serve, and richer than what most modern diners like to eat. But I am here to tell you none of that is true. A butter sauce is one of the easiest sauces to master, and while it is indeed buttery—it's a butter sauce, after all—you don't need to flood your dish with it. A generous drizzle is usually plenty.

A well-made butter sauce has an exquisite flavor tension between acid and butter. The sauce tastes at once bright and mellow, tangy and rich. It's a dynamic and compelling combination. In other words, I often find myself eating a spoonful directly from the saucepan.

I also like the process of making this sauce. It is a beautiful thing to watch as hunks of cold butter relax into a creamy, satiny liquid. Indeed, it makes you feel like a genius cook.

Beurre blanc is a classic accompaniment to fish dishes or to mild vegetables such as asparagus, and that is generally how I use it. But some of my gutsier butter sauces, such as Soy-Ginger Butter Sauce (page 105), Balsamic Beurre Rouge (page 96), or Orange-Rosemary Balsamic Butter Sauce (page 102), pair well with pork and beef, too.

Butter sauces have two main components: a base made from reducing one or two acidic liquids and the butter. Aromatics or other flavorings are also usually involved, but they are merely delicious additions and are not essential to the architecture of the sauce.

The reduction phase is a matter of letting the liquids boil down until only a tablespoon or two of syrupy liquid are left in the pan. As this happens, I like to scrape down the sides of the pan with a heat-resistant rubber spatula (one of my top kitchen utensils!) to incorporate any splashes back into the main volume. That simple action helps develop the flavor of the sauce because the small droplets on the pan sides are reducing even faster and getting lightly caramelized or toasted. When they are blended back into the main sauce base, they bring that flavor with them.

The butter phase is what gives people anxiety. The idea is to add cold butter to the reduced acidic liquid in such a way that you encourage the butter to melt but also remain emulsified and creamy (rather than melt to the point where the butterfat separates and it becomes oily). Most recipes instruct you to do this over very low heat, adding one small chunk of butter at a time and avoiding boiling at all costs. You can do it that way, but I think it's easier and the emulsion is more stable (so your sauce won't separate as it sits) if you add the butter all at once over medium-high heat and let the sauce actually boil. This method has the added benefit of producing a hotter sauce, as well. Chef Chambrette, my favorite teacher at La Varenne cooking school, taught me to make beurre blanc this way, and I've never looked back.

Using pristine, best-quality butter is, of course, important for the success of a butter sauce. Although I like salted butter for eating, unsalted is best here so that you can control the amount of salt in the sauce. If you have access to specialty butters, such as a cultured European-style butter or a seasonal butter from a local dairy, by all means use them in your butter sauces. But even if you are using supermarket butter, be sure it is as fresh as possible. If you notice a darker outer layer when you cut into a stick, the butter has gotten old and oxidized. Replace it with a fresh package.

The French have a rather more limited view of this type of sauce than I do. They make butter sauces two ways: the classic beurre blanc, made with white wine and white wine vinegar, and a red wine–vinegar version, called beurre rouge. But don't let French rules stand in your way.

The method for making a butter sauce is wide open for improvisation, and you can make your butter sauces based on just about anything acidic that you can think of, from balsamic vinegar to lemon juice to apple cider to soy sauce or even beer. Anything will work that can be reduced to an acidic and flavorful base to which the cold butter can be added.

## WHAT CAN GO WRONG AND HOW CAN I FIX IT?

In general, only two things can go wrong with a butter sauce. First, you let your liquids reduce too much. It is easy to do: walk over to the fridge to get the butter and when you return your pan is totally dry. But wait! If the liquid has totally evaporated but the dry glaze has not burned at all, just pull the pan off the heat and add 2 tablespoons of water to "reconstitute" it—no worries. If you can see or smell that the reduction has started to caramelize or even burn, however, you should start over because the flavor of the sauce will be compromised.

Second, once you add the butter, the emulsion breaks and your sauce separates. This happens for two reasons: you're trying to whisk in too much butter and the emulsification can't hold it all, or you let the sauce get too hot and the butter melts incorrectly. The remedy is the same: if your sauce looks fine right up until the end and then you suddenly see droplets of butterfat forming, pull it off the heat and whisk in a teaspoon or two of cold water or heavy cream.

You can preemptively avoid a broken sauce by adding some cream to the reduction before you add the butter. Many chefs do this as a matter of course, especially if they're making the sauce for a restaurant, where it needs to sit, well behaved, throughout the dinner service. I prefer to use cream only when I want a truly creamy dimension to the sauce; I don't use it to prevent breakage. Even a little bit of extra cream can mute the subtle dynamic between the acid and butter, which I like, but it's a perfectly good trick to use if you're feeling less than confident.

## HOW MUCH SAUCE PER SERVING?

Usually 2 tablespoons per person is the average serving, though it will depend on what the sauce accompanies.

## SPECIAL EQUIPMENT

A Windsor pan, which has sloped sides, is perfect for making butter sauces. The wider top encourages quick evaporation and the narrower base helps keep your reduction from spreading out too far and scorching. You can use a whisk to mix in the butter, but since you're not trying to incorporate any air, a heat-resistant rubber spatula is a good choice. If you want a perfectly smooth sauce, use a fine-mesh sieve to strain out the shallots and other aromatic additions. And if you make the sauce ahead, like for a dinner party, you can keep it warm in a thermos or over hot water (no hotter than 110°F/43°C) in a double boiler.

## STORAGE

Butter sauces are ephemeral—quick to make and meant to be enjoyed soon thereafter. You can easily hold a butter sauce for a couple of hours, but once it has cooled—which means the butter has resolidified—it is not easy to bring it back to life. If you have leftover butter sauce, refrigerate it and then just scoop out a spoonful to dollop onto cooked vegetables. Don't try to re-create the satiny fluid texture of the original sauce.

# BEURRE FONDU (MELTED BUTTER)

This sauce, which is sometimes called drawn butter, is simply melted butter and lemon juice. But leave it to the French to refine a simple thing into a creamy sauce that beautifully cloaks food, distributing the butter and lemon flavors evenly. Use this as a dip for Dungeness crab or lobster or as a sauce for tender spring vegetables, especially asparagus, fava beans, or baby carrots.

¼ cup/60 ml water

½ cup/115 g very cold unsalted butter in one piece

1 tsp fresh lemon juice, plus more if needed

Kosher salt

**MAKES ABOUT ½ CUP/120 ML**

**STORAGE** This sauce must be served the moment it is ready.

In a small saucepan, bring the water to a boil over medium-high heat. Add the butter and start stirring it around in circles with a whisk, a fork, a wooden spoon, or anything that lets you "stab" the hunk of butter so that you can move it around easily. The butter will start to melt and the mixture will bubble and boil around the edges. The melted butter should look creamy, rather than melted and oily. Keep stirring and blending until almost all of the butter is incorporated, then remove the pan from the heat as you work in the last bit. Add the lemon juice and ¼ tsp salt. Taste and add more lemon juice or salt if needed. Serve right away.

# CLASSIC BEURRE BLANC (WHITE BUTTER SAUCE)

A beurre blanc (pronounced *buhr blahnk*) is like an elegant version of melted butter and lemon, and it's just about as easy to make. The texture here is as important as the flavor—in fact, the texture contributes to the smooth flavor—so pay attention when incorporating the butter to make sure that it blends well and emulsifies into a creamy sauce. My method accomplishes this over high heat, but if you're nervous working over high heat, you can cut the butter into several pieces and work in the pieces one by one over low heat.

A beurre blanc is at once light and rich, so it is best on lighter foods, such as fish and shellfish, chicken, and vegetables. This classic version is straightforward and a perfect canvas for fresh herbs, if you want to dress it up a bit.

¼ cup/60 ml dry white wine such as Sauvignon Blanc

¼ cup/60 ml white wine vinegar

1 tbsp minced shallot

½ cup/115 g very cold unsalted butter in one piece, plus ½ tbsp if needed

1 tsp fresh lemon juice

Kosher salt and freshly ground white pepper

MAKES ABOUT ½ CUP/120 ML

**STORAGE** To keep the sauce warm, hold it in the saucepan for a few minutes. For longer keeping, transfer it to a bowl set over a saucepan of hot water (the water should be no hotter than 110°F/43°C). You can also keep the sauce in a thermos for up to 2 hours. The sauce cannot be stored in the refrigerator, as it will separate when reheated.

**QUICK CHANGE** Add 1 tbsp chopped fresh tender herb such as parsley, basil, chervil, chives, cilantro, dill, or tarragon, or a mixture.

In a small saucepan, combine the wine, vinegar, and shallot and bring to a simmer over medium-high heat. Cook, stirring and scraping the sides of the pan occasionally with a heat-resistant rubber spatula, until the liquid is reduced to about 2 tbsp, 4 to 5 minutes.

Add the butter and start stirring it around in circles with a whisk, a fork, a wooden spoon, or anything that lets you "stab" the hunk of butter so that you can move it around easily. The butter will start to melt and the mixture will bubble and boil around the edges. The melted butter should look creamy, rather than melted and oily. Keep stirring and blending until almost all of the butter is incorporated, then remove the pan from the heat as you work in the last bit. Add the lemon juice, ¼ tsp salt, and a pinch of pepper. Taste and adjust the seasoning with salt and pepper if needed. If the sauce is still very sharp, whisk in another ½ tbsp cold butter.

For a perfectly smooth sauce, strain it through a fine-mesh sieve. If you are okay with the shallot, serve as is. If possible, serve right away.

# BALSAMIC BEURRE ROUGE (BALSAMIC–RED WINE BUTTER SAUCE)

I find that the red wine in beurre rouge can make the sauce overly tannic, so I like to blend balsamic vinegar with the wine to add a touch of sweetness and to round out the sauce. Although this sauce is just as elegant as beurre blanc and a lovely partner for meaty fish such as halibut or salmon, it's gutsy enough to drizzle over medallions of beef or pork, too.

¾ cup/180 ml fruity (but not oaky) red wine such as Pinot Noir, Syrah, or Tempranillo

1 tbsp minced shallot

1 fresh thyme sprig

¼ cup/60 ml balsamic vinegar

½ cup/115 g very cold unsalted butter in one piece, plus ½ tbsp if needed

½ tsp fresh lemon juice, plus more if needed

Kosher salt  and freshly ground black pepper

**MAKES ABOUT ⅔ CUP/165 ML**

**STORAGE** To keep the sauce warm, hold it in the saucepan for a few minutes. For longer keeping, transfer it to a bowl set over a saucepan of hot water (the water should be no hotter than 110°F/43°C). You can also keep the sauce in a thermos for up to 2 hours. The sauce cannot be stored in the refrigerator, as it will separate when reheated.

**QUICK CHANGE** Substitute ½ cup/120 ml ruby port for all of the red wine.

In a small saucepan, combine the wine, shallot, and thyme and bring to a simmer over medium-high heat. Boil until reduced by half, about 4 minutes. Add the vinegar and continue to simmer, stirring and scraping the sides of the pan occasionally with a heat-resistant rubber spatula, until the liquid is reduced to about 2 tbsp, 4 to 5 minutes.

Add the butter and start stirring it around in circles with a whisk, a fork, a wooden spoon, or anything that lets you "stab" the hunk of butter so that you can move it around easily. The butter will start to melt and the mixture will bubble and boil around the edges. The melted butter should look creamy, rather than melted and oily. Keep stirring and blending until almost all of the butter is incorporated, then remove the pan from the heat as you work in the last bit.

Pluck out and discard the thyme, and add the lemon juice, ¼ tsp salt, and a few generous grinds of pepper. Taste and adjust the seasoning with lemon juice, salt, and pepper if needed. If the sauce is still very sharp, whisk in another ½ tbsp cold butter. If it is flat, whisk in more lemon juice.

For a perfectly smooth sauce, strain it through a fine-mesh sieve. If you're okay with the shallot, serve as is. If possible, serve right away.

# CREAMY, LEMONY BUTTER SAUCE

Some chefs add heavy cream or crème fraîche to their butter sauces to ensure a stable emulsion (meaning the sauce will be less likely to separate if it's kept warm for a while before serving). The only time I add cream is when I want the flavor and texture of the addition to be part of the character of the sauce. Here, the cream helps take the sharp edge off the wine-vinegar reduction, which means that you can use a bit less butter . . . so you can think of this as a low-fat sauce!

¼ cup/60 ml fresh lemon juice, plus more if needed

¼ cup/60 ml white wine vinegar

1 tbsp minced shallot

¼ cup/60 ml crème fraîche or heavy cream

4 tbsp/55 g very cold unsalted butter in one piece, plus ½ tbsp if needed

Kosher salt and freshly ground white pepper

**MAKES ABOUT ½ CUP/120 ML**

**STORAGE** To keep the sauce warm, hold it in the saucepan for a few minutes. For longer keeping, transfer it to a bowl set over a saucepan of hot water (the water should be no hotter than 110°F/43°C). You can also keep the sauce in a thermos for up to 2 hours. The sauce cannot be stored in the refrigerator, as it will separate when reheated.

**QUICK CHANGE** Use Meyer lemon juice instead of the regular lemon juice and add ½ tsp lightly packed finely grated Meyer lemon zest after adding the butter.

In a small saucepan, combine the lemon juice, vinegar, and shallot and bring to a simmer over medium-high heat. Cook, stirring and scraping the sides of the pan occasionally with a heat-resistant rubber spatula, until the liquid is reduced to about 2 tbsp, 4 to 5 minutes. Add the crème fraîche, bring to a simmer, and simmer until slightly reduced, about 30 seconds.

Add the butter and start stirring it around in circles with a whisk, a fork, a wooden spoon, or anything that lets you "stab" the hunk of butter so that you can move it around easily. The butter will start to melt and the mixture will bubble and boil around the edges. The melted butter should look creamy, rather than melted and oily. Keep stirring and blending until almost all of the butter is incorporated, then remove the pan from the heat as you work in the last bit. Add ¼ tsp salt and a pinch of pepper. Taste and adjust the seasoning with salt and pepper if needed. If the sauce is still very sharp, whisk in another ½ tbsp cold butter.

For a perfectly smooth sauce, strain it through a fine-mesh sieve. If you are okay with the shallot, serve as is. If possible, serve right away.

# LEMON-CAPER BUTTER SAUCE

I only need to read the name of this sauce and I see the fillets of sole in the hot sauté pan, delicate and golden around the edges, the perfect sweet partner for this zesty but elegant sauce. Or, to make a slightly lighter dish, I might cook the sole *en papillote*— seasoned with salt and pepper, wrapped in parchment (or aluminum foil, let's make things easy), and baked with no added fat. Bake the packets on a large rimmed baking sheet in a 400°F/200°C/gas 6 oven for 5 to 8 minutes, depending on the thickness of the fish. It's so simple and delicious. The sauce is also excellent on braised or grilled leeks, or as a dipping sauce for steamed artichoke.

¼ cup/60 ml fresh lemon juice, plus more if needed

1 tbsp white wine vinegar

1 tbsp minced shallot

½ cup/115 g very cold unsalted butter in one piece, plus ½ tbsp if needed

1 tbsp drained capers, chopped

1 tbsp chopped fresh flat-leaf parsley

2 tsp lightly packed finely grated lemon zest

Kosher salt and freshly ground black pepper

**MAKES ABOUT ½ CUP/120 ML**

**STORAGE** To keep the sauce warm, hold it in the saucepan for a few minutes. For longer keeping, transfer it to a bowl set over a saucepan of hot water (the water should be no hotter than 110°F/43°C). You can also keep the sauce in a thermos for up to 2 hours. The sauce cannot be stored in the refrigerator, as it will separate when reheated.

**QUICK CHANGE** Omit the parsley and add 1 tbsp chopped fresh dill and 2 tsp finely diced cornichon with the capers.

In a small saucepan, combine the lemon juice, vinegar, and shallot and bring to a simmer over medium-high heat. Cook, stirring and scraping the sides of the pan occasionally with a heat-resistant rubber spatula, until the liquid is reduced to about 2 tbsp, 4 to 5 minutes.

Add the butter and start stirring it around in circles with a whisk, a fork, a wooden spoon, or anything that lets you "stab" the hunk of butter so that you can move it around easily. The butter will start to melt and the mixture will bubble and boil around the edges. The melted butter should look creamy, rather than melted and oily. Keep stirring and blending until almost all of the butter is incorporated, then remove the pan from the heat as you work in the last bit. Whisk in the capers, parsley, lemon zest, ¼ tsp salt, and a few generous grinds of pepper. Taste and adjust the seasoning with salt and pepper if needed. If the sauce is still very sharp, whisk in another ½ tbsp cold butter. If possible, serve right away.

# JALAPEÑO-LIME-GINGER BUTTER SAUCE

This sauce embodies the concept of sprightly: it's light, bright, and refreshing, and boasts some definite zing from the chiles and ginger. It is beautiful drizzled over stir-fried vegetables, grilled shrimp, or the chicken cutlet on page 108.

¼ cup/60 ml fresh lime juice, plus more if needed

2 tbsp white wine vinegar

1 tbsp minced shallot or yellow onion

1 tsp minced jalapeño or other fresh hot chile

1 tsp peeled and grated fresh ginger

4 tbsp/55 g very cold unsalted butter in one piece

Kosher salt

**MAKES ⅓ CUP/75 ML**

**STORAGE** To keep the sauce warm, hold it in the saucepan for a few minutes. For longer keeping, transfer it to a bowl set over a saucepan of hot water (the water should be no hotter than 110°F/43°C). You can also keep the sauce in a thermos for up to 2 hours. The sauce cannot be stored in the refrigerator, as it will separate when reheated.

**QUICK CHANGE** Add 1 clove garlic, minced, with the shallot, and finish with 2 tsp chopped fresh cilantro.

In a small, heavy saucepan, combine the lime juice, vinegar, shallot, jalapeño, and ginger and bring to a simmer over medium-high heat. Cook, stirring and scraping the sides of the pan occasionally with a heat-resistant rubber spatula, until the liquid is reduced to about 2 tbsp, 4 to 5 minutes.

Add the butter and start stirring it around in circles with a whisk, a fork, a wooden spoon, or anything that lets you "stab" the hunk of butter so that you can move it around easily. The butter will start to melt and the mixture will bubble and boil around the edges. The melted butter should look creamy, rather than melted and oily. Keep stirring and blending until almost all of the butter is incorporated, then remove the pan from the heat as you work in the last bit. Whisk in ¼ tsp salt, then taste and adjust with more salt or a touch more lime juice.

For a perfectly smooth sauce, strain it through a fine-mesh sieve, though it's fine to leave all the aromatics. If possible, serve right away.

# GRAPEFRUIT-CORIANDER BUTTER SAUCE

Grapefruit is my favorite fruit, and my perfect grapefruit variety is a Rio Star red grapefruit from Texas, harvested in March. I find the end-of-season fruit intensely sweet and perfumed, but always with the subtle, intriguing grapefruit tickle of bitter and sour. I am using the zest, juice, and flesh of the fruit in this sauce, so it's a real celebration of this refreshing fruit. The small amount of ground coriander and ginger underscores the fruit flavor, and the slight anise flavor in the basil is a beautiful accent. Try this on big, fat seared sea scallops, grilled mackerel, grilled chicken breast, or steamed asparagus spears.

1 large grapefruit (about 1 lb/455 g), preferably a red variety such as Rio Star

¼ cup/60 ml white wine vinegar

1 tbsp minced shallot

6 tbsp/85 g very cold unsalted butter in one piece, plus ½ tbsp if needed

⅛ tsp ground coriander

⅛ tsp ground ginger

Kosher salt and freshly ground black pepper

½ tsp fresh lemon juice, or more if needed

1 tbsp finely sliced fresh basil

**MAKES ABOUT ½ CUP/120 ML**

**STORAGE** To keep the sauce warm, hold it in the saucepan for a few minutes. For longer keeping, transfer it to a bowl set over a saucepan of hot water (the water should be no hotter than 110°F/43°C). You can also keep the sauce in a thermos for up to 2 hours. The sauce cannot be stored in the refrigerator, as it will separate when reheated.

**QUICK CHANGE** Use a mix of orange and lime juice and segments in place of the grapefruit juice and segments.

Using a rasp-type grater, finely grate 1 tsp zest from the grapefruit and set the zest aside. Cut a slice off each end of the grapefruit to reveal the flesh. Stand the grapefruit on a flat end on a work surface. Using a sharp knife, slice away the peel, including all of the white pith, cutting from the top to the bottom and following the contour of the fruit. Take your time and work in wide strips. If any white pith remains, just slice it off.

Cut out half of the grapefruit segments by holding the fruit in one hand and cutting along both sides of each segment to release it from the membrane, until you've worked your way around half of the fruit. Chop the segments into ¼-in/6-mm pieces; set aside.

Holding the unsegmented grapefruit half over a small saucepan, squeeze the juice from it into the pan. You should have about ½ cup/120 ml (you can also add any juice that has accumulated from the segments). Add the vinegar and shallot to the pan and bring to a simmer over medium-high heat. Cook, stirring and scraping the sides of the pan occasionally with a heat-resistant rubber spatula, until the liquid is reduced to about 2 tbsp, 6 to 8 minutes.

Add the butter and start stirring it around in circles with a whisk, a fork, a wooden spoon, or anything that lets you "stab" the hunk of butter so that you can move it around easily. The butter will start to melt and the mixture will bubble and boil around the edges. The melted butter should look creamy, rather than melted and oily. Keep stirring and blending until almost all of the butter is incorporated, then remove the pan from the heat as you work in the last bit.

Add the coriander, ginger, ¼ tsp salt, a few grinds of pepper, and the lemon juice, then gently stir in the chopped grapefruit. Taste and adjust the seasoning with more salt if needed. If the sauce is still very sharp, whisk in another ½ tbsp cold butter. If it's flat, add more lemon juice. Stir in the basil. If possible, serve right away.

# ORANGE-ROSEMARY BALSAMIC BUTTER SAUCE

This sauce is so delicious that I found myself eating it with a spoon during the testing sessions for this book, but really it's meant to be drizzled around a sautéed pork medallion (see page 109) or seared scallop. The concentrated balsamic vinegar turns the sauce a lovely, glossy brown, almost like a chocolate sauce. Use a decent vinegar but not an artisanal one. I like Lucini brand, they charge a fair price for a good-quality balsamic vinegar to use for cooking, rather than as a condiment.

¼ cup/60 ml balsamic vinegar

¼ cup/60 ml fresh orange juice

1 tsp minced shallot or yellow onion

1 fresh rosemary sprig, 4 in/10 cm long

4 to 5 tbsp very cold unsalted butter in one large piece, plus ½ tbsp if needed

Kosher salt

MAKES ABOUT ½ CUP/120 ML

STORAGE To keep the sauce warm, hold it in the saucepan for a few minutes. For longer keeping, transfer it to a bowl set over a saucepan of hot water (the water should be no hotter than 110°F/43°C). You can also keep the sauce in a thermos for up to 2 hours. The sauce cannot be stored in the refrigerator, as it will separate when reheated.

QUICK CHANGE Add 2 tbsp finely diced roasted red pepper after adding the butter.

In a small saucepan, combine the vinegar, orange juice, shallot, and rosemary and bring to a simmer over medium-high heat. Cook, stirring and scraping the sides of the pan occasionally with a heat-resistant rubber spatula, until the liquid is reduced to 3 tbsp, 3 to 5 minutes.

Add the butter and start stirring it around in circles with a whisk, a fork, a wooden spoon, or anything that lets you "stab" the hunk of butter so that you can move it around easily. The butter will start to melt and the mixture will bubble and boil around the edges. The melted butter should look creamy, rather than melted and oily. Keep stirring and blending until almost all of the butter is incorporated, then remove the pan from the heat as you work in the last bit.

Remove and discard the rosemary sprig (squeegee the sauce off it with your fingers so you don't lose a drop) and whisk in ¼ tsp salt. Taste and adjust the seasoning with salt if needed. If the sauce is still very sharp, whisk in another ½ tbsp cold butter.

For a perfectly smooth sauce, strain it through a fine-mesh sieve. If you are okay with the shallot, serve as is. If possible, serve right away.

# APPLE CIDER–CHILE BUTTER SAUCE

A little of this sauce goes a long way, which is why the recipe yields only ¼ cup/60 milli-liters. It doubles easily, however, if you want to make more of it. The key is to balance the sweet, tang, salt, and spicy heat. You don't want the sauce to tip too far to the buttery, sweet-apple side or it will seem like a dessert sauce. But if you want a dessert sauce, you can have that, too, by leaving out the shallot and chile powder and adding only a pinch of salt.

As a savory sauce, drizzle it over a fried ham steak, grilled sausages served with braised cabbage and onions, or the roasted Brussels sprouts on page 110. For a rustic dessert, drizzle it over *fromage frais* spread on those lovely British cookies called wheatmeal digestive biscuits; McVitie's brand is especially good.

1 cup/240 ml unfiltered apple cider

1 tbsp minced shallot or yellow onion

Big pinch of Espelette pepper (see ingredient note), coarsely ground Aleppo chile (see ingredient note, page 44), cayenne pepper, or other chile powder, plus more if needed

2 tbsp very cold unsalted butter in one piece, plus more if needed

Kosher salt

**MAKES ABOUT ¼ CUP/60 ML**

**STORAGE** To keep the sauce warm, hold it in the saucepan for a few minutes. For longer keeping, transfer it to a bowl set over a saucepan of hot water (the water should be no hotter than 110°F/43°C). You can also keep the sauce in a thermos for up to 2 hours. The sauce cannot be stored in the refrigerator, as it will separate when reheated.

**QUICK CHANGE**

Use pear cider or a mix of apple cider and unsweetened cranberry juice (not cranberry "cocktail") instead of the apple cider.

Add 1 fresh rosemary sprig, 1 tsp balsamic vinegar, or 1 clove garlic, chopped, to the first addition of cider.

In a small saucepan, combine the cider, shallot, and pepper and bring to a simmer over medium-high heat. Cook, stirring and scraping the sides of the pan occasionally with a heat-resistant rubber spatula, until the liquid is reduced to about 2 tbsp, 15 to 20 minutes.

Add the butter and start stirring it around in circles with a whisk, a fork, a wooden spoon, or anything that lets you "stab" the hunk of butter so that you can move it around easily. The butter will start to melt and the mixture will bubble and boil around the edges. The melted butter should look creamy, rather than melted and oily. Keep stirring and blending until almost all of the butter is incorporated, then remove the pan from the heat as you work in the last bit.

Whisk in ¼ tsp salt, then taste and adjust the seasoning with more salt, pepper, or a touch more butter. For a perfectly smooth sauce, strain it through a fine-mesh sieve. If you are okay with the shallot, serve as is. If possible, serve right away.

**INGREDIENT NOTE:** *The Espelette pepper is cultivated in the commune of Espelette in the Basque region of southwestern France. It is a mild chile and is typically dried and ground. Look for it in specialty food shops or from online sources.*

# SAVORY TOMATO–RED WINE BUTTER SAUCE

This is a big-flavored butter sauce that wants to be served with poultry or meat. I panfry hamburgers and serve them with this sauce as though they were little steaks: no buns, just juicy meat and a more glamorous ketchup.

1 tsp extra-virgin olive oil

1 tsp minced garlic

1 tbsp minced shallot

3 whole canned tomatoes

1 fresh rosemary sprig, 3 in/7.5 cm long

½ cup/120 ml fruity (but not oaky) red wine such as Pinot Noir, Syrah, or Tempranillo

¼ cup/60 ml sherry vinegar, plus more if needed

1 tsp Worcestershire sauce

¼ tsp granulated sugar

Kosher salt

6 tbsp/85 g very cold unsalted butter in one piece, plus ½ tbsp if needed

**MAKES ABOUT ⅔ CUP/165 ML**

**STORAGE** To keep the sauce warm, hold it in the saucepan for a few minutes. For longer keeping, transfer it to a bowl set over a saucepan of hot water (the water should be no hotter than 110°F/43°C). You can also keep the sauce in a thermos for up to 2 hours. The sauce cannot be stored in the refrigerator, as it will separate when reheated.

**QUICK CHANGE** Substitute 1 tbsp minced, seeded fresh hot chile for the shallot.

In a small saucepan, heat the olive oil over medium heat. Add the garlic and shallot and cook, stirring constantly, until beginning to soften, about 1 minute. Do not allow them to brown. Raise the heat to medium-high and add the tomatoes and rosemary. Smash the tomatoes with a wooden spoon to collapse them into a pulp and then cook, stirring constantly, until the tomatoes are thick and starting to stick and brown on the bottom of the pan, 3 to 4 minutes.

Add the wine, vinegar, and Worcestershire sauce, bring to a boil, and boil until the mixture is very thick and reduced to the consistency of tomato jam, about 10 minutes. Stir in the sugar and ¼ tsp salt.

Add the butter and start stirring it around in circles with a whisk, a fork, a wooden spoon, or anything that lets you "stab" the hunk of butter so that you can move it around easily. The butter will start to melt and the mixture will bubble and boil around the edges. The melted butter should look creamy, rather than melted and oily. Keep stirring and blending until almost all of the butter is incorporated, then remove the pan from the heat as you work in the last bit.

Strain the sauce through a fine-mesh sieve, pushing on the tomatoes to squeeze out all of the juice. Taste and adjust the seasoning with salt if needed. If the sauce is still very sharp, whisk in another ½ tbsp cold butter. If it's flat, add a drop or two of vinegar. If possible, serve right away.

# SOY-GINGER BUTTER SAUCE

This sauce surprised me when I first made it. I intended to make something fairly light, with a bright, gingery kick. Instead, I ended up with a deep, savory, and slightly mysterious sauce with a distinctly "meaty" flavor. This is because as the soy sauce reduces, it starts to toast a bit, deepening its umami flavors. Use a good-quality soy sauce, such as Kikkoman brand. At my house, we call this sauce vegetarian gravy. We're not actually vegetarian, so we'll drizzle the sauce on slices of rare flank steak or leg of lamb. It's also delicious tossed with green vegetables such as green beans, broccoli, or broccoli rabe.

¼ cup/60 ml rice vinegar

¼ cup/60 ml mirin

4 tbsp/60 ml soy sauce

1 small clove garlic, minced

2 tbsp peeled and chopped fresh ginger (from 1-oz/30-g piece)

4 tbsp/55 g very cold unsalted butter in one piece, plus ½ tbsp if needed

1 tsp fresh lime juice

4 drops hot-pepper sauce such as Sriracha

**MAKES ABOUT ¼ CUP/60 ML**

**STORAGE** To keep the sauce warm, hold it in the saucepan for a few minutes. For longer keeping, transfer it to a bowl set over a saucepan of hot water (the water should be no hotter than 110°F/43°C). You can also keep the sauce in a thermos for up to 2 hours. The sauce cannot be stored in the refrigerator, as it will separate when reheated.

**QUICK CHANGE** Add ½ tsp finely minced hot red chile with the ginger.

In a small saucepan, combine the vinegar, mirin, 2 tbsp of the soy sauce, the garlic, and ginger and bring to a simmer over medium heat. Cook, stirring and scraping the sides of the pan occasionally with a heat-resistant rubber spatula, until the liquid is reduced to about 2 tbsp, about 10 minutes. (I simmer the mixture over a lower heat than in my other recipes because I want to allow enough time for the ginger to infuse into the liquids.)

Add the remaining 2 tbsp soy sauce and simmer, stirring occasionally, until reduced to about 3 tbsp, 2 to 3 minutes more.

Raise the heat to medium-high, add the butter, and start stirring it around in circles with a whisk, a fork, a wooden spoon, or anything that lets you "stab" the hunk of butter so that you can move it around easily. The butter will start to melt and the mixture will bubble and boil around the edges. The melted butter should look creamy, rather than melted and oily. Keep stirring and blending until almost all of the butter is incorporated, then remove the pan from the heat as you work in the last bit.

Whisk in the lime juice and hot-pepper sauce. Taste and adjust the seasoning if needed. If the sauce is still very sharp, whisk in another ½ tbsp cold butter.

Strain through a fine-mesh sieve, pushing on the ginger pieces to squeeze out all their juice. If possible, serve right away.

# ANCHOVY BUTTER SAUCE

This is a sauce for anchovy lovers; the flavor is quite pronounced. But it is also a sauce that could recruit people who are tentative about anchovies, because the lemon and butter temper the anchovy assertiveness in a truly delicious way.

Anchovies oxidize quickly after the can or jar is opened (even when stored in the refrigerator), so use a fresh supply for this recipe. This sauce is fantastic on grilled red peppers or eggplant, as a dip for raw endive spears or steamed asparagus or artichokes, or drizzled over thinly sliced grilled skirt or flank steak.

¼ cup/60 ml fresh lemon juice, plus more if needed

¼ cup/60 ml white wine vinegar

4 tbsp/55 g very cold unsalted butter in one piece, plus ½ tbsp if needed

3 to 4 olive oil-packed anchovy fillets (see ingredient note, page 27), finely chopped and then mashed with a fork to a coarse paste

1 tbsp finely chopped fresh flat-leaf parsley

1 tsp lightly packed finely grated lemon zest

Kosher salt and freshly ground black pepper

**MAKES ABOUT ½ CUP/120 ML**

**STORAGE** To keep the sauce warm, hold it in the saucepan for a few minutes. For longer keeping, transfer it to a bowl set over a saucepan of hot water (the water should be no hotter than 110°F/43°C). You can also keep the sauce in a thermos for up to 2 hours. The sauce cannot be stored in the refrigerator, as it will separate when reheated.

**QUICK CHANGE** Add 1 tbsp finely chopped, pitted Kalamata olive or 2 tsp black olive tapenade with the anchovies.

In a small saucepan, combine the lemon juice and vinegar and bring to a simmer over medium-high heat. Cook, stirring and scraping the sides of the pan occasionally with a heat-resistant rubber spatula, until the liquid is reduced to about 2 tbsp, 4 to 5 minutes.

Add the butter and start stirring it around in circles with a whisk, a fork, a wooden spoon, or anything that lets you "stab" the hunk of butter so that you can move it around easily. The butter will start to melt and the mixture will bubble and boil around the edges. The melted butter should look creamy, rather than melted and oily. Keep stirring and blending until almost all of the butter is incorporated, then remove the pan from the heat as you work in the last bit.

Add the anchovies and stir vigorously to help them dissolve. Whisk in the parsley, lemon zest, ⅛ tsp salt, and a few generous grinds of pepper. Taste and adjust the seasoning with salt and pepper if needed. If the sauce is still very sharp, whisk in another ½ tbsp cold butter. If it's flat, whisk in more lemon juice. If possible, serve right away.

# POTATO-TOPPED HALIBUT FILLET
## with BALSAMIC BEURRE ROUGE

Adding a crunchy potato topping and a drizzle of rich, tangy sauce is an easy way to "upgrade" a plain fish fillet to first-class status. This is a great dinner-party main dish because much of the prep can be done ahead. Boil and chill the potato that afternoon, but don't grate it until it's time to cook or it will darken. And season the fillets with the mustard ahead, too. Make the sauce right before people come over and keep it warm as directed in the recipe. All that will be left to do is pat on the potato topping, bake, and serve.

1 waxy potato, about 5 oz/140 g

Kosher salt and freshly ground black pepper

2 tbsp unsalted butter, melted

Four 6-oz/170-g skinless halibut, salmon, or cod fillets, about 1 in/ 2.5 cm thick

2 tbsp Dijon mustard

½ cup/120 ml Balsamic Beurre Rouge (page 96)

In a small saucepan, combine the potato with salted water to cover by 1 in/ 2.5 cm and bring to a boil over high heat. Reduce the heat to maintain a vigorous simmer and cook until just tender when pierced with a fork, about 20 minutes. Do not cook to the point of mushiness or it will be too hard to grate. Drain the potato in a sieve, let cool, chill, and then peel away the skin.

Heat the oven to 400°F/200°C/gas 6. Line a rimmed baking sheet with parchment paper or aluminum foil.

Grate the potato on the large holes of a box grater. As you work, don't apply too much pressure, as you want fairly thin shavings. Season the grated potato with salt and pepper and toss with the melted butter.

If the fish fillets are thick on one end, thin on the other, fold the thin end under to make neat fillets of uniform thickness. Spread an equal amount of the mustard on top of each fillet and season with a little salt and pepper. Divide the potato evenly among the fillets, gently patting it on top and pressing lightly so it sticks.

Arrange the fillets on the prepared baking sheet. Bake until the fish is just opaque at the center when tested with a knife and the potatoes are golden brown and crisp around the edges, 15 to 18 minutes. If the fish is almost cooked but the potato topping isn't crisp, switch the oven to broil for the last few minutes.

Transfer the fillets to warmed individual plates and spoon a ribbon of the beurre rouge around each fillet. Serve right away.

SERVES 4

# COCONUT-SESAME CHICKEN BREASTS
## with JALAPEÑO-LIME-GINGER BUTTER SAUCE

Sometimes it's nice to have someone else do the cooking, even in your own cookbook, so I invited my friend, food writer and awesome recipe developer, Matthew Card to think of something excellent to go with this sauce. He certainly hit the mark with this quick and easy crunchy-on-the-outside, tender-on-the-inside chicken dish.

Panko, crisp Japanese-style bread crumbs, is stocked in the Asian-food aisle of many supermarkets. The crust works equally well on thick-cut halibut fillets. Keep in mind that nowadays some chicken breast halves are enormous. I have bought skinless, boneless half breasts that weigh 12 ounces/340 grams each. This recipe calls for 6-ounce/170-gram breast halves. If you can only find larger ones, cut them in half.

½ cup/65 g all-purpose flour

Kosher salt and freshly ground black pepper

2 large eggs

1½ tsp hot-pepper sauce such as Sriracha

½ cup/35 g panko

½ cup/50 g unsweetened shredded dried coconut

2 tbsp sesame seeds

Finely grated zest of 1 lime

4 small skinless, boneless chicken breast halves, about 6 oz/170 g each, patted dry

3 tbsp unsalted butter

5 tbsp/75 ml canola or other neutral vegetable oil

⅓ cup/75 ml Jalapeño-Lime-Ginger Butter Sauce (page 99)

Have ready three small, shallow bowls. In the first bowl, season the flour generously with salt and pepper. In the second bowl, whisk together the eggs and hot-pepper sauce until blended. In the third bowl, stir together the bread crumbs, coconut, sesame seeds, and lime zest and season with salt and pepper.

Working with one piece of chicken at a time, pound the thicker end lightly with a meat mallet or a heavy frying pan to create a uniform thickness. Using tongs, dip the chicken piece into the flour mixture, coating it thoroughly and then shaking it to remove the excess flour. Next, dip it into the egg mixture, allowing the excess to drip back into the bowl. Finally, lay the coated chicken in the coconut mixture, turn to coat thickly and evenly, and press firmly to ensure the coconut layer adheres to the chicken. Transfer to a rack. Repeat with the remaining chicken. Let the chicken sit for 10 minutes before cooking so the crust firms up.

In a large frying pan, melt the butter with the oil over medium-high heat. After the butter foams and the bubbles subside and the oil is shimmering, place the chicken pieces in the pan, arranging them so they are not touching one another. Cook until well browned on the first side, 3 to 5 minutes. Using tongs, flip and cook the second side until browned and the chicken is just cooked through, about 2 minutes longer.

Transfer the chicken pieces to a clean rack and blot with paper towels. Serve right away with the butter sauce.

SERVES 4

# PORK TENDERLOIN MEDALLIONS with WILTED SPINACH and ORANGE-ROSEMARY BALSAMIC BUTTER SAUCE

Pork tenderloin is one of the easiest meats to prepare and cook, and its sweet flavor and tender texture are appreciated by nearly all meat eaters. Choose good-quality natural pork, not one that's been "enhanced" with a flavored brine—I hate the flavor and texture of those.

In this dish, I like the contrast of the slightly earthy, tannic greens with the mild meat and fruity-tangy-herbal sauce. You could make this same dish with turkey cutlets in place of the pork or with Swiss chard instead of spinach. If you opt for the chard, allow a bit more time for it to cook.

One 14- to 16-oz/400- to 455-g pork tenderloin

Kosher salt and freshly ground black pepper

2 tbsp olive oil

10 oz/300 g spinach, large stems removed, washed well, with water still clinging to leaves

½ cup/120 ml Orange-Rosemary Balsamic Butter Sauce (page 102)

SERVES 2

With a very sharp knife, trim away any patches of silver skin and big pieces of fat from the tenderloin. Cut into slices 1 in/2.5 cm thick. Flatten each slice lightly with the heel of your hand. Season both sides of each slice generously with salt and pepper.

Heat a large frying pan over medium-high, add 1 tbsp of the oil, and then add the pork. The pork should sizzle as soon as it touches the pan. If it doesn't, hold off for another minute to let the pan get properly hot. If all of the pork will not fit in a single layer without crowding, use two pans or cook it in batches. Sauté the pork until nicely browned on the first side, 2 to 3 minutes. Flip and finish cooking until browned on the second side and still pink in the center, another 1 to 2 minutes. Transfer to a plate, tent with aluminum foil, and let rest while you cook the spinach.

If there's a lot of fat in the pan, pour it off, but don't rinse the pan. Drop the spinach into the pan and quickly toss it around to encourage it to wilt. Season with a bit of salt and pepper and keep cooking until it's tender and most of the liquid has evaporated off, 30 seconds to 1 minute. Some spinach gives off a lot of water, so if it's getting tender but is still quite wet, just pour off the excess water from the pan, pressing on the spinach with tongs or a spoon to release even more. Taste and adjust the seasoning.

Arrange a nice pile of wilted spinach on each warmed plate and top with the pork medallions. Pour any accumulated pork juices over the pork and spinach, then drizzle a thick ribbon of the butter sauce around the base of the spinach, reserving a little of the sauce to pass at the table. Serve right away.

# BRUSSELS SPROUTS with TOASTED WALNUTS and APPLE CIDER–CHILE BUTTER SAUCE

A big platter of these Brussels sprouts makes a delicious centerpiece for a fall dinner party. If you have a pork roast or a roasted chicken to serve with them, all the better, but the vegetables themselves may just steal the spotlight.

1 lb/455 g medium Brussels sprouts, trimmed and halved or quartered lengthwise if large

3 tbsp extra-virgin olive oil

½ tsp chopped fresh rosemary

Kosher salt and freshly ground black pepper

¼ cup/30 g coarsely chopped walnuts

¼ cup/60 ml Apple Cider–Chile Butter Sauce (page 103)

Heat the oven to 400°F/200°C/gas 6.

In a large bowl, toss the sprouts with the olive oil, and rosemary and season with salt and pepper. Spread them in a single layer on a large rimmed baking sheet. Roast until just tender, 15 to 18 minutes. The single leaves that fall away should be dark and crisp, and the sprouts should be tender when pierced with a knife but not mushy. Take a bite, to be sure.

During the last 5 minutes or so of roasting, spread the walnuts on a small baking sheet or pie pan and slide them into the oven. Cook until lightly toasted, about 5 minutes. Pour onto a plate and reserve.

Mound the sprouts on a platter and drizzle the butter sauce over the top. Start with a small amount; you can always pass more at the table. Sprinkle the walnuts over the top and serve right away.

SERVES 4

# CREAM SAUCES

WHEN YOU HEAR *CREAM SAUCE*, YOU MAY THINK "NOT FOR ME ANYMORE, THANKS," BELIEVING THAT ALL CREAM SAUCES ARE CREAMY, RICH, AND HEAVY—AND OLD-FASHIONED.

But I am using *cream sauce* as an umbrella term for a range of sauces that includes everything from a workaday béchamel made mostly with milk to a sauce for pasta that uses broth as the base with a finish of cream to a full-on heavy cream reduced to a luxurious rivulet of dairy goodness—many styles, many levels of richness, many different uses.

A tiny but perfect filet mignon draped with a porcini cream sauce, tender egg pappardelle cloaked in a lemony Parmesan sauce tossed with spring vegetables, or slices of grilled pork tenderloin drizzled with a bracing mustardy cream sauce—these are all dishes we love to eat from time to time, even in today's olive oil–worshipping cuisine. And although it is true that all cream sauces carry a generous amount of fat and calories, a well-made sauce enhanced with sweet cream or nutty-tangy crème fraîche is worth the splurge.

In this chapter, I'm lumping together some classic French sauces as well as sauces that don't fit a traditional mold but rather are just made with methods that I've developed. I've divided all of the sauces into two types: those that get their body by thickening with a roux and those that are thickened by boiling down the cream and other liquids to reduce and concentrate them.

A roux (pronounced roo) is made by whisking together flour and fat, usually butter, to make a smooth paste into which you whisk a liquid. For a béchamel (also called a white sauce), the liquid is either milk or milk and cream. Some versions include onion, clove, bay leaf, and black peppercorns for flavoring. Every former home-economics teacher is probably confident that he or she knows the correct way to make the sauce, but in the end, all of the sauces are essentially the same.

A béchamel is pleasingly bland—if you can imagine such a thing—with a creamy texture but a light flavor. Cooks in the past used it as a stand-alone sauce, as witnessed by my mother's 1942 Fannie Farmer cookbook. The book had many versions of white sauce, including one in which you boil "oyster crabs" to add some flavor. (I learned through a 1913 *New York Times* article that oyster crabs are tiny crabs that live inside an oyster, a delicacy that was rare a century ago and, as far as I know, is nonexistent today.)

Today, béchamel is like a helping verb: it's the sauce that lets you build a cheese soufflé, gratin of greens, or classic lasagna. Your goal when making it is to avoid lumps; to cook both the roux and the sauce long enough to develop some nice nutty flavors, rather than the taste of raw flour and milk; and to balance the seasoning, accomplished by tasting and adjusting.

Velouté sauce, a cousin of béchamel, also starts with a roux, but it calls for broth as the primary liquid. Like béchamel, velouté is not typically served as is, anymore. Instead, it is a binder for potpie and crepe fillings and for the base of luxurious puréed vegetable soups.

In the non–roux-thickened category, you have lighter cream sauces and not-so-light versions. The lighter specimens are the most versatile, complex, and fun to make. These are sauces in which you lay down layers of flavor by sequentially reducing liquids. For example, you might start with ½ cup/120 milliliters white wine that you cook down to just a tablespoon or two; that produces a flavor nugget of acidity and fruitiness. Then you add chicken broth, which you reduce by about three-fourths. The broth dissolves the wine glaze, becomes concentrated and savory, and starts to develop some body, especially if you're using homemade broth that contains a lot of collagen and other natural thickeners.

Pay attention to the "tide rings" of reduced broth that develop along the sides of the pan as the broth evaporates. They become more fully reduced and sort of "toasted," creating even more complex flavors, so be sure to scrape them into the sauce as they form. Some chefs will deliberately provoke this intensified reduction by adding broth to the pan, reducing it way down, adding more broth, and reducing again (at school, the chefs called this *remouiller*, or "remoistening").

The final layer is the cream or crème fraîche, which you also reduce so it gains viscosity and flavor intensity. Along the way, you may add other ingredients, such as a mirepoix (chopped aromatic vegetables), herbs and spices, mushrooms, and mustards.

The result of all this reduction (which often takes only minutes, depending on the volume) is a sauce that is creamy and beautiful feeling on your tongue, with subtle, complex flavors.

The richest and creamiest of my cream sauces is just that: cream that has been reduced along with flavorings until it is quite thick and clings languorously to whatever it's poured over. This is indeed an indulgence, but it is also quick and easy to make and great for improvising.

## WHAT CAN GO WRONG AND HOW CAN I FIX IT?

With roux-thickened sauces, the big threat is lumps. Avoiding them is a matter of adding the liquid fast enough to keep up with the thickening power of the roux. If you add the liquid too slowly, the sauce in the pan gets so thick that it is hard to incorporate more liquid without lumps forming. But adding the liquid all at once makes it hard to blend smoothly, too.

I get the most control if I pull the pan from the heat once the roux is cooked, add about one-fourth of my liquid, whisk like mad, and then return the sauce to the heat, add the rest, and continue whisking as the mixture comes to a simmer and thickens.

If you do get lumps, you can usually whisk them away or smash them into submission with a wooden spoon or heat-resistant rubber spatula. But for stubborn lumps, you will need to push your sauce through a fine-mesh sieve.

With the light cream sauces, the only threat is that the flavors are out of balance. Take care not to use too much wine, or a wine with lots of oak or tannin, because when the sauce is reduced, those flavors get strong and unpleasant and you can actually feel the tannins on your tongue. My basic white wine for cooking is an unoaked Sauvignon Blanc, though not a super-grapefruity one such as those from the Marlborough region of New Zealand. For a red, I like a Syrah from southern France. Whatever wine you use, be sure to reduce it thoroughly. Splashing some wine into a sauce may feel *joie de vivre*-ish, but you'll only give your sauce an unwelcome *je ne sais quoi* of raw alcohol and acid.

The ultra cream sauce is also mostly trouble free, though if you overreduce the cream, the water can get out of whack with the butterfat and your sauce can separate. If you see that happening—the first sign is little beads of butterfat appearing around the edges of the pan—just whisk in a few drops of water or broth and perhaps a touch of fresh cream.

### HOW MUCH SAUCE PER SERVING?

I can't tell you an average amount of béchamel or velouté, since those will most likely be components of any number of other recipes. An average serving of lighter cream sauce might be ⅓ cup/80 milliliters per person. The richest sauces are best in modest portions of ¼ cup/60 milliliters.

### SPECIAL EQUIPMENT

My preferred pan is a heavy, stainless steel–lined copper Windsor pan, which has sloped sides. (The same pan I describe on page 92 for making butter sauces.) The copper doesn't really matter, other than for emotional reasons. What's important is the weight and heat-transferring capacity of the pan. Copper and aluminum, such as the aluminum core in three-ply cookware, are good choices. I would not use a tin-lined copper pan, however, because the tin wears out quickly, leaving exposed copper that can develop a mildly toxic oxide, and the tin can react with the stainless tines of a whisk and turn your sauces a pale gray. The sloped sides are important because they allow for maximum evaporation—reduction—even with a small amount of liquid. Plus, they make it easy for your whisk, wooden spoon, or (my favorite) heat-resistant rubber spatula to reach the angles at the bottom of the pan.

A fine-mesh sieve is useful for losing lumps but also for straining out aromatics, herbs, and the like. A whisk is important too, especially for the roux-based sauces. May

I say boo-yah to the inventor of the whisk, whoever he or she may be?

### STORAGE

Cream sauces can be stored in an airtight container in the refrigerator, though I find that the flour-thickened ones get a touch tired after 3 or 4 days. I think cream sauces are meant to be made and used for a specific purpose, unlike a vinaigrette or caramel sauce, which can stand by in the fridge for all sorts of impromptu uses. All of these sauces can be reheated using very gentle heat, whether stove top or microwave.

# ACTUALLY TASTY BÉCHAMEL SAUCE

Béchamel is a home-economics-class sauce. You learn to make it, but you never conceive of using it again. But a good béchamel has its place in the world, though mostly as a supporting player rather than a star. You can't make a cheese soufflé without béchamel, some delicious lasagnas are made moist with béchamel (called *besciamella* in Italian), and real mac and cheese is all about the sauce, which starts with béchamel. Many béchamels are made with only milk, but I'm adding 30 percent cream because I like the depth of flavor it imparts. Don't be tempted to add a lot of nutmeg. It's fun to grate, but it can call unwanted attention to itself.

2 tbsp unsalted butter

2 tbsp all-purpose flour

1¼ cups/300 ml whole milk

½ cup/120 ml heavy cream or crème fraîche

¼ tsp kosher salt

Freshly ground black pepper

4 or 5 scrapes of fresh nutmeg

**MAKES ABOUT 1¼ CUPS/300 ML**

**STORAGE** Refrigerate in an air-tight container for up to 3 days. The sauce does not freeze well.

**QUICK CHANGE** Add ¼ yellow onion and 1 fresh thyme sprig after whisking in the milk and cream. Remove before serving.

In a medium saucepan, combine the butter and flour over medium-high heat and whisk to blend as the butter melts. Cook, whisking a lot, for about 1 minute. This will give the flour a nutty, rather than floury, flavor.

Pull the pan off the heat and pour in about ¼ cup/60 ml of the milk. Whisk like crazy to form a smooth paste, then whisk in the remaining 1 cup/240 ml milk and the cream.

Return the pan to medium-high heat and bring to a simmer, whisking frequently and making sure to get into the angles of the pan where the thick roux can accumulate.

Simmer, giving the sauce an occasional whisk, until smooth and glossy and no taste of flour remains, 8 to 10 minutes. As it simmers, be sure to scrape down the sides of the pan where the sauce builds up and whisk into the sauce; otherwise you will end up with lumps.

Add the salt, several grinds of pepper, and the nutmeg, then taste and adjust the seasoning. Serve right away or keep warm over low heat.

# ALMOST CREAMLESS CREAMY VELOUTÉ SAUCE

A traditional velouté sauce is broth thickened with a roux, but the texture is so smooth and velvety (which is what *velouté* means) that it's hard to believe that it doesn't contain cream. Because the sauce is all about the broth, use a homemade one, or buy a good-quality broth from a gourmet store. Everyday canned broth won't cut it for this recipe. Choose the type—chicken, fish, or veal—depending on what you intend to do with the sauce, though I find that chicken broth is all-purpose and will even complement seafood. I like to add a good splash of cream at the end to round out the flavors.

4 tbsp/55 g unsalted butter

¼ cup/30 g all-purpose flour

4 cups/960 ml homemade or store-bought good-quality reduced-sodium chicken, fish, or veal broth

¼ cup/60 ml heavy cream or crème fraîche

Kosher salt and freshly ground black pepper

MAKES 3 CUPS/720 ML

STORAGE Refrigerate in an air-tight container for up to 5 days. The sauce does not freeze well.

QUICK CHANGE Add 2 tbsp dry sherry with the cream and simmer for an extra 2 or 3 minutes to cook off the alcohol.

In a medium saucepan, combine the butter and flour over medium-high heat and whisk to blend as the butter melts. Cook, whisking a lot, for about 1 minute. This will give the flour a nutty, rather than floury, flavor.

Pull the pan off the heat and pour in about ¼ cup/60 ml of the broth. Whisk like crazy until smooth, then whisk in the remaining 3¾ cups/900 ml broth.

Return the pan to medium-high heat and bring to a simmer, whisking frequently and making sure to get into the angles of the pan where the thick roux can accumulate. Simmer, giving the sauce an occasional whisk, until reduced by about one-quarter and the sauce is smooth and glossy, 15 to 20 minutes. As it simmers, be sure to scrape down the sides of the pan where the sauce builds up and whisk into the sauce; otherwise you will end up with lumps.

Add the cream and simmer for 1 minute more, then season with salt and pepper. Serve right away or keep warm over low heat.

# SHARP CHEDDAR SAUCE

This sauce, which is essentially a Mornay sauce, is either comforting or sophisticated, depending on how you use it. It's the sauce for mac and cheese—comfort!—or the base of a soufflé—sophistication! I also like it on steamed cauliflower and broccoli for something in between. Feel free to play with different types of cheese, too. This recipe is a blank slate.

3 tbsp unsalted butter

3 tbsp all-purpose flour

2¼ cups/540 ml whole milk if making a sauce, or 1½ cups/360 ml if making a soufflé base

1 cup/115 g lightly packed grated extra-sharp aged Cheddar cheese

¼ cup/30 g finely grated Parmigiano-Reggiano cheese

½ tsp kosher salt

⅛ tsp freshly ground black pepper

Pinch of cayenne pepper

Pinch of freshly grated or ground nutmeg

**MAKES ABOUT 3 CUPS/720 ML SAUCE OR 2⅓ CUPS/560 ML SOUFFLÉ BASE**

**STORAGE** Refrigerate in an air-tight container for up to 3 days. Reheat very gently to ensure the sauce doesn't separate. The sauce does not freeze well.

**QUICK CHANGE** Use another cheese in place of the Cheddar. I like aged Gouda, smoked Cheddar, or Roquefort or other blue. If using a blue or other strong-flavored cheese, start with half the quantity listed and add more to taste. But for all of the variations, keep the Parmigiano-Reggiano, which boosts the overall intensity level.

In a medium saucepan, combine the butter and flour over medium-high heat and whisk to blend as the butter melts. Cook, whisking a lot, for about 1 minute. This will give the flour a nutty, rather than floury, flavor.

Pull the pan off the heat and pour in about ¼ cup/60 ml of the milk. Whisk like crazy to form a smooth paste, then whisk in the remaining milk (2 cups/480 ml if making a sauce or 1¼ cups/300 ml if make a soufflé base).

Return the pan to medium-high heat and bring to a simmer, whisking frequently and making sure to get into the angles of the pan where the thick roux can accumulate. Simmer, whisking often, until smooth and glossy and no taste of flour remains, 8 to 10 minutes. As it simmers, be sure to scrape down the sides of the pan where the sauce builds up and whisk it into the sauce; otherwise you will end up with lumps.

Turn the heat to low, add the cheeses, and whisk until completely melted. Add the salt, black pepper, cayenne, and nutmeg, then taste and adjust the seasoning. Serve right away.

# LIGHT, LEMONY CREAM SAUCE

This sauce is all about the layers of flavor that you create by reduction, so take your time to simmer the liquids down to concentrate their flavors. Once you get the basic architecture of this sauce, you can improvise like crazy—a little saffron, some herbs, different cheese—and you can use it on many different pastas, on light fish dishes, and on green vegetables such as asparagus and broccoli.

½ tsp unsalted butter

1 tbsp minced shallot or sliced green onion (white and light green parts only)

½ cup/120 ml dry (but not oaky) white wine

1¾ cups/420 ml homemade turkey broth (see page 165), chicken broth, or canned reduced-sodium chicken broth

1 fresh thyme sprig (optional)

¾ cup/180 ml heavy cream or crème fraîche

1 tsp lightly packed finely grated lemon zest

1 tbsp grated Parmigiano-Reggiano cheese

Kosher salt and freshly ground black pepper

**MAKES ¾ CUP/180 ML**

**STORAGE** Refrigerate in an air-tight container for up to 4 days. The sauce does not freeze well.

**QUICK CHANGE** Add ¼ cup/7 g finely chopped fresh herb such as tarragon, dill, or flat-leaf parsley, or a mixture, when you add the lemon zest and cheese.

In a medium, heavy sauté pan, melt the butter over medium-high heat. Add the shallot and cook, stirring occasionally, until soft and fragrant but not browned, about 1 minute. Add the wine, raise the heat to high, and boil until reduced to about 1 tbsp, 4 to 6 minutes. Add the broth and the thyme (if using) and boil until reduced to about ½ cup/120 ml, another 8 to 10 minutes.

Now add the cream and continue to boil until reduced to about ¾ cup/180 ml, 9 to 12 minutes longer. Remove the pan from the heat, remove the thyme, and add the lemon zest and cheese. Season with salt and pepper. (If using canned broth, you may not need much or any salt.) Serve right away.

# DIJON-COGNAC CREAM SAUCE

This is a classic sauce that wants a classic accompaniment. A filet mignon or strip steak is my first choice, but I think we could make a new classic by pairing the sauce with halibut or cod. You can make this sauce in the same pan that you cook the main ingredient in, capturing the cooking juices, but making the sauce separately eliminates some of the timing juggling.

2 tsp unsalted butter

1 tbsp minced shallot or yellow onion

⅓ cup/75 ml Cognac or brandy

¾ cup/180 ml homemade turkey broth (see page 165), chicken broth, or canned reduced-sodium chicken broth

¾ cup/180 ml heavy cream or crème fraîche

3 fresh sage leaves

1 fresh thyme sprig

2 tbsp whole-grain Dijon mustard (*moutarde à l'ancienne*)

½ tsp lemon juice

1 tbsp unsalted butter (optional)

Kosher salt and freshly ground black pepper

MAKES ¾ CUP/180 ML

STORAGE Refrigerate in an air-tight container for up to 4 days. The sauce does not freeze well.

QUICK CHANGE Add 2 tbsp drained brined green peppercorns with the mustard.

In a medium, heavy saucepan, melt the butter over medium-high heat. Add the shallot and cook until soft and fragrant but not browned, about 1 minute. Add the Cognac, raise the heat to high, and simmer until reduced to about 1 tbsp, 2 to 3 minutes. Add the broth and boil until reduced to about ¼ cup/ 60 ml, 4 to 5 minutes.

Now add the cream, sage leaves, and thyme; reduce the heat to medum-high; and continue to boil, whisking frequently, until you have about ¾ cup/180 ml, 9 to 11 minutes longer. Strain the sauce through a fine-mesh sieve to remove the herbs and the shallot, or simply pluck out the herbs and leave the shallot in. Return the sauce to the pan over low heat and whisk in the mustard, lemon juice, and the butter (if using). Season well with salt and pepper. (If using canned broth, you may not need much or any salt.) Serve right away.

# SPICY SAFFRON–RED PEPPER CREAM SAUCE

The French pair saffron and seafood beautifully in a variety of dishes, such as bouillabaisse and *soupe de poissons*, and I'm doing it here in a sauce that's fantastic with seafood and pasta. I call for a mix of chicken or turkey broth and fish stock or bottled clam juice, but if you have good homemade fish stock, use only that. Bottled clam juice adds a briny ocean flavor, but it can be salty, so take special care to taste before your final seasoning—as you should with every dish.

2 tsp olive oil

1 cup/160 g finely chopped red bell pepper

1 tbsp finely chopped fresh hot chile such as jalapeño

1 clove garlic, minced

Medium pinch of saffron threads (about 12 threads)

½ cup/120 ml dry (but not oaky) white wine

½ cup/120 ml homemade turkey broth (see page 165), chicken broth, or canned reduced-sodium chicken broth

½ cup/120 ml fish stock or bottled clam juice

1 fresh rosemary sprig

1 cup/240 ml heavy cream or crème fraîche

2 tsp fresh lemon juice

1 tsp lightly packed finely grated lemon zest

Kosher salt and freshly ground black pepper

Hot-pepper sauce such as Sriracha

MAKES 1 CUP/240 ML

**STORAGE** Refrigerate in an airtight container for up to 4 days. The sauce does not freeze well.

**QUICK CHANGE** Add 2 tbsp pastis or other anise-flavored liqueur with the white wine and ½ cup/20 g finely sliced fresh basil with the lemon zest.

In a medium, heavy sauté pan, heat the oil over medium heat. Add the bell pepper and chile, cover the pan, reduce the heat to low, and cook, stirring occasionally, until very soft, fragrant, and lightly browned, 15 to 20 minutes. Add the garlic and cook for 1 minute longer. Add the saffron and cook, stirring frequently, for about 30 seconds. Pour in the wine, raise the heat to high, and simmer until the liquid has reduced to about 1 tbsp (the bell pepper and other solids will take up more volume than 1 tbsp, of course), 4 to 6 minutes. Add the broth, fish stock, and rosemary and boil until reduced to about ½ cup/120 ml liquid, 8 to 10 minutes.

Now add the cream and continue to boil until reduced to about 1 cup/240 ml liquid, 9 to 12 minutes longer. Strain the sauce through a fine-mesh sieve, pressing on the solids to extract all of the juice. Return the sauce to the pan over low heat and add the lemon juice and zest; heat until quite warm. Season with salt, pepper, and hot-pepper sauce. (If using canned broth and/or clam juice, you may not need much or any salt.) Serve right away.

# CHEATER'S CARBONARA SAUCE

True spaghetti carbonara is one of those alchemical dishes in which simple ingredients come together in a perfect moment of harmony and lusciousness—wonderful to eat but not that easy to pull off. Here, I'm referencing the flavors in a carbonara—pancetta or guanciale (two forms of cured pork related to bacon but not smoked), fresh eggs, pecorino, and freshly cracked black pepper—but I'm uniting them all with cream, which allows me to make an actual sauce that can wait patiently until I'm ready to mix it with the pasta. This sauce is also good on steamed asparagus or sautéed chicken breasts, or both, and the recipe is easily doubled.

1 oz/30 g pancetta, diced

2 tsp unsalted butter

1 clove garlic, minced

⅛ tsp red pepper flakes

½ cup/120 ml heavy cream or crème fraîche

1 egg yolk

1 tbsp water

¼ cup/30 g grated pecorino romano cheese

¼ cup/30 g grated Parmigiano-Reggiano cheese

Kosher salt and freshly ground black pepper

MAKES A SCANT 1 CUP/240 ML

**STORAGE** Refrigerate in an airtight container for up to 2 days. Reheat very gently so the egg yolk doesn't curdle. The sauce does not freeze well.

**QUICK CHANGE** Use prosciutto instead of pancetta and increase the butter to 1 tbsp.

In a medium saucepan, combine the pancetta, butter, garlic, and red pepper flakes over medium heat and cook until the pancetta has rendered its fat and is lightly browned around the edges, 4 to 6 minutes. Add the cream, bring to a simmer, and cook until slightly reduced, about 1 minute longer.

In a small bowl, whisk together the egg yolk and water until blended. Ladle in a few spoonfuls of the sauce and whisk immediately so the yolk doesn't coagulate. Pull the sauce off the heat and whisk the yolk mixture into it, along with both cheeses. Return the pan to very low heat and cook, stirring occasionally, until slightly thickened, 2 to 3 minutes. Taste and season generously with salt and black pepper. Keep warm until ready to serve.

# WILD MUSHROOM CREAM SAUCE

This sauce is lovely on poached chicken breasts served with rice and a green vegetable, a meal that recalls old-fashioned hotel restaurant food. It's also beautiful with veal meatballs. I usually strain the sauce, but it's luscious with the mushrooms left in, too.

½ oz/15 g dried porcini, morels, or other flavorful wild mushrooms

1 cup/240 ml hot water

2 tbsp unsalted butter

2 tbsp minced shallot

¼ cup/40 g finely chopped celery

4 oz/115 g fresh cremini mushrooms, trimmed and finely chopped

Kosher salt and freshly ground black pepper

⅓ cup/160 ml dry white wine

½ cup/120 ml homemade turkey broth (see page 165), chicken broth, or canned reduced-sodium chicken broth

1 cup/240 ml heavy cream or crème fraîche

1 tsp fresh lemon juice

1 tbsp finely grated Parmigiano-Reggiano cheese (optional)

MAKES ¾ CUP/180 ML

**STORAGE** Refrigerate in an airtight container for up to 4 days. The sauce does not freeze well.

**QUICK CHANGE** Add 1 tsp Hungarian sweet paprika and 2 tbsp chopped fresh dill to the sauce during the final heating.

In a small bowl, combine the dried mushrooms and the hot water and soak until the mushrooms are soft, about 1 hour. Scoop them out, leaving any grit in the bottom of the bowl. Chop the mushrooms and set aside

In a medium, heavy saucepan, melt the butter over medium-high heat. Add the shallot and celery and cook, stirring frequently, until soft but not browned, 2 to 3 minutes. Add the cremini and rehydrated mushrooms, season lightly with salt, and cook, stirring and scraping the pan frequently, until the mushrooms give off most of their liquid and the liquid has evaporated, 4 to 6 minutes. The mushrooms should smell very mushroomy and be getting nicely browned.

Add the white wine and stir to dissolve any brown bits on the pan bottom. Raise the heat to high and simmer until reduced to about 1 tbsp, 2 to 3 minutes. Add the broth and boil until reduced to about 1 tbsp, 4 to 6 minutes.

Now add the cream and simmer over medium-high heat until thick enough to coat the back of a spoon, 2 to 4 minutes longer. Take the pan from the heat and strain the sauce through a fine-mesh sieve, pushing on the mushrooms to extract all of the juices. Return the sauce to the pan over low heat and add the lemon juice. Heat until quite warm. Season with salt and pepper. (If using canned broth, you may not need much or any salt.) If you want to give the sauce one more boost of savoriness, stir in the Parmigiano-Reggiano. Keep warm until ready to serve.

# PERFECT CHEESE SOUFFLÉ

I love the fact that a lot of people think soufflés are temperamental, slightly risky dishes to make, because they aren't, of course, but I want to keep the mystique going! The most critical part of making a soufflé is to make sure that not even a speck of yolk gets into the whites when you separate the eggs. Soufflés can even be prepped hours ahead and baked at the last minute (ready the base completely, then whip the egg whites and fold them in just before the whole thing goes in the oven), which is fortunate because they make an unexpected and splendid first course for a dinner party.

I supercharge this soufflé with an amount of cheese beyond what a French cook might add, but I like the way it tastes, and if you're lucky enough to have leftovers, they're scrumptious at room temperature with a green salad.

Unsalted butter for the soufflé mold

2⅓ cups/560 ml Sharp Cheddar Sauce (page 118) made with 1½ cups/360 ml whole milk

½ cup/55 g shredded extra-sharp aged Cheddar cheese

Kosher salt and freshly ground black pepper

6 large eggs, separated

SERVES 4 TO 6

Heat the oven to 375°F/190°C/gas 5. Generously butter the bottom and sides of an 8-cup/2-L soufflé mold or other tall-sided baking dish.

In a medium saucepan, gently warm the sauce over medium heat. Add the cheese and stir until melted. Taste the sauce for seasoning and add salt and pepper if needed. The sauce should be highly seasoned and very cheesy to stand up to the bland eggs. Take the pan from the heat, stir the egg yolks into the sauce until blended and set aside.

Using a stand mixer fitted with the whisk attachment, or a large bowl and a handheld electric mixer, whip the egg whites, slowly at first until they are foamy and then increase the speed to high. Continue to whip until the whites are thick and pillowy and definite—though still soft and droopy—peaks form.

Put a big scoop of whites into the cheese sauce and carefully fold the two together with a rubber spatula. Continue adding whites and folding them into the sauce, scooping from the bottom of the pan and gently rolling the mixtures together to preserve as much volume as possible, until all of the whites are added. Don't worry about blending every last streak of white. Gently pour the soufflé batter into the prepared mold and put it in the hot oven.

Bake the soufflé until it is very high, deep golden brown on the top, and still moves slightly when you shake the mold but doesn't seem liquidy inside, 22 to 30 minutes. You can double-check by inserting a thin-bladed knife into the center of the soufflé; if the knife comes out with liquid batter on it, keep cooking. If you want to show the soufflé off, carry it to the table quickly, because it will deflate slightly as it cools. The flavor is better when it's not too hot.

# CLASSIC MACARONI and CHEESE
## with CRISP CRUMB TOPPING

No innovation here, just a great mac and cheese. Even though the dish is a major comfort food, it shouldn't be bland, so I use a good sharp Cheddar and a booster of Parmigiano-Reggiano. The crumb topping also keeps things interesting; you could add ½ teaspoon fresh thyme leaves to the crumbs if you wanted to get fancy, and, of course, the pasta will always welcome some bits of ham or sausage or a handful of steamed broccoli florets.

3 cups/720 ml Sharp Cheddar Sauce (page 118)

½ cup/55 g grated Parmigiano-Reggiano cheese

1 cup/55 g coarse fresh bread crumbs

2 tbsp unsalted butter, melted

10 oz/280 g elbow macaroni or other short pasta

2 tbsp kosher salt

Heat the oven to 400°F/200°C/gas 6. Bring a large pot of water to a boil.

While the water is heating, in a medium saucepan, gently heat the sauce over low heat. Add the cheese and stir until melted. Keep warm. In a small bowl, toss the bread crumbs with the butter and set aside.

Add the macaroni and salt to the boiling water, stir, and cook until al dente, according to the package instructions. Drain well, return the macaroni to the pot, add the sauce, and toss to coat evenly. Pour the sauced macaroni into an 8-in/20-cm square baking dish. Sprinkle evenly with the crumbs.

Bake until the surface is browned and bubbling, about 20 minutes. Let rest for about 15 minutes before serving.

SERVES 3 TO 4

# PASTA with SPRING VEGETABLES in LIGHT, LEMONY CREAM SAUCE

A handful of dishes make up my core repertoire—the ones I can make in my sleep, which are flexible enough to deal with whatever's in the fridge or garden, and are endlessly satisfying. This pasta is one of those dishes. I call for spring vegetables here, but you can use whatever you like, as long as the vegetables aren't too watery, such as tomatoes. And here's a case where the trick of finishing the pasta with a bit of cooking water is crucial—the starchy water emulsifies with the added cheese to give the dish the right amount of sloppy, but not gloppy, creaminess, so please don't skip it.

Kosher salt and freshly ground black pepper

2 carrots, peeled and cut into slices ⅛ in/3 mm thick

½ fennel bulb, trimmed and cut into ¼-in/6-mm dice

12 asparagus spears, woody ends snapped off and cut into 1-in/2.5-cm lengths

1 cup/145 g shelled fresh or frozen English peas (from about 1 lb/455 g in the pod)

8 oz/225 g dried pasta such as penne, linguine, or farfalle

¾ cup/180 ml Light, Lemony Cream Sauce (page 119), heated

1 cup/115 g grated Parmigiano-Reggiano cheese, plus more for serving (optional)

1 tbsp chopped fresh mild-flavored herb such as parsley, dill, mint, tarragon, or basil

Bring a large pot of water to a boil over high heat and add 2 tbsp salt. Have ready a sieve or a large slotted spoon. Add the carrots, fennel, and asparagus to the boiling water and boil for 1 minute. Add the peas and boil for 1 minute longer. Scoop out all of the vegetables with the sieve or spoon, shake off the water, and put them in a bowl. Set aside and keep warm.

Let the water come back to a boil, add the pasta, and cook until al dente, according to the package instructions. Just before the pasta is ready, scoop out about 1 cup/240 ml of the cooking water and set aside. Drain the pasta well and return it to the pot.

Pour in the sauce, add the vegetables and the cheese, and toss well, coating the pasta evenly and melting the cheese. Let the pasta sit for a minute, so it can absorb the liquid. It should be fairly liquidy at first, but as it sits, it will firm up, so check the consistency again just before serving and add a few spoonfuls of the reserved cooking water to get the consistency correct. Finally, toss in the herb and season with salt and pepper. Serve right away and pass more cheese at the table, if you like.

SERVES 4 AS A FIRST COURSE
OR 2 AS A MAIN COURSE

# SAUTÉED CALVES' LIVER with CRISPY SHALLOTS, MASHED POTATOES, and DIJON-COGNAC CREAM SAUCE

Liver doesn't win many popularity contests, but for those of us who like it, this is a wonderful way to enjoy its deep flavor and tender but dense texture. The slight mustard bite of the sauce is a good foil for the liver, and the crispy shallots are my nod to the more traditional fried onions. Warning: The shallots make a great snack, so you might want to make a double batch of them. Do your best to cut them as evenly as possible so that you don't have thick and thin pieces in the same batch, which would cook unevenly.

## SHALLOTS

About 1½ cups/360 ml vegetable oil, for frying

2 large shallots, peeled and cut into ¹⁄₁₆-in/1.5-mm thick (or slightly thinner) rounds and separated into rings

Kosher salt

## POTATOES

1 lb/455 g starchy potatoes, such as russet, peeled and cut into large chunks

½ cup/120 ml milk or cream

3 tbsp butter

Kosher salt and freshly ground black pepper

## LIVER

2 tbsp butter

Two 4-oz/120-g thin liver cutlets, patted dry on paper towels

About ½ cup/60 g flour, for dredging

Kosher salt and freshly ground black pepper

½ cup/120 ml Dijon-Cognac Cream Sauce (page 120), warmed

SERVES 2

**TO FRY THE SHALLOTS,** arrange a double layer of paper towels on a plate for draining the shallots. Pour the oil into a medium saucepan; it should come to a depth of about ¾ in/18 mm. (It's important to use a deep pan and fairly shallow oil so there's no danger of the oil boiling over as you fry.) Attach a candy thermometer to the side of the pan. Heat over medium-high heat until the thermometer reads 350°F/180°C. Add about a quarter of the shallots and fry, stirring almost constantly with a slotted metal spoon or a skimmer, until pale brown (the color of a grocery bag—any darker and the shallots will be bitter), about 60 seconds. (If you don't have a thermometer, test the oil temperature by just starting with a few shallots.) With the slotted spoon, quickly scoop out the shallots and drain on the plate of paper towels. They'll crisp up as they cool. Repeat with the remaining shallots in three more batches, transferring each batch to the plate when done. Allow the oil to return to 350°F/180°C before each batch. If burned bits accumulate in the oil, scoop them out before adding a new batch. Sprinkle generously with salt and set aside. (You can fry the shallots several hours ahead. Once cool, transfer to an airtight container.)

**TO MAKE THE POTATOES,** put the potatoes in a medium pot, cover with water by about 2 in/5 cm, add 2 tbsp salt, and bring to a boil. Adjust the heat to a lively boil and cook until the potatoes are thoroughly tender when pierced with a knife. Drain in a colander. Put the milk and butter into the pot, return to low heat, add the potatoes, and mash with a potato masher, a large fork, or a big wooden spoon. (If you want your potatoes really smooth, use a ricer or food mill, but I'm okay with a few chunks.) Add more milk or butter until you get the consistency you like. Season generosly with salt and pepper, and keep warm in the pan.

**TO COOK THE LIVER,** heat a medium skillet over medium-high and add the butter. When it begins to sizzle, quickly dredge the liver in flour, arrange in the pan, and season generously with salt and pepper. Cook until the first side is nicely browned, about 2 minutes, flip to the second side, season again, and cook just until browned, another 1 minute. Do not overcook liver—it should be rosy pink inside—so check by cutting a piece.

Spoon a nice bed of the warm potatoes on each plate, arrange the liver on the potatoes, drizzle both with the cream sauce, and top with a tangle of fried shallots. Serve right away.

# FARFALLE with SHRIMP and SCALLOPS in SPICY SAFFRON–RED PEPPER CREAM SAUCE

This is a delicious dish, but also rich, so I like to serve it as a first course (smaller portions!) for special dinners. My philosophy of menu planning is to serve a first and a last course with fanfare and fuss and make the middle courses simpler. For the cook, this isn't a fussy dish, however, because you can make the sauce ahead of time and keep it warm, and then cook the seafood in the sauce just before you combine it with the pasta. If you want to keep things even simpler, make the dish with only one of the shellfish in the title.

4 oz/115 g dry-pack bay scallops or sea scallops

1 cup/240 ml Spicy Saffron–Red Pepper Cream Sauce (page 121)

6 oz/180 g medium shrimp, peeled and deveined

1 tsp lightly packed finely grated lemon zest

2 tbsp finely chopped fresh basil

2 tbsp kosher salt

6 oz/180 g farfalle pasta or similar pasta shapes

Bring a large pot of water to a boil over high heat. If using sea scallops, cut away or pull off the tough muscle on the side of each scallop and quarter the scallop.

While the water is heating, bring the cream sauce to a gentle simmer, add the shrimp, and simmer for a minute or so. Add the scallops and simmer until the shrimp and scallops are cooked, 2 to 3 minutes longer, depending on their size. Keep the sauce warm. In a small bowl, mix together the lemon zest and basil.

When the water is boiling, add the salt and pasta, stir, and cook until al dente, according to the package instructions. Just before the pasta is ready, scoop out about 1 cup/240 ml of the cooking water and set aside. Drain the pasta well and return it to the pot.

Add the seafood sauce to the pasta and toss gently but thoroughly to mix. If the mixture seems at all dry or clumpy, add a few spoonfuls of the reserved cooking water, knowing that the pasta will continue to drink up sauce as it sits.

Arrange a neat mound of pasta in each warmed bowl and top with the zest-basil mixture, dividing it evenly. Serve right away.

SERVES 2 AS A FIRST COURSE

# MAYONNAISE SAUCES

MOST OF US HAVE BEEN CONDITIONED TO THINK OF MAYONNAISE AS A CONDIMENT THAT COMES FROM A JAR, one that is mostly functional rather than flavorful. It glues tuna and celery together to make tuna salad, it helps lettuce stick to bread in countless sandwiches, and it moistens yolks in deviled eggs.

But mayonnaise is much more than that. A well-made, from-scratch mayonnaise isn't a mere condiment. It's a spoonful of unctuousness that's mellow and rich as a sauce on its own, or rich and creamy as a base for other ingredients. One taste of homemade mayonnaise—especially one made with farm-fresh eggs—and you'll understand why the French consider it a true sauce. A classic mayo, or one spiked with herbs, spices, or other flavorings, makes a beautiful dip for raw or steamed vegetables, plays a deliciously considered role in a good sandwich, pairs with cold roast chicken or red meat, and forms the base of the famous French rouille, a red pepper sauce that enriches fish soups and stews. It's versatile, and indispensable.

### WHAT'S GOING ON IN THIS SAUCE?

Mayonnaise is made from egg yolks seasoned with a touch of acidity (usually lemon juice, vinegar, or both), which are then whipped with oil to form a voluminous emulsion. The consistency of homemade mayonnaise will be different from that of the jarred stuff. When you make it with a whisk, it will be loose and almost pourable. If you use a blender or food processor, it will be firmer and more puddinglike, because generally more air is whipped into it. Which style you make depends on what you plan to do with it: drizzle it, slather it, or fold it.

### WHAT CAN GO WRONG AND HOW CAN I FIX IT?

The egg yolks and oil must be close to room temperature rather than cold. I often ignore that kind of instruction in a recipe because I'm too lazy or impatient to plan ahead, but in this case, temperature is critical. The emulsion won't come together with cold yolks and you'll be left with a liquidy mess. This doesn't happen every time, but it happens enough that you don't want to take the risk. (Tip: To warm eggs quickly to room temperature, immerse the whole eggs in a bowl of warm water for a few minutes.)

You also need to know when to stop adding oil. Add too much, too fast and the emulsion will break, causing the mayonnaise to separate or curdle. The best way to avoid this is to add the oil a drop at a time in the beginning of whisking, and then slowly add the oil in a more steady stream as it comes together.

Some cooks suggest fixing a broken mayonnaise by whisking together another egg yolk and some mustard, and then gradually whisking the broken sauce into it. That works, but it's easier and usually just as effective to put 1 tablespoon of warm water in another bowl and gradually whisk the broken sauce into the water.

### HOW MUCH SAUCE PER SERVING?

Portion size for mayonnaise depends on where the sauce is being used. For most uses, such as a dip or on a sandwich, a couple of tablespoons are plenty.

### SPECIAL EQUIPMENT

A large bowl and a whisk are all you need, but a food processor makes the job easy, and a rubber spatula helps corral all of the ingredients.

### STORAGE

Even though the French chefs at my cooking school would leave a bowl of mayonnaise on the counter for days, it's important to refrigerate mayonnaise because it's made with raw egg yolks. And if you have any concerns about eating or serving raw yolks (folks who are pregnant, elderly, very young, or have a compromised immune system should avoid them), use pasteurized eggs. Or, just use commercial mayonnaise and add the flavoring elements in the recipes. It's okay to cheat sometimes! Most mayonnaises will keep in an airtight container in the refrigerator for up to 5 days.

# CLASSIC MAYONNAISE

Grocery-store eggs make perfectly good mayonnaise, but taste mayo made with fresh, flavorful eggs from the farmers' market, or maybe from your own chickens, and you'll understand why it's regarded as an important sauce.

Sometimes farmers' market eggs are smaller or larger than a "large" egg from the supermarket, so pay attention to their size and adjust your other ingredients as needed. The other critical element here is the oil, which must also be fresh. And this is not the time to use an olive oil with a big flavor. A neutral-flavored vegetable or seed oil or a mild and fruity extra-virgin olive oil allows the creamy flavor to stay balanced.

2 egg yolks

2 tsp white wine vinegar

¼ tsp Dijon mustard

Kosher salt

1 to 1¼ cups/240 to 360 ml mild extra-virgin olive oil or canola, grapeseed, or a mixture

1 tbsp fresh lemon juice, plus more if needed

**MAKES ABOUT 1½ CUPS/360 ML**

**STORAGE** Refrigerate in an air-tight container for up to 5 days.

**QUICK CHANGE** Add ¼ cup/ 7 g finely chopped fresh tender herb, such as flat-leaf parsley, chervil, chives, dill, basil, mint, or cilantro, or a mixture, with the lemon juice.

**WHISK METHOD:** Shape a kitchen towel into a ring on your work surface and set a medium bowl in the center of the ring. This will stabilize the bowl so that you can whisk with one hand and pour in the oil with the other hand.

Put the egg yolks, vinegar, mustard, and ½ tsp salt in the bowl and whisk vigorously to combine. As you continue to whisk, begin adding the oil a drop at a time and whisk until the sauce begins to emulsify. Continue whisking, and as the mayonnaise gets thicker, you can add the oil a little faster. When you have incorporated almost all of the oil, slow down with adding the remaining oil and watch the sauce closely. If you see oil starting to separate out, stop adding oil; the yolks have absorbed enough. Whisk in the lemon juice. Taste and adjust with more salt and lemon juice if needed.

**FOOD PROCESSOR METHOD:** Put the yolks, vinegar, mustard, and ½ tsp salt in a food processor and pulse until well blended. The yolks will likely be sprayed on the sides of the bowl, so scrape them down with a rubber spatula. With the motor running, begin adding the oil in a very slow stream. You may need to stop and scrape again. As the mayonnaise gets thicker, you can add the oil faster. When you have incorporated almost all of the oil, slow down and watch the sauce closely. If you see oil starting to separate out, stop adding oil; the yolks have absorbed enough. Whirl in the lemon juice and a few drops of water, if the sauce looks too thick. Taste and adjust the seasoning with salt and lemon juice if needed.

# ROSEMARY-MINT MAYONNAISE

Rosemary is one of my favorite herbs, but its assertive flavor and wiry texture means that I rarely use it in uncooked dishes. Here I infuse the oil with the rosemary flavor, taking texture out of the equation. The mayonnaise is excellent with cold roast lamb, as a dip for little lamb sliders, or slathered onto a roast beef sandwich.

1 to 1¼ cups/240 to 300 ml mild extra-virgin olive oil, canola, grapeseed, or a mixture

2 fresh rosemary sprigs, 4 in/10 cm long

½ cup/10 g very lightly packed fresh mint leaves

½ cup/15 g lightly packed fresh flat-leaf parsley leaves

2 egg yolks

2 tsp white wine vinegar, plus more if needed

½ tsp granulated sugar

¼ tsp Dijon mustard

Kosher salt

**MAKES ABOUT 1½ CUPS/360 ML**

**STORAGE** Refrigerate in an air-tight container for up to 5 days.

**QUICK CHANGE** Heat 2 large fresh thyme sprigs in the oil along with the rosemary and substitute basil for the parsley.

In a small saucepan, heat 1 cup/240 ml of the oil and the rosemary over low heat until the oil gets quite hot but the rosemary does not start to sizzle (check the oil temperature with an instant-read thermometer, if you have one; aim for 140°F/60°C). Keep the oil at this temperature on the heat for about 10 minutes, then remove the pan from the heat and let the rosemary steep for another 20 to 30 minutes. Taste the oil; it should be fragrant and flavored but not bitter. Remove and discard the rosemary sprigs. Let the oil cool completely.

Bring a small saucepan of water to a boil over high heat. Add the mint and parsley leaves, stir for 2 to 3 seconds, and then drain the herbs in a colander. Immediately rinse the herbs with very cold water to stop the cooking. Drain well and blot them completely dry with paper towels.

In a food processor, combine the egg yolks, vinegar, sugar, mustard, and 1 tsp salt and pulse until well blended. The yolks will likely be sprayed on the sides of the bowl, so scrape them down with a rubber spatula. With the motor running, begin adding the rosemary oil in a very slow stream. You may need to stop and scrape again. As the mayonnaise gets thicker, you can add the oil faster. When you have incorporated almost all of the oil, slow down and watch the sauce closely. If you see oil starting to separate out, stop adding oil; the yolks have absorbed enough. If you think you can still add more oil, add the final ¼ cup/60 ml or so of unflavored oil.

Add the mint and parsley and process until well combined into the mayonnaise. Taste and adjust the seasoning with salt and vinegar if needed.

# SWEET ONION–CURRY MAYONNAISE

This is my ultimate mayo for chicken salad, whether the salad ends up between slices of bread or as the center of a composed salad plate (see page 141). The mayo is also good with slices of cold roasted turkey breast or oven-fried sweet potatoes, or as a dip for crudités, especially carrots, cauliflower, and tender celery hearts.

2 tbsp canola or other neutral vegetable oil, plus ¾ cup/180 ml

1 cup/140 g chopped sweet onion such as Walla Walla or Vidalia or yellow onion

Kosher salt

1 tbsp mild curry powder

1 tsp peeled and finely chopped fresh ginger

1 tbsp fresh lime juice, plus more if needed

2 tsp cider, rice, or white wine vinegar

1 tsp granulated sugar, plus more if needed

¼ tsp dry mustard

3 egg yolks

**MAKES ABOUT 1¼ CUPS/300 ML**

**STORAGE**: Refrigerate in an air-tight container for up to 5 days.

**QUICK CHANGE**: Add 1 small jalapeño chile, stemmed, seeded (if desired), and minced, to the pan with the onion.

In a medium frying pan, heat the 2 tbsp oil over medium-high heat. Add the onion and ¼ tsp salt and cook, stirring, until the onion begins to soften, about 1 minute. Reduce the heat to low and continue to cook, stirring often, until the onion is very soft, fragrant, and deeply golden but not browned, 12 to 15 minutes. Add the curry powder and ginger and cook for 1 minute more. Transfer the onion mixture to a plate and let cool completely.

In a food processor, combine the cooled onion mixture, lime juice, vinegar, sugar, mustard, and ½ tsp salt and pulse until well blended. Add the egg yolks and process until the mixture is mostly puréed. With the motor running, begin adding the remaining ¾ cup/180 ml oil in a very slow stream. You may need to stop and scrape again. As the mayonnaise gets thicker, you can add the oil faster. When you have incorporated almost all of the oil, slow down and watch the sauce closely. If you see oil starting to separate out, stop adding oil; the yolks have absorbed enough. Taste and adjust the seasoning with salt, sugar, and lime juice if needed.

# SMOKY RED PEPPER MAYONNAISE

Spanish smoked paprika, or *pimentón de la Vera*, comes in sweet, bittersweet, and hot varieties. I like using the sweet here because it plays well off the sweet roasted red pepper, but feel free to use whichever kind you like best. If you're pressed for time and opt for a jarred roasted red pepper, be sure to rinse and dry it before adding it to the mayonnaise. This crimson sauce, which is a bit like the French rouille, is wonderful on grilled vegetable and mozzarella sandwiches or as a dip for seared or steamed green beans.

2 egg yolks

2 tsp sherry vinegar or red wine vinegar

¼ tsp Dijon mustard

1 or 2 cloves garlic

Kosher salt

1 to 1¼ cups/240 to 300 ml canola, grapeseed, or mild extra-virgin olive oil, or a mixture

1 tsp Spanish sweet smoked paprika (see ingredient note, page 24)

1 red bell pepper, roasted, peeled, stemmed, seeded, and cut into a few pieces

Hot-pepper sauce such as Sriracha

MAKES ABOUT 2 CUPS/480 ML

**STORAGE** Refrigerate in an air-tight container for up to 5 days.

**QUICK CHANGE** Soak a small pinch (about 8 threads) of saffron threads in 1 tbsp warm water for 10 minutes and add the saffron and soaking water with the egg yolk mixture.

In a food processor, combine the egg yolks, vinegar, mustard, garlic, and ½ tsp salt and pulse until well blended. The yolks will likely be sprayed on the sides of the bowl, so scrape them down with a rubber spatula. With the motor running, begin adding the oil in a very slow stream. You may need to stop and scrape again. As the mayonnaise gets thicker, you can add the oil faster. When you have incorporated almost all of the oil, slow down and watch the sauce closely. If you see oil starting to separate out, stop adding oil; the yolks have absorbed enough.

With the motor running, add the paprika, roasted pepper, and a few dashes of hot-pepper sauce. Taste and adjust the seasoning with salt and hot-pepper sauce if needed.

# AVOCADO-LIME MAYONNAISE

This recipe is doubly rich, with puréed avocado taking the place of some of the oil. And although it's not a low-fat sauce by any means, the fats in avocado are so beneficial that I think it's safe to consider this jade green sauce a health food.

1 ripe avocado, halved, pitted, peeled, and cut into about 8 pieces

2 tbsp fresh lime juice, plus more if needed

2 egg yolks

Kosher salt

1 cup/240 ml avocado, canola, grapeseed, or mild extra-virgin olive oil, or a mixture

1 tsp lightly packed finely grated lime zest

**MAKES ABOUT 1½ CUPS/340 ML**

**STORAGE** Refrigerate in an airtight container for up to 5 days.

**QUICK CHANGE** Add 2 tbsp chopped canned mild green chiles and ¼ cup/10 g chopped fresh cilantro with the last of the avocado chunks.

In a small bowl, toss the avocado with 2 tsp of the lime juice to prevent browning; set aside.

In a food processor, combine the egg yolks, the remaining 4 tsp lime juice, and ½ tsp salt and pulse until well blended. The yolks will likely be sprayed on the sides of the bowl, so scrape them down with a rubber spatula. With the motor running, begin adding the oil in a very slow stream. You may need to stop and scrape again. As the mayonnaise gets thicker, you can add the oil faster. When you have incorporated almost all of the oil, slow down and watch the sauce closely. If you see oil starting to separate out, stop adding oil; the yolks have absorbed enough.

When all of the oil is incorporated, add the avocado, a few chunks at a time, processing until the mayonnaise is smooth and light. Whirl in the lime zest. Taste and adjust the seasoning with salt and lime juice if needed.

# VITELLO TONNATO MAYONNAISE

*Vitello tonnato* is an Italian dish of cold sliced veal slathered in an irresistible tuna-anchovy mayonnaise. The veal is just a vehicle for the tasty mayonnaise, so I'm skipping it here and focusing on the sauce. In this version, I'm using some reduced broth as a quick substitute. You can serve this mayonnaise on any type of cold leftover roasted meat or chicken, on grilled vegetables (see the green beans on page 145), on crostini, or on seared fresh tuna—redundant, perhaps, but delicious.

½ cup/120 ml homemade turkey broth (see page 165), chicken broth, or canned reduced-sodium chicken broth

1 cup/240 ml canola, grapeseed, or mild extra-virgin olive oil, or a mixture

¼ cup/60 ml fruity extra-virgin olive oil

2 egg yolks

2 tsp white wine vinegar

¼ tsp Dijon mustard

1 small clove garlic

Kosher salt

One 5-oz/140-g can olive oil–packed tuna, drained

4 olive oil–packed anchovy fillets (see ingredient note, page 27), rinsed

1 tbsp drained capers

1 tbsp fresh lemon juice, plus more if needed

2 tbsp crème fraîche (optional)

**MAKES ABOUT 2 CUPS/480 ML**

**STORAGE** Refrigerate in an airtight container for up to 5 days.

**QUICK CHANGE** Add ¼ cup/ 10 g finely chopped tender fresh herb such as flat-leaf parsley, chervil, chives, dill, basil, mint, or cilantro, or a mixture, with the crème fraîche.

In a small saucepan, bring the broth to a simmer over medium-high heat. Simmer until reduced to about 2 tbsp, 6 to 8 minutes. Set aside to cool completely.

Pour both oils into a measuring cup; set aside. In a food processor, combine the egg yolks, vinegar, mustard, garlic, and ½ tsp salt and pulse until well blended. The yolks will likely be sprayed on the sides of the bowl, so scrape them down with a rubber spatula. With the motor running, begin adding the oil in a very slow stream. You may need to stop and scrape again. As the mayonnaise gets thicker, you can add the oil faster. When you have incorporated almost all of the oil, slow down and watch the sauce closely. If you see oil starting to separate out, stop adding oil; the yolks have absorbed enough.

With the motor running, add the tuna, anchovies, capers, lemon juice, and reduced broth and process until quite smooth. If using the crème fraîche, add to the mixture and pulse to combine. Taste and adjust the seasoning with salt and lemon juice if needed (if using canned broth, you probably won't need more salt).

# MELLOW GARLIC CONFIT AIOLI

Aioli, a garlic-infused version of mayonnaise, is a wonderful way to add Mediterranean flavor to any dish. But I think my taste buds must be more Swedish than Mediterranean because most of the aioli I taste is too harshly garlicky for me. This version tempers that bite but still delivers full garlic flavor in two forms: oil-poached cloves (or garlic confit) and garlic-flavored oil. You can use this sauce with lightly steamed or grilled vegetables, fried shrimp, or crab cakes, or you can stir it into a seafood stew at the last minute for a creamy note (but don't let it boil).

10 large cloves garlic, smashed

½ cup/120 ml canola or other neutral vegetable oil

½ cup/120 ml fruity extra-virgin olive oil, plus more if needed

2 egg yolks

1 tbsp white wine vinegar

Kosher salt and freshly ground black pepper

1 tbsp fresh lemon juice, plus more if needed

½ tsp lightly packed finely grated lemon zest

**MAKES ABOUT 1½ CUPS/360 ML**

**STORAGE** Refrigerate in an air-tight container for up to 5 days.

**QUICK CHANGE** Add ¼ cup/ 30 g finely chopped, pitted black olives such as Kalamata with the lemon juice and zest.

In a small saucepan, heat the garlic and both oils over medium heat just until the garlic begins to sizzle the tiniest bit. Reduce the heat to low and continue to cook, swirling the oil in the pan occasionally, until the cloves are completely soft, 5 to 7 minutes. Don't let the garlic brown at all. Remove the pan from the heat and let the oil cool completely. Scoop out the garlic and reserve the garlic and the oil separately.

In a food processor, combine the egg yolks, garlic, vinegar, and ¼ tsp salt and pulse until well blended. The yolks will likely be sprayed on the sides of the bowl, so scrape them down with a rubber spatula. With the motor running, begin adding the reserved garlic oil in a very slow stream. You may need to stop and scrape again. As the mayonnaise gets thicker, you can add the oil faster. When you have incorporated almost all of the oil, slow down and watch the sauce closely. If you see oil starting to separate out, stop adding oil; the yolks have absorbed enough. Whirl in the lemon juice and zest. Season with pepper, then taste and adjust the seasoning with salt and lemon juice if needed.

# UPDATED "FRY SAUCE"

At the risk of upsetting fry-sauce cultists, I think this is a more delicious version than the classic, rather simple mayo-ketchup french fry sauce that is revered in parts of the West. It retains the creamy-zesty balance of the original, but the umami factor is much stronger thanks to soy and Worcestershire sauce. This sauce is yummy paired with salty-fatty french fries or just about any other fried food.

½ cup/120 ml Classic Mayonnaise (page 133)

¼ cup/60 ml ketchup

2 tsp Worcestershire sauce

2 tsp fresh lemon juice

2 tsp soy sauce

4 drops hot-pepper sauce such as Sriracha

**MAKES ABOUT ¾ CUP/180 ML**

**STORAGE** Refrigerate in an airtight container for up to 5 days.

**QUICK CHANGE** Add 1 tsp minced chipotle chile in adobo.

In a small bowl, stir together the mayonnaise, ketchup, Worcestershire sauce, lemon juice, soy sauce, and hot-pepper sauce. Taste and adjust the seasoning with additional lemon juice, soy sauce, and hot-pepper sauce until the sauce is zesty but balanced.

# CHICKEN, APPLE, and HAZELNUT SALAD
## with SWEET ONION–CURRY MAYONNAISE

I've never lost my love for what I think of as ladies luncheon chicken salad, which is tender chicken with apples or grapes and some kind of crunchy nut, all bound together with mayonnaise. Tuck some of this salad into a croissant and you have a classic sandwich (and to my mind, the only sandwich that should be allowed on a croissant). I call for purchased rotisserie chicken here, but you can also use home-roasted chicken. Almonds, pecans, or walnuts are a fine substitute for hazelnuts.

2 cups/280 g shredded or diced cooked chicken; a store-bought rotisserie chicken is fine

2 cups/240 g diced crisp, tart apple such as Braeburn, Pink Lady, or Fuji, peeled or not, as you prefer

1 cup/160 g finely diced celery

¼ cup/20 g thinly sliced green onion (white and light green parts only)

½ to ¾ cup/120 to 180 ml Sweet Onion–Curry Mayonnaise (page 135)

Kosher salt and freshly ground black pepper

½ cup/55 g coarsely chopped, lightly toasted hazelnuts

Pretty lettuce leaves or 4 all-butter croissants, split, for serving

In a large bowl, gently fold together the chicken, apple, celery, green onion, and mayonnaise. Season with salt and pepper. Sprinkle with the hazelnuts.

Arrange the chicken salad on the lettuce on serving plates, or use the croissants to make sandwiches. Serve right away.

SERVES 4

# SIMPLE SEAFOOD STEW with
# GRILLED BREAD and SMOKY RED PEPPER MAYONNAISE

This dish is delicious as written here, but the recipe is also a starting point for whatever calls to me when I'm shopping on the day I'm cooking it: sweet summer corn, chunks of firm zucchini, or fat white beans. You can turn this simple stew into a feast by adding shrimp, mussels, and clams.

5 tbsp/75 ml extra-virgin olive oil

1 small jalapeño chile, stemmed, seeded, and minced

1½ tbsp chopped garlic

Two 28-oz/795-g cans whole peeled tomatoes, coarsely chopped, with juices, or 4 cups/600 g peeled, seeded, and chopped fresh tomatoes

1 cup/240 ml dry white wine

4 slices artisanal white bread such as ciabatta or *pain au levain*

3 cups/720 ml fish stock, bottled clam juice, homemade turkey broth (see page 165), chicken broth, or canned reduced-sodium chicken broth

Large pinch of saffron threads (about 15 threads)

1 lb/455 g halibut, cod, or other firm white fish, cut into 1-in/2.5-cm chunks

Kosher salt

Hot-pepper sauce such as Sriracha

⅔ cup/165 ml Smoky Red Pepper Mayonnaise (page 136)

2 tbsp chopped fresh flat-leaf parsley

In a large soup pot or Dutch oven, heat 3 tbsp of the oil over medium heat. Add the chile and cook, stirring occasionally, until soft and fragrant, about 1 minute. Add the garlic and cook, stirring, until fragrant, another 30 seconds or so. Add the tomatoes and wine, raise the heat to medium-high, and simmer vigorously until the tomatoes have broken down and the mixture is slightly soupy, about 15 minutes.

While the soup is simmering, prepare a medium fire in a charcoal or gas grill. Or, position an oven rack about 5 in/12 cm from the broiler element and heat the broiler. If using a grill, the fire is ready when you can comfortably hold your hand, palm-side down, 2 to 3 in/5 to 7.5 cm above the grill rack for 4 seconds. Brush the grill rack so that it is perfectly clean.

Brush the bread slices on both sides with the remaining 2 tbsp oil. Place on the grill rack or on a baking sheet under the broiler and grill or broil, turning once, until nicely toasted on both sides. Set aside.

Pour the stock into the tomato mixture and crumble in the saffron. Simmer to reduce the liquid slightly and concentrate the flavors, about 5 minutes. Add the fish chunks, stir to make sure they are completely covered by liquid, and simmer until the fish is opaque throughout, 3 to 5 minutes more. Season with salt and hot-pepper sauce.

Put one slice of the grilled bread in each of four wide soup bowls, ladle some of the stew over each slice, and top with a big spoonful of the mayonnaise. Or, top the grilled bread generously with mayonnaise and serve on the side, for dipping. Sprinkle with the parsley and serve immediately, with a knife and fork as well as a spoon.

SERVES 4

# QUICK FISH TACOS with
# AVOCADO-LIME MAYONNAISE and SALSA VERDE

At the risk of getting busted by the gourmet police, I am going to proclaim that I love frozen fish sticks. When I was a kid, my parents frequently went out on Friday nights, which meant I could fix my own fish-stick dinner and my affection for the bland and crunchy things has remained to this day. I like the way they taste in fish tacos, too.

But I do have standards, which means I look for the "whole fillet" sticks, usually haddock, which are miles better than the compressed bits. A box of fish sticks in the freezer means it's a cinch to make these tacos. Of course, if you want to use fresh fish, that's great. Just dust the fish fillets in flour seasoned with salt and pepper and sauté until golden and cooked through. Many stores sell shredded cabbage, sometimes labeled "angel hair." If you prefer to slice your own, cut a whole cabbage into quarters and slice part of a quarter into very thin shreds. Wrap the remaining cabbage and store in the crisper drawer for up to two weeks.

4 tbsp/60 ml fresh lime juice

1½ tsp granulated sugar

½ tsp kosher salt

1½ cups/100 g finely shredded green cabbage

8 whole pieces frozen breaded fish fillets

Eight 6-in/15-cm corn tortillas

½ cup/120 ml Avocado-Lime Mayonnaise (page 137)

⅓ cup/7 g coarsely chopped fresh cilantro

½ cup/120 ml salsa verde, homemade Roasted Green Chile and Tomatillo Sauce (page 82), made without avocado, or purchased

½ cup/55 g crumbled Cotija (see headnote, page 88) or feta cheese

In a medium bowl, stir together 3 tbsp of the lime juice, the sugar, and salt. Add the cabbage and toss to coat evenly. As you fix the rest of the dish, toss the cabbage occasionally so it softens slightly.

Heat the oven and bake the fish as directed on the package. Just before serving, wrap the tortillas in aluminum foil and warm in the oven for 5 to 7 minutes, or wrap them in paper towels and heat in the microwave on high for 1 minute.

To assemble each taco, lay a fish fillet on a tortilla (cut the fish in half if it fits better that way). Top with some cabbage, mayonnaise, cilantro, salsa, and cheese and fold loosely. Serve right away.

SERVES 4

# GRILLED GREEN BEANS with
# VITELLO TONNATO MAYONNAISE

This is the kind of appetizer that sneaks up on you. You're chatting, sipping your wine, munching on the occasional green bean dipped in the sauce . . . and before you know it, you've devoured the platter. They're that good.

1 tbsp Dijon mustard

1 tbsp extra-virgin olive oil

¼ tsp chili powder

½ tsp kosher salt

1 lb/455 g fresh green beans, ends trimmed

1 cup/240 ml Vitello Tonnato Mayonnaise (page 138)

In a medium bowl, whisk together the mustard, olive oil, chili powder, and salt. Add the beans and toss well to coat.

Prepare a medium-hot fire in a charcoal or gas grill or heat a stove-top grill pan over medium-high heat. If using a grill, the fire is ready when you can comfortably hold your hand, palm-side down, 2 to 3 in/5 to 7.5 cm above the grill rack for 2 to 3 seconds. Brush the grill rack so that it is perfectly clean.

Arrange the beans on the grill rack or grill pan, positioning them perpendicular to the bars so they don't fall through. (Yes, I know it's obvious, but it doesn't hurt to be reminded.) Grill, turning frequently, until the beans are nicely blackened and blistered, 5 to 10 minutes, depending on the size and age of the beans.

Transfer the beans to a platter and serve right away with the mayonnaise in a bowl for dipping.

SERVES 4

# HOLLANDAISE SAUCES

IF THE ONLY HOLLANDAISE SAUCE YOU'VE EVER TASTED IS THAT SORRY YELLOW PASTE FROM A PACKET, YOU WON'T YET UNDERSTAND MY JOY AT MAKING HOME-MADE HOLLANDAISE.
But once you've tried it yourself, you will. It isn't difficult, but it does require proper technique and a little attention. And the resulting sauce is a true French treasure: light and billowy, lemony, and rich with butter and egg, tasting of neither but rather of something all its own.

Hollandaise is traditionally used to sauce that Sunday-brunch staple, eggs Benedict, a slightly odd dish because you are putting an egg sauce on top of eggs. I adore it anyway, and I have updated it in this chapter for a delicious change of pace. But I think hollandaise comes into its glory when paired with green vegetables, because its richness is countered by fresh wholesomeness. Steamed asparagus, broccoli, or even slightly bitter broccoli rabe are fantastic with a lemony hollandaise, and dipping artichoke leaves into the Saffron–Red Pepper Hollandaise on page 152 would be a lovely way to spend a summer evening.

### WHAT'S GOING ON IN THIS SAUCE?

Making hollandaise sauce really feels like you're participating in French cuisine. First, you whisk egg yolks and a small amount of a flavoring liquid over low heat. This gently cooks the yolks, thickening them and allowing them to capture the air bubbles that are introduced as you whisk. Once this yolk foam develops, you whisk in melted butter to make an emulsion that turns thick, very glossy, and unctuous. The more gentle the temperature, the longer it will take, but that's a good thing. It gives you more control over the texture of the eggs and lets you whisk in lots of air for a lovely, fluffy consistency.

### WHAT CAN GO WRONG AND HOW CAN I FIX IT?

There are three potential trouble spots when making a hollandaise. The first is to avoid scrambling or overcooking the yolks by whisking them over heat that is too high. This is easily solved by using a double boiler (and paying attention). Although I've seen chefs make hollandaise in a saucepan in direct contact with a burner, the gentler heat of a double boiler (a bowl set over a pan of simmering water) gives you lots of control and confidence—just go slow and have patience.

The second potential trouble spot is failing to achieve an emulsion between the egg yolks and the butter. If you add the melted butter too quickly or add too much, the yolks won't be able to absorb it all and the sauce will "break" and look oily and separated. By adding the butter slowly, you will see the point at which it is no longer being absorbed well and you can just slow down or stop there.

The third trouble spot has to do with ingredients, not technique. A hollandaise sauce is rich, of course, but its flavor is actually quite delicate. And delicate can become bland very quickly if you aren't careful. How many uninspired servings of eggs Benedict have we all endured? I prefer eggs from the farmers' market because they have real eggy flavor but if I buy eggs for this sauce in the supermarket, I pick the latest "sell by" date I can find. It's also worth using fresh, premium butter. You can't get around the fact that hollandaise is an indulgent sauce, so just celebrate the ingredients instead. I use plenty of citrus in the sauce, too—adding grated zest as well as juice—and sometimes I brown the butter for even more flavor.

I know it's classic to prepare clarified butter for making a hollandaise. This is when you melt butter and separate the clear butterfat from the water and the milk solids that settle on the bottom of the pan. And it's fine if you want to make a batch of clarified butter. But I don't like to fuss too much when I cook, so I just melt the butter and pour directly from the pan into my sauce, and if a little of its water and milk solids come along, that's okay.

### HOW MUCH SAUCE PER SERVING?

Hollandaise is rich, so ¼ cup/60 milliliters per person will be plenty in most cases.

### SPECIAL EQUIPMENT

You need a medium, wide, stainless-steel bowl and a medium saucepan to sit below it as its double-boiler mate. You also need a good whisk and a strong arm or a handheld electric mixer. I like having a heat-resistant rubber spatula handy for scraping the sides of the bowl as I'm whisking.

### STORAGE

Although a hollandaise sauce is lofty and delicate, it does have the ability to hold nicely for an hour or so if you leave it in the double boiler over very low heat, or if you pour it into a large thermos. When I have leftover hollandaise, I like to use it as part of a topping for toasted crostini because it's delicious and browns beautifully under the broiler. Refrigerate leftovers in an airtight container for up to 3 days.

---

#### BLENDER HOLLANDAISE, PERHAPS

Making hollandaise in a blender is a quick way to get where you're going. You put the egg yolks and lemon juice in the blender, and then you slowly pour in the hot melted butter as the blender blades whirl. The advantage of this method is that by not cooking the egg yolks on the stove top, you don't run the risk of overcooking them.

The merit in this method is its quickness, but I've never gotten results that rival a handmade hollandaise. The consistency always seems runny to me, and I don't think it's that hard to whisk egg yolks in a double boiler.

A compromise position could be to use a handheld mixer to whisk your yolks and butter in the double boiler, sparing yourself some of the elbow grease but still properly cooking the yolks and getting that iconic light, fluffy texture.

# CLASSIC (BUT LEMONY) HOLLANDAISE

The classic sauce is incredibly delicate in flavor. I prefer a slightly zingier version, however, so I amp up the flavor here with lemon juice and lemon zest. If you're lucky enough to have your own hens or to buy eggs at a farmers' market, this sauce is the perfect destination for them. A yolk from a standard large supermarket egg weighs about ⅔ ounce/18 grams, so if your farm egg yolks are smaller than that, add another half a yolk or so.

6 oz/170 g unsalted butter

2 egg yolks

1 tbsp fresh lemon juice, plus more if needed

1 tbsp water

Kosher salt

½ tsp lightly packed finely grated lemon zest

**MAKES ABOUT 1 CUP/240 ML**

**STORAGE** Hollandaise is best eaten right after you make it, but you can hold it in the double boiler over very low heat or in a thermos for up to 1 hour. Refrigerate left-overs in an airtight container for up to 3 days.

**QUICK CHANGE** Fold 2 tbsp finely chopped preserved lemon peel into the finished sauce.

In a small saucepan, melt the butter over medium heat. Don't stir as it melts. You want the milky solids to fall to the bottom and the butterfat to float to the top. Keep warm.

Pour water to a depth of 1 to 2 in/2.5 to 5 cm into a medium saucepan and place over medium heat. Rest a medium stainless-steel bowl in the pan over (not touching) the water. Put the egg yolks, lemon juice, water, and ¼ tsp salt in the bowl and start whisking. As the bowl heats up, the yolks will begin to thicken. Whisk vigorously, scraping around the bowl with a heat-resistant rubber spatula from time to time so that bits of yolk don't get stuck to the sides and overcook. Beat until thick and frothy but not quite fluffy, 3 to 4 minutes. The whisk will start leaving a clear space on the bottom of the bowl. Remove the bowl from the heat and whisk for another 30 seconds or so to stabilize the sauce and let the bowl cool down.

Continue whisking as you slowly drizzle in the warm melted butter, taking care not to add too much of the milky-watery layer from the bottom of the pan. As you pour and whisk, make sure the yolks are accepting the butter and the yolks and butter are emulsifying. If the sauce looks at all broken or "curdly," stop adding butter and just whisk for a few seconds. Only resume adding butter once you've whisked the sauce into creaminess again.

Once all of the butter has been added, whisk in the lemon zest. Taste and adjust the seasoning with salt and lemon juice if needed. If possible, serve right away.

# LIME–BROWN BUTTER HOLLANDAISE

Here, the butter flavor of the hollandaise is amplified thanks to browning. The butter develops a lovely nuttiness that tastes especially good in the sauce. This is a gorgeous partner for crab cakes and other seafood, grilled chicken breasts, and just about any vegetable, but especially asparagus.

¾ cup/170 g unsalted butter

2 egg yolks

2 tbsp fresh lime juice, plus more if needed

Kosher salt

½ tsp lightly packed finely grated lime zest

Dash of hot-pepper sauce such as Sriracha

**MAKES ABOUT 1 CUP/240 ML**

**STORAGE** This sauce is best eaten right after you make it, but you can hold it in the double boiler over very low heat or in a thermos for up to 1 hour. Refrigerate leftovers in an airtight container for up to 3 days.

**QUICK CHANGE** Fold in 2 tbsp finely chopped fresh cilantro just before serving.

In a small, heavy saucepan or frying pan, melt the butter over medium heat. Once the butter has melted, keep cooking it. It will sizzle and foam as the water cooks off. Keep cooking, scraping the bottom of the pan with a heat-resistant rubber spatula or wooden spoon as the milk solids in the butter turn a light golden brown, 4 to 5 minutes. Once the butter becomes very fragrant and smells toasty, remove the pan from the heat and let the butter cool slightly.

Pour water to a depth of 1 to 2 in/2.5 to 5 cm into a medium saucepan and place over medium heat. Rest a medium stainless-steel bowl in the pan over (not touching) the water. Put the egg yolks, lime juice, and ¼ tsp salt in the bowl and start whisking. As the bowl heats up, the yolks will begin to thicken. Whisk vigorously, scraping around the bowl with a heat-resistant rubber spatula from time to time so that bits of yolk don't get stuck and overcook. Beat until thick and frothy but not quite fluffy, 3 to 4 minutes. The whisk will start leaving a clear space on the bottom of the bowl. Remove the bowl from the heat and whisk for another 30 seconds or so to stabilize the sauce and let the bowl cool down.

Continue whisking as you slowly drizzle in the browned butter. Unlike with classic hollandaise, go ahead and add all of the milk solids at the bottom of the pan. They carry most of the "browned" flavor. As you pour and whisk, make sure the yolks are accepting the butter and the yolks and butter are emulsifying. If the sauce looks at all broken or "curdly," stop adding butter and just whisk for a few seconds. Only resume adding butter once you've whisked the sauce into creaminess again.

Once all of the butter has been added, whisk in the lime zest and hot-pepper sauce. Taste and adjust the seasoning with salt, lime juice, and hot-pepper sauce if needed. If possible, serve right away.

# "STEAK SAUCE" HOLLANDAISE

I wanted to pump up the umami flavor of my classic hollandaise, so I added soy sauce, Worcestershire, and sherry vinegar. If I had pan drippings from a roast beef, I would whisk them in, too. I pair this with steak and garlicky fried potatoes (see page 158).

¾ cup/170 g unsalted butter

1 tsp soy sauce

1 tsp Worcestershire sauce

Hot-pepper sauce such as Sriracha

2 egg yolks

1 tbsp sherry vinegar, plus more if needed

1 tbsp water

Kosher salt

½ tsp lightly packed finely grated lemon zest

**MAKES ABOUT 1 CUP/240 ML**

**STORAGE:** This sauce is best eaten right after you make it, but you can hold it in the double boiler over very low heat or in a thermos for up to 1 hour. Refrigerate leftovers in an airtight container for up to 3 days.

**QUICK CHANGE:** Fold in 2 tbsp chopped fresh tarragon with the lemon zest.

In a small saucepan, melt the butter over medium heat. Don't stir as it melts. You want the milky solids to fall to the bottom and the butterfat to float to the top. Keep warm.

In a small bowl, stir together the soy sauce, Worcestershire sauce, and a few dashes of hot-pepper sauce; set aside.

Pour water to a depth of 1 to 2 in/2.5 to 5 cm into a medium saucepan and place over medium heat. Rest a medium stainless-steel bowl in the pan over (not touching) the water. Put the egg yolks, vinegar, water, and ¼ tsp salt in the bowl and start whisking. As the bowl heats up, the yolks will begin to thicken. Whisk vigorously, scraping around the bowl with a heat-resistant rubber spatula from time to time so that bits of yolk don't get stuck and overcook. Beat until thick and frothy but not quite fluffy, 3 to 4 minutes. The whisk will start leaving a clear space on the bottom of the bowl. Remove the bowl from the heat and whisk for another 30 seconds or so to stabilize the sauce and let the bowl cool down.

Continue whisking as you slowly drizzle in the warm melted butter, taking care not to add the milky-watery layer from the bottom of the pan. As you pour and whisk, make sure the yolks are accepting the butter and the yolks and butter are emulsifying. If the sauce looks at all broken or "curdly," stop adding butter and just whisk for a few seconds. Only resume adding butter once you've whisked the sauce into creaminess again.

Once all of the butter has been added, whisk in the soy sauce mixture and lemon zest. Taste and adjust the seasoning with salt and vinegar if needed. If possible, serve right away.

# SAFFRON–RED PEPPER HOLLANDAISE

I doubt if any Provençal cook has ever made this version of hollandaise, but I liked the way the flavors in it conjured up a south-of-France feeling as I made it, so I'm projecting a Provençal connection here. Use a nice, fruity extra-virgin olive oil to extend the Mediterranean note. This sauce begs to be served with seafood, especially hot and sizzling from the grill, and it's crazy good on a gutsier version of eggs Florentine (see page 156).

Jarred Spanish piquillo peppers are excellent in this sauce. You'll need about three peppers. Or, you can use regular jarred roasted red peppers, in which case one medium pepper should be sufficient. And, of course, you can roast and peel a fresh pepper.

½ cup/115 g unsalted butter

2 oz/55 g roasted red peppers

2 tbsp fruity extra-virgin olive oil

2 tbsp fresh orange juice, plus more if needed

1 tbsp water

Kosher salt

Large pinch of saffron threads (about 15 threads)

2 egg yolks

½ tsp lightly packed finely grated orange zest

⅛ tsp hot-pepper sauce such as Sriracha

**MAKES ABOUT 1 CUP/240 ML**

**STORAGE** This sauce is best eaten right after you make it, but you can hold it in the double boiler over very low heat or in a thermos for up to 1 hour. Refrigerate leftovers in an airtight container for up to 3 days.

**QUICK CHANGE** Add 1 tsp Spanish sweet smoked paprika (see ingredient note, page 24) to the pepper purée.

In a small saucepan, melt the butter over medium heat. Don't stir as it melts. You want the milky solids to fall to the bottom and the butterfat to float to the top. Keep warm.

In a food processor, combine the red peppers and olive oil and process until a smooth purée forms. You want to emulsify the oil with the peppers; the mixture should look creamy and combined.

Pour water to a depth of 1 to 2 in/2.5 to 5 cm into a medium saucepan and place over medium heat. Rest a medium stainless-steel bowl in the pan over (not touching) the water. Put the orange juice, water, ¼ tsp salt, and saffron into the bowl and let sit over the heat for a few minutes so the saffron infuses the liquid. When you can smell the saffron, add the egg yolks and start whisking. As the bowl heats up, the yolks will begin to thicken. Whisk vigorously, scraping around the bowl with a heat-resistant rubber spatula from time to time so that bits of yolk don't get stuck and overcook. Beat until thick and frothy but not quite fluffy, 3 to 4 minutes. The whisk will start leaving a clear space on the bottom of the bowl. Remove the bowl from the heat and whisk for another 30 seconds or so to stabilize the sauce and let the bowl cool down.

Continue whisking as you slowly drizzle in the warm melted butter, taking care not to add too much of the milky-watery layer from the bottom of the pan. As you pour and whisk, make sure the yolks are accepting the butter and the yolks and butter are emulsifying. If the sauce looks at all broken or "curdly," stop adding butter and just whisk for a few seconds. Only resume adding butter once you've whisked the sauce into creaminess again.

Once all of the butter has been added, whisk in the pepper purée, the orange zest, and hot-pepper sauce. Taste and adjust the seasoning with salt, hot-pepper sauce, and orange juice if needed. If possible, serve right away.

### DO I NEED TO WORRY ABOUT THE EGG YOLKS?

I'd love to be able to say unequivocally that it's always safe to eat a hollandaise sauce, but I'm afraid I can't do it. There will always be a small risk of salmonella in foods with egg yolks that reach only about 140°F/60°C when the sauce is finished cooking. The temperature for ultimate food safety is 160°F/70°C. With that said, unless you're pregnant, very young, very old, or have a compromised immune system, the yolks in a hollandaise are sufficiently cooked and the risk of a foodborne illness is minimal. If you're worried, you can use pasteurized eggs, but the flavor and texture of the finished sauce won't be the same. Another way to minimize the risk is to buy the freshest eggs you can find, refrigerate them the moment you get them home, and serve the finished sauce right away.

# BÉARNAISE SAUCE

Béarnaise is a close relative of hollandaise, but it includes very French ingredients such as tarragon, wine, and shallot. Be sure to chop tarragon with a very sharp knife, as it bruises easily. Béarnaise is classically paired with steak, but it's also marvelous with salmon, crab cakes, and even plain-Jane chicken breasts.

¼ cup/60 ml white wine vinegar

¼ cup/60 ml dry white wine

1 tbsp minced shallot or yellow onion

1 fresh tarragon sprig, plus 1 tbsp finely chopped leaves, plus more if needed

⅔ to ¾ cup/140 to 170 g unsalted butter

2 egg yolks

Kosher salt and freshly ground black pepper

**MAKES ABOUT 1 CUP/240 ML**

**STORAGE** Béarnaise is best eaten right after you make it, but you can hold it in the double boiler over very low heat or in a thermos for up to 1 hour. Refrigerate left-overs in an airtight container for up to 3 days.

**QUICK CHANGE** Add 1 tbsp pastis or other anise-flavored liqueur to the reduced vinegar mixture.

In a small saucepan. combine the vinegar, wine, shallot, and tarragon sprig and bring to a boil over medium-high heat. Boil until reduced to about 1 tbsp, 7 to 9 minutes. Strain through a fine-mesh sieve into a medium bowl, pressing on the herbs and shallot with a rubber spatula to squeeze out all of the flavor.

In a small saucepan, melt the butter over medium heat. Don't stir as it melts. You want the milky solids to fall to the bottom and the butterfat to float to the top. Keep warm.

Pour water to a depth of 1 to 2 in/2.5 to 5 cm into a medium saucepan and place over medium heat. Rest a medium stainless-steel bowl in the pan over (not touching) the water. Put the egg yolks, vinegar reduction, and ¼ tsp salt in the bowl and start whisking. As the bowl heats up, the yolks will thicken. Whisk vigorously, scraping around the bowl with a heat-resistant rubber spatula from time to time so that bits of yolk don't get stuck and overcook. Beat until thick and frothy but not fluffy, 3 to 4 minutes. The whisk will start leaving a clear space on the bottom of the bowl. Remove the bowl from the heat and whisk for another 30 seconds to stabilize the sauce and let the bowl cool down.

Continue whisking as you slowly drizzle in the melted butter, taking care not to add too much of the milky-watery layer. As you pour and whisk, make sure the yolks are accepting the butter and the yolks and butter are emulsifying. If the sauce looks broken or "curdly," stop adding butter and whisk for a few seconds. Resume adding butter once you've whisked the sauce into creaminess again.

Once all of the butter has been added, whisk in the chopped tarragon. Season with salt, pepper, and with more tarragon if needed. If possible, serve right away.

# SMOKED-SALMON BENEDICT BITES

I learned to make these addictive hors d'oeuvres during my one and only restaurant job, working as a cook in a small café in Denver. We did a thriving Sunday brunch business and usually had leftover hollandaise at the end of the shift, which we put to excellent use in these buttery-crisp snacks. I call for my version of classic hollandaise, but any of the sauces in this chapter would work well with this recipe. These hors d'oeuvres freeze beautifully, too, so they're ideal for make-ahead entertaining.

½ cup/120 ml Classic (but Lemony) Hollandaise (page 149), chilled

½ cup/65 g flaked hot-smoked salmon

½ cup/55 g shredded Fontina or Havarti cheese

1 tbsp finely chopped fresh chives

Freshly ground black pepper

16 baguette slices, ½ in/12 mm thick

Position an oven rack about 5 in/12 cm from the broiler element and heat the broiler.

In a small bowl, gently fold together the hollandaise, smoked salmon, cheese, and chives. Season well with pepper.

Arrange the baguette slices on a large rimmed baking sheet and broil until lightly toasted on one side, 1 to 2 minutes. Remove the pan from the oven, flip the toasts, and let them cool.

Spread about 1 tbsp of the salmon mixture on each cooled toast, mounding the mixture slightly. Return the pan to the broiler and cook until the salmon is bubbling and golden brown, about 1 minute. Serve right away.

To make ahead: After topping the toasts with the salmon mixture, refrigerate until very firm, about 30 minutes. Individually wrap each chilled toast in plastic wrap, transfer them all to a ziplock freezer bag, and freeze for up to 2 months. To serve, arrange the toasts, straight from the freezer, in a single layer on a rimmed baking sheet and bake in a 400°F/200°C/gas 6 oven until heated through and toasty, 20 to 22 minutes. If they need more browning, finish them under the broiler for another minute.

MAKES 16 HORS D'OEUVRES

# FRIED EGGS with GARLICKY CHARD and SAFFRON–RED PEPPER HOLLANDAISE

Here is another recipe created by my friend Matthew Card. It's a riff on eggs Florentine (eggs Benedict but with spinach instead of Canadian bacon or ham) and, like every dish he makes, it is turbocharged with flavor. It would also be delicious with any of the other sauces in this chapter, so feel free to experiment.

Avoid using a hard-crusted bread here. If you can't find focaccia, substitute something tender and flavorful, such as brioche or a soft Italian loaf. Peppadew peppers, which originated in South Africa, are sweet, tangy, and only modestly hot. They are pickled and sold in jars in the deli section of well-stocked grocery stores.

Kosher salt

1 large bunch Rainbow or Bright Lights Swiss chard (12 oz/340 g), leaves and stems separated and stems cut crosswise into slices ¼ in/6 mm thick

4 tbsp/60 ml extra-virgin olive oil

3 cloves garlic, minced

Pinch of Espelette pepper (see ingredient note, page 103) or red pepper flakes

½ cup/80 g thinly sliced jarred roasted red pepper

4 tsp minced pickled Peppadew pepper

4 large eggs

4 pieces focaccia, toasted

1 cup/240 ml Saffron–Red Pepper Hollandaise (page 152)

Bring a large pot of salted water to a boil. Add the chard leaves (not the stems) and cook, stirring occasionally, until just tender, 3 to 5 minutes. Drain, rinse well with cold water, and squeeze out as much excess water as possible. Chop coarsely and set aside.

In a large frying pan over medium-high heat, heat 3 tbsp of the olive oil over medium-high heat. Add the chard stems and a large pinch of salt and cook, stirring occasionally, until tender and lightly browned, 6 to 9 minutes. Add the garlic and Espelette pepper and cook, stirring, until very fragrant, about 30 seconds. Stir in the cooked chard leaves, roasted pepper, and Peppadew pepper. Cook, stirring often, until the flavors are blended and the chard is hot, about 2 minutes. Transfer to a medium bowl and cover to keep warm. Do not rinse the pan.

Break each egg into a small teacup. Return the frying pan to low heat and add the remaining 1 tbsp oil. Carefully slide the eggs from the teacups into the pan so they stay whole. Season them with salt, cover the pan, and cook until the eggs are just set, 2 to 3 minutes.

Place a piece of focaccia on each plate, divide the chard mixture evenly among the focaccia, top with an egg, and then spoon a generous blanket of the warm hollandaise over the top. Serve right away.

SERVES 4

# SEARED SKIRT STEAK with GARLICKY FRIED POTATOES and "STEAK SAUCE" HOLLANDAISE

Next to rib eye, skirt steak is my favorite cut of beef for its beefy flavor and appealing texture, which is tender and chewy at the same time. The muscle fibers in skirt steak are very long and loose, which creates a particularly juicy consistency. But take care not to overcook it, because that juiciness will disappear quickly.

The twice-cooked method for the potatoes here is borrowed from classic french fry–making technique. The first round of cooking makes the potatoes tender and the second makes them crisp. This dish is a perfect bistro-at-home dinner, so serve it with a simple green salad and a glass of Beaujolais or Côtes du Rhône.

12 oz/340 g medium Yukon gold potatoes, sliced ⅛ in/3 mm thick

4 tbsp/60 ml extra-virgin olive oil

Kosher salt and freshly ground black pepper

12 oz/340 g skirt steak

2 cloves garlic, minced

2 tbsp chopped fresh flat-leaf parsley

½ cup/120 ml "Steak Sauce" Hollandaise (page 151), or more if you like

**SERVES 2**

Spread a few paper towels or a large, clean dish towel (not dried with fabric softener!) on a work surface, arrange the potato slices on the towel(s) in a single layer, and pat dry thoroughly. Leave the towel(s) on the work surface.

In one large or two medium frying pans, heat 2 tbsp of the oil over medium-high heat. When the oil is shimmering, carefully add the potato slices in more or less a single layer. Season with ½ tsp salt and ¼ tsp pepper. Reduce the heat to medium and cook undisturbed until the underside of the slices is just beginning to turn golden, 1 to 2 minutes. Flip the potatoes over, season them lightly again, and continue to cook until they are tender when you bite into a slice but are not too browned, another 1 to 2 minutes. With a slotted spatula or tongs, transfer the potato slices to the towel(s) to drain. Do not rinse the pan.

In another large frying pan, preferably cast-iron, heat 1 tbsp of the remaining oil. While the oil is heating, cut the steak into two or three pieces, depending on what fits best in the pan. Season the steak pieces generously with salt and pepper. When the oil is shimmering, add the steak pieces and cook, undisturbed, until nicely browned on the underside, about 3 minutes. Flip the steaks, reduce the heat to medium-high, and continue to cook for 1 minute longer for rare, 2 to 3 minutes longer for medium-rare, or until done to your liking. (I hope that's no more done than medium-rare.) Transfer the steaks to a plate and tent with aluminum foil to keep warm.

Return the potato frying pan(s) to medium-high heat, add the remaining 1 tbsp oil, and heat until shimmering. Add the potatoes and cook them a second time, flipping them when they are nicely browned on the first side, about 1 minute. Sprinkle the garlic over all of the slices and cook until the potatoes are nicely browned on the second side, about 1 minute longer. Sprinkle with the parsley and divide between two warmed dinner plates.

Slice the steak on the diagonal across the grain and divide the slices between the plates. Spoon a nice dollop of the warm hollandaise over the meat. Pour any accumulated juices from the steak over the sauce and serve right away.

# GRAVY, JUS, AND PAN SAUCE

GROWING UP, MY FAMILY'S HOLIDAY DIN-
NERS ALWAYS FEATURED A ROAST BEEF
OR A LEG OF LAMB. The gravy was a highly treasured compo-
nent of the meal.

I learned the method for gravy from my mother, and by the time I was in college, I had mastered it and was anointed the official gravy maker. And it was
pretty easy to make: pour off the fat; scrape up the drippings; add a little flour,
a little broth, and a shake of Kitchen Bouquet (hey, it makes the color great);
and voilà, you have a deeply flavored, savory sauce. Easy.

It stopped being easy the year there were no drippings. When the roast came out
of the oven, the pan looked like it had been through the dishwasher rather than
through two hours of cradling a juicy roast. That experience taught me an extremely
useful lesson: a gravy, jus, or pan sauce isn't hard to make in terms of what the
cook has to do, but it is totally dependent on what the roast beef, chicken, duck,
or the like does first. It's impossible to predict and even similar cuts of meat
won't behave the same way twice. The backbone of any of these sauces is the
concentrated flavor contributed by the food's juices, and if you don't have
enough, you either don't have a sauce or you have to find the flavor elsewhere.

I'm structuring this chapter differently from the others because I think the most
useful information to share is the basic method for making each of these sauces.
So, here you will find a master recipe for gravy, jus, and pan sauce and ideas for
creatively flavoring them.

## GRAVY

I'm defining gravy as a sauce made from pan drippings, fat from the main ingredient, a thickener such as flour, and liquid, with the thickening the defining feature. Gravies accompany big roasted things, such as an Easter leg of lamb, Thanksgiving turkey, Christmas roast beef—meat or poultry that is in the oven long enough to give off flavorful juices that become more so as they roast in the bottom of the pan. The word *gravy* can seem down-market, like what might be congealed on a blue-plate special in a diner. But a well-made gravy fashioned from roast turkey or roast beef drippings can be as exquisite as any demi-glace sauce at a restaurant. At the same time, it is satisfyingly familiar and comforting in its simplicity.

### GRAVY COMPONENTS

The components are essentially the same whether you're roasting a chicken, turkey, pork loin, sirloin roast, or leg of lamb. Read through each step carefully so that you are familiar with all the "moving parts" of a gravy and can more easily make judgments about them while you're cooking. All of the sauces in this chapter have an element of urgency to them, though with a gravy you need to let your roast rest anyway, which gives you a comfortable window in which to perform the alchemy.

**THE ROASTING PAN**  Ideally, a roasting pan is heavy and *not* nonstick. It should also not be so large that there's a big area of exposed surface around whatever you're roasting where juices can evaporate too quickly or burn. If the only pan you have is too big, surround whatever you're cooking with some onion, carrot, celery, fennel, or other aromatic vegetable that will complement the gravy and will act as a buffer for the pan. Should you use a roasting rack? That is subjective. I know some expert cooks who insist on a rack and others who don't. I don't use a rack because I am lazy.

**THE AROMATICS**  In addition to protecting against the evaporation and burning of juices, aromatic vegetables can add flavor to the final gravy, so you might want to include some anyway. A few lemon slices, garlic cloves, or sprigs of thyme or rosemary are nice accents, too. Don't go overboard or your gravy will end up tasting like vegetable soup. Plan on about 1 cup/140 grams diced aromatic vegetables for a 3- to 4-pound/1.4- to 1.8-kilogram roast.

You can also fill open space in your roasting pan with meat scraps or meaty bones, which will amplify the savory quotient of your gravy. An extra turkey neck; some chicken necks, backs, or wings; some pork ribs; or some beef ribs or meaty soup bones are all fairly inexpensive and good insurance. Turkey and chicken necks yield succulent bits of meat (stand-ins for giblets without the taste of organ meats for those who don't like the latter) to add to a poultry gravy.

**THE LIQUID**  A good broth is the main ingredient of a gravy. Make it from scratch if you can; it will keep for weeks in your freezer. I think turkey broth is a great all-purpose liquid for just about any gravy, so it is my standard and I'm including a recipe for it in this chapter (see page 165). I am not opposed to using good store-bought broth, but be sure to choose a reduced-sodium one, and I use chicken broth even for roasted meats. I have yet to find a commercial beef broth that has a good flavor. Water is just fine, too, though only if you have superior drippings to provide the flavor.

Cognac, port and other wines, and certain other spirits can add a nice dimension to gravy, but only in moderation, as they can overwhelm any gravy easily. Anything with alcohol needs to simmer long enough to cook off most of the alcohol. Wines need to be reduced by at least three-fourths for them not to taste thin and sour in a sauce, so I prefer to use wine in a jus, where the reduction doesn't interfere with the thickening. Apple cider can be lovely in a turkey or pork gravy, and a touch of cream to finish can be nice.

**THE FAT**  Most of the fat comes from the drippings of the roast, but if you like, you can incorporate other fats, such as butter, bacon fat, or duck fat, for flavor or to make up volume. You will have the most control over the amount of fat if you first pour it all off and then measure back the amount you need. Save any extra fat to use for cooking other dishes later.

**THE PAN JUICES**  These are the drippings that are still liquid. You don't always get a lot of them, though one Thanksgiving in London I roasted a 14-pound/6.5-kilogram turkey that produced about 1 quart/1 liter of delectable pan juices—amazing.

**THE BROWN BITS**  These are the drippings that have cooked onto the bottom of the pan, where they become concentrated and caramelized. They are the flavor power-plants of your gravy and must be protected from burning and from the cook wanting to snack on them.

**THE THICKENER**  I always use all-purpose flour because it's handy, but some cooks swear by Wondra flour, a brand of so-called instant flour engineered not to form lumps, and other cooks use cornstarch. I don't like the way cornstarch sets—slightly gel-like—so, again, all-purpose flour works best for me.

## THE METHOD

Read through these steps a few times before you embark on making gravy so that you understand how the steps flow from one to the other. After that, you can use this "cheat sheet" to remind you of what to do next.

1. Set the meat or poultry roast on a platter that allows you to capture more juices, which are sure to flow. Or, put it on a cutting board resting on a rimmed baking sheet. Tent the roast with aluminum foil.

2. Without scraping or disturbing anything, gently pour off the juices and fat into a gravy separator or tall measuring cup. Avoid vigorous movement that will create turbulence that can emulsify the fat into the juices. You want them to remain as separate as possible.

   Leave the juices and fat to settle, then spoon or pour off the fat into another container.

3. Put your roasting pan over a couple of stove-top burners and turn the heat to medium. If your pan fits over only one, be sure to slide it around as needed to heat all of the surfaces evenly. Bring things to a gentle sizzle before adding anything. This allows any lingering free-running juice to caramelize, too. The French call this *pincer les sucs* (paan say lay SOOK), or roughly "to tighten the meat juices."

4. Add the measured amount of fat to the pan. Use 1 tbsp fat per 1 cup/240 ml liquid. Now add the flour (1½ tbsp per 1 cup/240 ml liquid). Whisk the fat and flour together rapidly, incorporating the brown bits that want to come along, but don't worry about scraping them all up. The rest of them will dissolve later. Just take care that nothing is burning. This is your roux.

   When the roux is smooth, turn the heat to low and cook, whisking constantly, for about 1 minute more, to develop some flavors in the flour.

5. Now begin pouring in the broth while whisking rapidly. The key is to stay ahead of the lumps, whisking so quickly that the roux absorbs and blends with the liquid before it has a chance to get too thick.

   If you do see lumps developing, don't worry. Just add a bit more liquid and whisk until you work them out. If they are intractable, you can strain them out later, so carry on with the rest of the liquid.

   At this point, all of the good brown bits should be dissolved. If they are not, give them a scrape to dislodge.

6. Pour in the defatted pan drippings that you collected earlier and simmer the gravy for a minute or two, then evaluate it.

---

### HOW MUCH FAT TO FLOUR TO LIQUID?

A nice serving of gravy is ⅓ cup/75 ml per person, meaning 1 cup/240 ml gravy serves three people.

For 1 cup gravy, you will need the following:
  1 tbsp fat
  1½ tbsp flour
  1 to 1½ cups/240 to 360 ml broth, depending on how much you need to reduce to achieve good flavor

Because I like having leftover gravy, which I use in all kinds of dishes (see page 164), my goal is always to make as much gravy as my pan drippings and broth supply will allow.

---

**HOW'S THE CONSISTENCY?** Too thick? Add more broth. Too thin? Simmer the gravy a little longer to concentrate and thicken it. Alternatively, thicken it by working in a slurry or beurre manié (see "Quick Thickeners," page 164). Lumpy? At the end of cooking, you can put it through a fine-mesh sieve.

**HOW'S THE FLAVOR?** You'll probably need to season with salt, unless the drippings were highly salted, which might be the case if the roast was brined or you used a canned broth that was salty. How's the meatiness? Is there enough depth of flavor? You can heighten the flavor by simmering the gravy to reduce and concentrate it. Be careful you don't cook off all of your volume, however, and end up with a spoonful of gravy.

If the juices were not sufficiently plentiful to give the gravy enough savoriness, it is fine to cheat. In fact, I encourage it. If you have some homemade broth, reduce it until it is powerfully concentrated and then add it to the gravy. (This isn't really cheating, of course, because the broth was made from scratch.) If you do not have homemade broth, use canned reduced-sodium chicken broth from the pantry.

Another option is a packaged demi-glace, such as More Than Gourmet's *glace de poulet* for poultry or *glace de viande* for meats. These are hard pastes that you dilute with water. I add a few teaspoons to the gravy and then taste.

I also like Savory Choice, which comes in small tubes like ketchup packets. The flavor of the chicken and the turkey is quite good, and I use them all of the time. The beef is

## QUICK THICKENERS

### BEURRE MANIÉ

Literally "worked butter," beurre manié (pronounced buhr mah NYAY) is slightly softened butter into which you have worked flour. I use a fork or my fingers to mash the butter and flour into a paste. You then whisk small bits of the paste into simmering gravy (or stew or whatever you want to thicken), stopping when you are happy with the consistency.

It takes a few minutes for the starch in the flour to absorb and expand, so give it some time before you add more. The downside of beurre manié is that you are adding more fat to the gravy, which isn't necessarily a bad thing, of course, but you need to keep it in mind. And once you have added the last bit, simmer the gravy for another minute or so to cook off any raw flour flavor before you declare it ready.

### SLURRY

This is water and flour or cornstarch mixed together and added to the gravy in the same way as you add beurre manié, with the gravy at a simmer and whisking in a small amount at a time until the consistency is good. Always allow a minute or so for the gravy to thicken before evaluating the consistency. And once the consistency is good, simmer the gravy for another minute or so to cook off any raw starch taste.

Slurries are simple to pull together, but they dilute the sauce by adding water. Cornstarch and water are easy to blend; flour and water can get lumpy if you are not careful. Despite the ease with cornstarch, as noted earlier, I prefer the consistency of flour-thickened gravy.

## WHAT TO DO WITH LEFTOVER GRAVY

Other than the obvious—hot turkey or roast beef sandwiches or reheating leftovers—I exploit my gravy good fortune in the following ways:

- as a binder and flavoring for hash, added to the potatoes, onions, and meat during the last few minutes of cooking, so it sizzles a bit
- as a pasta sauce, mixed with grated Parmigiano-Reggiano cheese, fresh lemon juice, fresh herbs, and a little pasta cooking water
- to enrich a vegetable soup such as minestrone
- to make a quick cassoulet, combining canned white beans, chopped canned tomatoes, and the gravy in a baking dish, tucking some good sausage into the beans, and baking until bubbling
- to flavor Classic Sherry Vinaigrette (page 17) for using on a green salad that accompanies cold roast poultry or meat or for using on warm smashed new potatoes

disappointing, so even with meat dishes, I use the turkey.

Finally, in a pinch, you can use a bouillon cube. Start with half a cube to make sure you don't end up with a gravy that is too salty or tastes like it has been artificially flavored. You can also boost the umami profile by adding a spoonful of dark miso or a few drops of soy sauce or Worcestershire sauce.

**DO YOU WANT TO ADD OTHER FLAVORS?** I am usually a purist when it comes to gravy, but here are a handful of enhancements that won't overpower its natural goodness:

- small amount of chopped fresh thyme or flat-leaf parsley, or a tiny bit of chopped fresh tarragon, especially with chicken
- splash of heavy cream or crème fraîche just to round off sharp edges and enhance the texture, but not to make it creamy—cream gravy is a whole thing of its own
- small spoonful of Dijon mustard
- few drops of Cognac
- squeeze of fresh lemon juice

**DO YOU NEED TO STRAIN?** I'm lazy and don't like to take unnecessary steps in the kitchen, so I only strain my gravy if it has flour-lump issues (which can happen even to an experienced cook). If it is a matter of a few bits of chicken skin or onion, I leave the gravy au natural. To strain, use a large fine-mesh sieve that can be positioned over a big liquid measuring cup or a bowl with a spout to make it easy to pour the final sauce into a gravy boat or pitcher.

## ALL-PURPOSE TURKEY BROTH

A few years ago, after repeated frustration from trying to make a chicken broth that tasted like something, I realized I was working with the wrong bird. Modern chickens—even their backs, necks, and wings—just don't have much flavor. Turkey seemed more promising, and when I learned that I could buy just turkey necks, I knew that was the way to go.

Turkey necks have a lovely, sweet flavor that is neutral enough to work in all kinds of recipes. And because the necks are full of cartilage, they give broth lots of body—so much body that the broth will gel once it is cold. If you can't find necks, you can use other turkey parts in this recipe, such as wings or drumsticks.

An aside on terminology: Some sources insist that the term *broth* is correct only when bones with some meat on them are used, and the term *stock* is correct when bones without meat are used. I have used the word *broth* throughout the book. For me, what is important is whether it tastes good and is not overly salty, so that you can use it in reduced sauces.

The bonus with turkey-neck broth is that the meat is delicious—moist and silky, though not easy to extract (time to use your fingers)—and is good in salads, soups, tacos, or risotto. And turkey necks are fairly inexpensive, so you can create superior homemade broth for about the price of canned.

I've created two versions of turkey broth here: a light one in which the turkey and vegetables start out raw, and a dark one in which you must roast or sauté everything before you simmer it in water.

I never feel wealthier than when I have a freezer full of homemade broth, packed in ziplock bags, labeled, and ready for action. Freeze the broth in amounts that make sense for your style of cooking, such as 1 cup/240 milliliters or 4 cups/960 milliliters. Be sure to label each bag with the quantity and the date.

## LIGHT TURKEY BROTH

3 lb/1.4 kg turkey necks

1 celery stalk

½ yellow onion

5 qt/4.7 L water

Kosher salt (optional)

In a large pot, combine the turkey necks, celery, onion, and water and bring to a boil over high heat. Immediately turn down the heat to a bare simmer and cook, uncovered, for 2½ to 3½ hours. During the first hour or so, you will notice foamy scum forming on the surface. Use a large spoon to skim it off. If you want to retrieve the turkey meat while it still has some flavor, use tongs to pull out the necks after about 2 hours, pick off the meat, and return the bones to the pot to finish simmering. The broth is ready when it has a good rich flavor.

Remove the pot from the heat. Pour or ladle the broth through a fine-mesh sieve placed over a clean container. You should have about 4 qt/3.8 L broth, which is a good intensity for an all-purpose broth. If you want to season the broth with salt, stir it in now. Let cool, skim off any visible fat, and transfer to storage containers. Cover and refrigerate for 1 week or freeze for up to 4 months.

**MAKES ABOUT 4 QT/3.8 L**

## DARK TURKEY BROTH

1 tbsp canola or other neutral vegetable oil

3 lb/1.4 kg turkey necks

1 celery stalk

½ yellow onion

5 qt/4.7 L water

Kosher salt (optional)

**TO SAUTÉ THE INGREDIENTS:** in a wide frying pan, heat the oil over medium-high heat. Add the turkey necks, reduce the heat to medium-low, add the vegetables, and cook, turning the necks and stirring and flipping the vegetables so they brown evenly, until everything is deeply browned, about 40 minutes.

**TO ROAST THE INGREDIENTS:** heat the oven to 400°F/200°C/gas 6. Drizzle the oil over a rimmed baking sheet or roasting pan, arrange the turkey necks and vegetables in the pan, and roast until everything is nicely browned, 40 to 50 minutes.

Transfer the sautéed or roasted turkey and vegetables to a big pot. Pour off the fat from the pan, add about ½ cup/120 ml of the water, and stir to dissolve the brown bits on the pan bottom. Pour the contents of the pan into the pot and add the remaining water. Bring to a boil over high heat, immediately turn down the heat to a bare simmer, and cook, uncovered, for 2½ to 3½ hours. During the first hour or so, you will notice foamy scum forming on the surface. Use a large spoon to skim it off. If you want to retrieve the turkey meat while it still has some flavor, use tongs to pull out the necks after about 2 hours, pick off the meat, and return the bones to the pot to finish simmering. The broth is ready when it has a good rich flavor.

Remove the pot from the heat. Pour or ladle the broth through a fine-mesh sieve placed over a clean container. You should have about 4 qt/3.8 L of broth, which is a good intensity for an all-purpose broth. If you want to season the broth with salt, stir it in now. Let cool, skim off any visible fat, and transfer to storage containers. Cover and refrigerate for 1 week or freeze for up to 4 months.

**MAKES ABOUT 4 QT/3.8 L**

## JUS

My definition of a jus is a sauce made by dissolving pan juices with another liquid. It could be as elemental as boiling a little water in the bottom of your roasting pan, or it can be a more complex jus for which you sauté an aromatic vegetable first, deglaze the pan with a wine or spirit, add broth, and finish with a little cream.

Unlike a starch-thickened gravy, a jus is thickened only by reduction and/or whisking in some cream or butter to finish, and generally it is so intense that you drizzle only a small amount onto your food—no mashed-potato swimming pools full of jus. I like to make a jus from a roast chicken or pork loin, for example, when my accompanying dishes don't include potatoes. A drizzle of jus from a lemony roast chicken or rosemary-scented pork loin can unite your roast and your side dishes and add a note of polish to the meal.

Many of the elements of a jus are the same as they are for a gravy, including the pan, the aromatics, the liquids, and the pan juices, so you should review that information on page 162. Two elements are different:

**THE FAT** Because you are not making a roux for thickening, you don't need extra fat in a jus. In fact, you want the jus to be as clean and fat free as possible, other than the butter or cream you might choose to add as a finish. So you must separate all of the fat from the drippings, perhaps saving it to use for cooking other dishes later, such as potatoes or beans.

**THE THICKENER** Because by definition a jus is not thickened, you do not need any flour, cornstarch, or other thickener.

### THE METHOD

Read through the gravy method (see page 163) and the modifications below a few times before you start to make a jus.

Follow steps 1 through 3 for making gravy, then skip step 4, which directs you to add fat and flour.

Follow step 5, but just add the broth without worrying about lumps, because there is no flour to get lumpy.

Follow step 6, but because a jus is meant to be thin, you need to use different criteria to evaluate the consistency. It should have some body so that it is more viscous than broth. To achieve this, simmer the liquid to reduce it, which concentrates the flavor, as well. You also can whisk in a little butter at the end to impart body without altering the intensity of the jus.

## PAN SAUCE

This is the sauce that you make in the sauté pan after you have cooked your main ingredient—a filet mignon, a chicken breast, some pork medallions. The goal is to capture the savory cooked-on juices left in the pan, which you do by deglazing, or dissolving with a liquid. This type of sauce is sometimes called *à la minute* (ah la mee NUTE), meaning instantly, and it is satisfying to make: it's quick, you don't need a second pan, and when it's well made, it offers a small amount of intensely flavored sauce that perfectly accents your main ingredient. And once you get comfortable with the process, you can have fun improvising. These are the sauces that make you feel like an accomplished cook, or as my friend Amy Albert always said, like a bloody genius.

As with a gravy, a pan sauce can include many other elements, such as aromatics, flavorful spirits or wines, broths, and enrichments such as cream, butter, or cheese, but usually no starch thickener.

The method and ingredients you use to make an à la minute pan sauce are similar to those for a beurre blanc (see page 95) or cream sauce (see page 116), but the difference is that you have pan juices, too, and you are trying to make the sauce quickly, in that pan, before your main ingredient cools too much.

### THE METHOD

1.  Sauté your ingredient. Perfect candidates for this type of cooking include boneless, skinless chicken breasts, duck breasts, pork chops, pork tenderloin medallions, small steaks, hamburgers, lamb chops, scallops, and shrimp. I like to dust the ingredient with seasoned flour, which helps create a nice browning on the food and the small amount of flour left in the pan has a subtle thickening action on the sauce. But a pan sauce can be made without using flour.

    For the fat, I use half butter and half oil. Butter encourages browning and imparts flavor, and oil keeps the butter from burning.

2.  Set your cooked meat (let's just call it that for simplicity's sake) on a plate or other dish that will catch any juices that run and tent with aluminum foil to keep warm. As you do this, don't leave the pan on the burner because you might burn the juices.

3.  Pour off any loose fat, but take care not to pour off any floating brown bits. Those are the tasty parts that are the keys to flavor in the sauce.

4.  Return the pan to medium-high heat.

5.  Add your aromatic ingredient, if using one, and sauté briefly so it softens but doesn't brown, 30 seconds to 1 minute. Then, add your first liquid, which will probably be something with a strong flavor—brandy, wine, port, or vinegar—an ingredient that needs to be tamed by reduction but will also provide a backbone of intense flavor to the sauce. Cook the liquid until it has evaporated—reduced—to just a spoonful or so. You want a flavorful essence without the harsh qualities of the original liquid.

6.  Now, add the next liquid. This is what will make up the bulk of the sauce. The most common liquid is some kind of broth. Homemade broth is best, of course, but if you use a canned broth, choose a reduced-sodium one. When you reduce any liquid that contains salt, the saltiness becomes more concentrated. Cook this liquid down by about two-thirds.

7.  Add some flavor accents. This might be Dijon mustard, fresh herbs, fresh fruit, black olives, green peppercorns, or the like. You want to use an ingredient that will taste great in the sauce but won't require a lot of transformation.

8.  Enrich the sauce with cream or butter. At this point, you have a lot of concentrated flavors, including some sharp ones, and you need to decide whether everything tastes good just as it is, or whether you need to polish off the sharp edges with cream or butter. Keep in mind that such fats don't just enrich a sauce, they also unlock and spread flavors, so that even a small amount can be a catalyst to the other flavors in the sauce.

9.  The last decision is whether you want to strain or not. I generally don't strain because I don't mind texture, but if you're looking for those few drops of perfectly smooth essence, then strain.

10. Taste and adjust your seasoning.

### GUIDELINE AMOUNTS FOR SAUCE INGREDIENTS

Because I think this type of sauce is all about improvising and responding to what you have in your sauté pan, I am not giving traditional recipes for pan sauces. Instead, I'm giving proportions of ingredients and ideas that you can play with to create interesting sauces. You will need to adjust and adapt, but some great starting points are on the following page.

For four chops, chicken breasts, steaks, or the like, use the following amounts:

**AROMATICS** 1 tablespoon finely chopped shallot, onion, leek, mushroom, or other mild aromatic and/or 1 teaspoon finely chopped garlic, fresh chile, peeled fresh ginger, or other strong aromatic

**LIQUIDS** ¼ cup/60 milliliters wine, spirits, vinegar, or other strong liquid and/or ¾ cup/180 milliliters home-made or canned reduced-sodium broth, fruit juice, hard cider, or other mild liquid

**ACCENTS** Fresh herb sprigs and/or 1 teaspoon to 1 table-spoon accent ingredient such as Dijon mustard, soy sauce, green peppercorns, capers, or chopped fresh herbs

**ENRICHMENTS** 1 to 4 tablespoons crème fraîche or heavy cream and/or 1 to 2 tablespoons unsalted butter

---

### TO GET YOU STARTED, HERE ARE TEN GREAT COMBINATIONS:

1. Chopped shallot
   Balsamic vinegar
   Turkey or chicken broth
   Dijon mustard, chopped fresh rosemary
   Unsalted butter

2. Minced garlic
   Madeira
   Turkey or chicken broth
   Sliced fresh basil
   Heavy cream

3. Thinly sliced yellow onion
   Calvados, then white wine
   Apple cider
   Dijon mustard, chopped fresh thyme
   Crème fraîche

4. Chopped shallot
   Fresh lemon juice
   Turkey or chicken broth
   Chopped fresh tarragon
   Crème fraîche

5. Chopped fresh chile, minced garlic
   Balsamic vinegar
   Fresh orange juice
   Unsalted butter

6. Chopped shallot
   Dry white wine
   Turkey or chicken broth
   Dijon mustard, capers, finely chopped cornichon, chopped fresh flat-leaf parsley
   Unsalted butter

7. Chopped shallot
   Cognac or brandy
   Turkey or chicken broth
   Dijon mustard, cracked green peppercorns
   Crème fraîche
   Lot of freshly ground black pepper

8. Chopped shallot and fresh chile
   Sherry vinegar, crushed fresh blackberries or raspberries
   Turkey or chicken broth
   Fresh rosemary sprig
   Unsalted butter

9. Chopped shallot and chile, minced garlic
   Dry white wine
   Turkey or chicken broth
   Peeled, seeded, and finely diced tomato
   Finely grated lime zest, chopped fresh cilantro
   Unsalted butter

10. Chopped shallot, finely chopped mushroom
    Cognac or brandy
    Dry red wine
    Turkey or chicken broth
    Dijon mustard
    Crème fraîche

11

# SABAYON SAUCES

sabayon gets its luscious, flowing consistency and rich flavor from whipping egg yolks over very low heat, just like hollandaise. But unlike hollandaise, sabayon does not include any butter. It is simply egg yolks, sugar (or honey), and traditionally a sweet fortified wine, such as Marsala. I love the slightly boozy character that comes with this kind of sauce, but I also like to make sabayon with flavorings that are not alcoholic.

Sabayon can be a dessert all on its own, eaten from a coupe or wineglass for a special touch. It is especially good when you fold in some whipped cream, pile the whole thing in a pretty glass, chill it, and then eat it like a mousse. Or, you can take that lightened sabayon and use it as a delicious and surprising alternative to plain whipped cream on a berry shortcake. As a sauce, however, it's gorgeous over fresh fruit, especially berries and stone fruits such as apricots, peaches, and plums, or as a complement to a fruit galette or tart.

## WHAT'S GOING ON IN THIS SAUCE?

A great sabayon is primarily about texture, and texture in this case is achieved by juggling time and temperature. You start by whisking egg yolks with sugar (or other sweetener) and fortified wine (or other flavorings) over low heat, usually in a double boiler (unless you're a daredevil). As the heat slowly cooks the yolks, they thicken and trap the air bubbles that you are incorporating with your vigorous whisking. The process should proceed at a pace that allows you to whisk in lots of air before the yolks are cooked to the point where they won't expand any more. If the heat is too low, your mixture will never thicken. And while the sugar and wine provide a certain amount of protection for the yolks, if the heat is too high, the yolks risk setting before they are at their loftiest. In the worst case, they'll "scramble."

## WHAT CAN GO WRONG AND HOW CAN I FIX IT?

If you find yourself with a sabayon that's too runny but you've already taken it off the heat, the best thing to do is fold in some firm whipped cream and pretend you wanted this style of sauce all along. I've never had success trying to recook a loose sabayon. If your problem is an over-cooked sabayon with bits of cooked yolk in it, you can push it through a fine-mesh sieve, though you will lose some volume doing that. You may want to boost it with some whipped cream, too.

## HOW MUCH SAUCE PER SERVING?

Sabayons are rich but they're also quite airy, so an average serving might be 2 to 3 tablespoons per person, and a bit more for sauces that have been enriched with whipped cream.

## SPECIAL EQUIPMENT

You need the same equipment for making a sabayon that you need for making its savory sister, hollandaise. That includes a double-boiler setup of a wide, medium stainless-steel bowl and a medium saucepan, a good whisk and a strong arm or a handheld electric mixer, and a heat-resistant rubber spatula for scraping the sides of the bowl as you whisk and to fold in any whipped cream.

## STORAGE

Warm sabayon won't hold for more than about 30 minutes in the double boiler over very low heat, so it is best made just before serving. A chilled sabayon lightened with whipped cream can be refrigerated in an airtight container for up to 24 hours.

# CLASSIC SABAYON

This sauce is perfect for whipping up on the spur of the moment for guests. I mean, you always have eggs and sugar in the kitchen, right? And a search through your cupboard where those rarely drunk spirits hang out is sure to yield something usable. Be sure to taste the wine or spirit first to determine how sweet it is and then adjust your sugar up or down accordingly.

4 egg yolks

¼ cup plus 1 tbsp/65 g granulated sugar

⅓ cup/75 ml sweet fortified wine such as Marsala, Madeira, or port

Pour water to a depth of 1 to 2 in/2.5 to 5 cm into a medium saucepan and place over medium heat. Rest a medium stainless-steel bowl in the pan over (not touching) the water. Put the egg yolks and sugar in the bowl and, using a whisk or a handheld electric mixer on medium-high speed, begin beating together the yolks and sugar. After about 1 minute, add the wine and continue beating. As the bowl heats up, the yolks will begin to thicken. Beat vigorously, scraping around the bowl with a heat-resistant rubber spatula from time to time so that bits of yolk don't get stuck and overcook. Beat until thick and frothy but not quite fluffy, 8 to 10 minutes by hand or 4 to 5 minutes with the mixer. It is ready when it forms a thick ribbon as it trails off the end of the whisk or beater. Remove the bowl from the heat and beat for another 30 seconds or so to stabilize the sauce and let the bowl cool down. If possible, serve right away.

MAKES 1¼ CUPS/300 ML

**STORAGE** The sabayon is best eaten right after you make it, but you can hold the sauce in the double boiler over very low heat for up to 30 minutes.

**QUICK CHANGE** To serve the sabayon cold, chill it. Whip ½ cup/ 120 ml heavy cream or crème fraîche until soft peaks form and fold the cream into the chilled sabayon just until combined. Chill again for a few minutes to set. Refrigerate any leftovers in an airtight container for up to 1 day.

# HONEY-GINGER-TANGERINE SABAYON

The flavor of tangerine is soft and lovely and is nicely amplified by the perfumed sweetness of honey, rather than sugar. I reduce most of the tangerine juice to concentrate its flavor and reserve the balance to deliver a superfresh note. This sabayon is lovely with berries or over a piece of flourless chocolate cake.

1 cup/240 ml fresh tangerine juice

2 tbsp peeled and coarsely chopped fresh ginger (from a 1-oz/30-g piece)

4 egg yolks

¼ cup plus 1 tbsp/75 ml honey

Pinch of kosher salt

In a small saucepan, combine ¾ cup/180 ml of the tangerine juice and the ginger and bring to a simmer over medium-high heat. Simmer until reduced to about 3 tbsp, 6 to 8 minutes. Remove from the heat and let cool slightly. Strain through a fine-mesh sieve into a small bowl, pushing on the ginger with a rubber spatula or wooden spoon to force out all of its juice.

Pour water to a depth of 1 to 2 in/2.5 to 5 cm into a medium saucepan and place over medium heat. Rest a medium stainless-steel bowl in the pan over (not touching) the water. Put the egg yolks and honey in the bowl and, using a whisk or a handheld electric mixer on medium-high speed, begin beating together the yolks and honey. After about 1 minute, add the reduced tangerine juice, the remaining ¼ cup fresh juice, and the salt and continue beating. As the bowl heats up, the yolks will begin to thicken. Beat vigorously, scraping around the bowl with a heat-resistant rubber spatula from time to time so that bits of yolk don't get stuck and overcook. Beat until thick and frothy but not quite fluffy, 8 to 10 minutes by hand or 4 to 5 minutes with the mixer. It is ready when it forms a thick ribbon as it trails off the end of the whisk or beater. Remove the bowl from the heat and beat for another 30 seconds or so to stabilize the sauce and let the bowl cool down. Serve right away.

**MAKES 1¼ CUPS/300 ML**

**STORAGE** The sabayon is best eaten right after you make it, but you can hold the sauce in the double boiler over very low heat for up to 30 minutes.

**QUICK CHANGE**

Use orange juice instead of tangerine juice; simmer 2 tbsp Grand Marnier or other orange liqueur with the citrus juice.

To serve the sabayon cold, chill it. Whip ½ cup/120 ml heavy cream or crème fraîche until soft peaks form and fold the cream into the chilled sabayon just until combined. Chill again for a few minutes to set. Refrigerate any leftovers in an airtight container for up to 1 day.

# MAPLE-RUM SABAYON

The deep, mellow sweetness of this sabayon is gorgeous with fall fruits such as baked apples and poached pears, and I especially love it with a prune and frangipane tart (see page 179) I learned to make from chef Claude Vauget at La Varenne cooking school. The French know how wonderful prunes can be.

Grade B maple syrup will give you the best flavor. I've never understood why the syrup that tastes the best gets the second-best grade.

4 egg yolks

¼ cup/60 ml grade B maple syrup

2 tbsp lightly packed dark brown sugar

Tiny pinch of kosher salt

¼ cup/60 ml dark rum

¼ tsp pure vanilla extract

**MAKES 1¼ CUPS/300 ML**

**STORAGE** The sabayon is best eaten right after you make it, but you can hold the sauce in the double boiler over very low heat for up to 30 minutes.

**QUICK CHANGE**

Use brandy, Cognac, or bourbon instead of the rum.

To serve the sabayon cold, chill it. Whip ½ cup/120 ml heavy cream or crème fraîche until soft peaks form and fold the cream into the chilled sabayon just until combined. Chill again for a few minutes to set. Refrigerate any leftovers in an airtight container for up to 1 day.

Pour water to a depth of 1 to 2 in/2.5 to 5 cm into a medium saucepan and place over medium heat. Rest a medium stainless-steel bowl in the pan over (not touching) the water. Put the egg yolks, maple syrup, brown sugar, and salt in the bowl and, using a whisk or a handheld electric mixer on medium-high speed, begin beating them together. After about 1 minute, add the rum and continue beating. As the bowl heats up, the yolks will begin to thicken. Beat vigorously, scraping around the sides of the bowl with a heat-resistant rubber spatula from time to time so that bits of yolk don't get stuck and overcook. Beat until thick and frothy but not quite fluffy, 8 to 10 minutes by hand or 4 to 5 minutes with the mixer. It is ready when it forms a thick ribbon as it trails off the end of the whisk or beater. Remove the bowl from the heat and beat for another 30 seconds or so to stabilize the sauce and let the bowl cool down. If possible, serve right away.

# GRILLED FIGS with CLASSIC SABAYON and BALSAMIC DRIZZLE

Here are the elements of a perfect August dinner party: a deck, some friends, a cold bottle (or three) of Grüner Veltliner, salumi, white beans in olive oil, platters of grilled vegetables, and then these figs, cooked over the slow warmth of the last embers in the grill.

You can reduce the balsamic ahead of time, but make the sabayon at the last minute. It is a fun sauce to make in front of an audience, and you can get your friends to help with the whisking.

½ cup/120 ml balsamic vinegar

18 to 24 ripe figs, halved lengthwise

2 tbsp canola or other neutral vegetable oil or a mild olive oil

2 tbsp granulated sugar

1¼ cups/300 ml Classic Sabayon (page 173)

6 to 8 amaretti, crumbled

In a small saucepan, bring the vinegar to a simmer over medium heat. Cook until reduced by about half, 5 to 7 minutes. Remove from the heat and let cool completely.

Prepare a medium fire in a charcoal or gas grill. Or, position an oven rack about 5 in/12 cm from the boiler element and heat the broiler. If using a grill, the fire is ready when you can comfortably hold your hand, palm-side down, 4 in/10 cm above the grill rack for 4 seconds. Brush the grill rack so that it is perfectly clean.

In a medium bowl, toss the figs with the oil, coating them evenly. Arrange them, cut-side up, on a large rimmed baking sheet. Sprinkle the cut sides with the sugar. If grilling, transfer the figs to the grill rack, sugared-side up, cover the grill, and grill the figs until they have softened slightly and the sugar starts to bubble a bit, 7 to 9 minutes. If broiling, place the figs on the baking sheet under the broiler and broil to the same end for the same amount of time.

Transfer the figs to a serving platter. Spoon the warm sabayon over the figs, drizzle the balsamic reduction over everything, and then sprinkle the amaretti over the top. Serve right away.

SERVES 6 TO 8

# JUMBLE OF BERRIES with
# GRATINÉED HONEY-GINGER-TANGERINE SABAYON

I like the warm-cool temperature contrast of this dish and the way the berry juices mingle with the rich sabayon on the plate. A mix of fresh summer berries will give you the most complexity here, but using just one or two types is lovely as well. If you are lucky enough to live in blackberry country, they are wonderful in this dish. Be sure to taste your berries first, and if they're tart, add a touch more sugar.

1½ lb/680 g mixed berries (if using strawberries, hull and halve length-wise if large)

2 tbsp granulated sugar

1 tsp lightly packed finely grated lemon or lime zest

1½ cups/300 ml Honey-Ginger-Tangerine Sabayon (page 174)

Position an oven rack about 5 in/12 cm from the broiler element and heat the broiler.

In a large bowl, toss the berries with half of the sugar and all of the lemon zest until combined. Transfer to a shallow 2-qt/2-L broiler-safe baking dish or gratin dish.

Evenly spread the warm sabayon over the berries and sprinkle evenly with the remaining sugar. Broil, rotating the dish from back to front after 1½ to 2½ minutes, until the sabayon is browned in spots, 3 to 5 minutes. Let cool briefly, then serve warm.

**SERVES 4 TO 6**

# RUM-SOAKED PRUNE and FRANGIPANE TART with MAPLE-RUM SABAYON

Prunes are underappreciated in the United States, and I have no idea why. Meaty, sweet, and complex, they're even more delicious when plumped up with some dark spirits such as rum, Cognac, or bourbon. I love those warm flavors paired with almonds, so I fill this tart shell with an almond frangipane and nestle the prunes inside. The touch of maple and the boozy bite in the sabayon marry perfectly with the other flavors.

24 to 30 meaty prunes, pitted

½ cup/120 ml dark rum such as Myers's

### CRUST

1½ cups/190 g unbleached all-purpose flour, plus more for rolling

½ cup/65 g cake flour

1 tbsp granulated sugar

1¼ tsp kosher salt

⅛ tsp ground cinnamon

⅔ cup/140 g cold unsalted butter, cut into small pieces, plus 1 tbsp, melted, for the pan

½ tsp pure vanilla extract

1 egg yolk

Ice water, as needed

### FRANGIPANE

7 tbsp/100 g unsalted butter, at warm room temperature

1 cup/100 g confectioners' sugar

1¼ cups/175 g blanched almonds, finely ground

2 large eggs

½ tsp pure vanilla extract

1¼ cups/300 ml Maple-Rum Sabayon (page 175)

---

**MAKES ONE 9-IN/23-CM TART; SERVES 6 TO 8**

---

In a medium saucepan, combine the prunes and rum and bring to a simmer over medium heat. Simmer for 2 to 3 minutes to cook off some of the alcohol, then remove from the heat. Leave the prunes to soak until they are quite soft, at least 2 hours or up to overnight.

**TO MAKE THE CRUST,** in a food processor, combine both flours, the granulated sugar, salt, and cinnamon and pulse until blended. Scatter the butter pieces over the top, add the vanilla, and pulse just until the mixture looks like coarse sand. Add the egg yolk and pulse briefly just to blend. The dough should be coming together.

Dump the dough onto a clean work surface and blend the ingredients further by pushing the dough, a little bit at a time, away from you with the heel of your hand, so that you "smear" the ingredients together on the work surface. (This technique is called *fraisage* in French, and it yields a very tender crust.) If the dough seems dry, sprinkle a tiny bit of ice water onto it as you smear. Using a rubber spatula or bench scraper and your hands, scrape the dough together and shape it into a flat disk. Wrap in plastic wrap and refrigerate until firm, about 30 minutes. (You can make the dough ahead and refrigerate it for up to 2 days or freeze it for up to 2 months. Thaw frozen dough in the refrigerator overnight.)

Brush the bottom and sides of a 9-in/23-cm tart pan with a removable bottom with the melted butter.

Remove the dough from the refrigerator and let it sit at room temperature to soften slightly. It should be cold and firm but not rock hard. Depending on how long the dough was refrigerated, this can take 5 to 20 minutes. Lightly flour the work surface, place the dough on it, and roll out into a round 12 in/30.5 cm in diameter and ⅛ in/3 mm thick. Gently roll the dough around the rolling pin and transfer it to the prepared tart pan, centering it over the pan. Unroll the dough from the pin, draping it gently so you can center it without stretching. Lift the outer edges of the dough to give you enough slack to line the sides of the pan without stretching the dough. Gently press the dough onto the bottom and sides of the pan. Trim the excess from the rim and press against the sides so the edges of the crust are neat and tall. Chill for at least 30 minutes or up to overnight.

*continued . . .*

(You can also wrap and freeze the crust for up to 1 month and then bake it later. When it's time to bake the crust, don't thaw it. Instead, just add a few minutes to the baking time.)

Heat the oven to 400°F/200°C/gas 6. If you have a heavy baking sheet, put it in the oven to heat, too; this will help the underside of the crust to brown.

Line the chilled tart crust with parchment paper or aluminum foil and fill it with pie weights or dried beans. Place on the heated baking sheet (if using) and bake until the edges seem firm, slightly dry, and are beginning to color (but don't let the crust actually brown), about 10 minutes.

Remove the tart pan from the oven and remove the pie weights and the parchment. Reduce the oven temperature to 325°F/165°C/gas 3 and return the crust to the oven. Bake until the center of the crust looks dry, about 10 minutes more. Let cool completely on a rack while you prepare the frangipane. Raise the oven temperature to 350°F/180°C/gas 4.

**TO MAKE THE FRANGIPANE,** in a food processor, combine the butter and confectioners' sugar and process until fluffy. Add the almonds and process until blended. Add the eggs and vanilla and process just until combined. Do not overprocess or the frangipane may separate.

Carefully and evenly spread the frangipane in the cooled tart crust. Drain the prunes and blot dry on a paper towel. Arrange the prunes in a pretty pattern over the frangipane, pressing them slightly to nestle them in it.

Bake the tart until the frangipane is light brown and puffy, 25 to 35 minutes. Let cool on a rack. Serve slightly warm or at room temperature. Remove the pan sides and slide the tart onto a serving plate. Cut into slices and place on individual plates. Spoon a thick ribbon of the warm sabayon around each slice.

12

# CUSTARD SAUCES

CUSTARD SAUCE HAS THE ENVIABLE ABILITY TO MOVE FROM HOMEY TO ELEGANT, DEPENDING ON WHAT IT'S BEING SERVED WITH AND WHAT NAME IT GOES BY. When it's called custard, it's comforting and old-fashioned, and you can almost see the English country cook in a striped apron pouring it over a slice of cake. When it's called crème anglaise, it's soignée and dressy, making any dessert plate feel like Limoges china.

The first time I tasted real custard—make that crème anglaise—was at cooking school in Paris, so for me this delicate concoction of egg yolks, sugar, and milk or cream is all about finesse. It's a rich but subtle finishing touch to any dessert.

### WHAT'S GOING ON IN THIS SAUCE?

Custards are all about protein coagulation. That doesn't sound too appetizing, of course, but it's what you want to happen. The coagulation of the proteins in eggs is what thickens a custard and is the key to getting the most appealing, satiny texture in this sauce. If the egg yolks get too hot, they'll coagulate too much, and you'll end up with a curdled texture or outright bits of cooked egg.

There are two steps to avoiding curdling and developing just the right degree of thickening. The first is to temper the yolks, which you've whisked together with sugar. This means gently introducing the yolks to heat by whisking a little hot milk or cream into them (so they don't overcook or cook too quickly). The hot liquid helps the egg proteins start to relax and uncoil, which is the first phase of thickening.

The second step is to add the tempered mixture back to the hot liquid and then slowly cook it together over low heat until thickened. The slower you cook the sauce, the more control you have and the better the final texture will be. Higher heat causes the egg proteins to grab one another and squeeze too tightly, which will take your sauce down the path of curdling.

You also need to stir almost constantly to ensure the sauce doesn't thicken unevenly along the bottom and at the edges of the pan. And custards thicken as they cool, so you have to stop cooking them before you reach the desired consistency.

You can test the doneness three different ways. You can take the temperature of the sauce. A sauce that registers 180°F/82°C on an instant-read thermometer has the thickness and consistency that I like. Or, use the "swipe" test: dip a wooden spoon or heat-resistant rubber spatula into the sauce, swipe your finger across the back of the spoon or one side of the spatula, and if your finger leaves a clear trail that doesn't fill in right away, the custard is ready.

With experience, you'll come to use the third testing method, which is to observe the way the sauce sloshes in the pan. As the sauce thickens, the movement will shift from loose and liquidy to a flow that just feels more languid. It's hard to describe, but pay attention as you use the other two methods for judging doneness and soon you'll learn to recognize when your custard is at just the right point.

A perfectionist cook always strains a custard sauce as a final step, but I'm lazy so I don't strain, unless I see unwanted bits of egg to banish.

### WHAT CAN GO WRONG AND HOW CAN I FIX IT?

The main danger with a custard sauce is that you overcook it and it becomes gloppy, curdled, or lumpy. A certain amount of overcooking can be remedied by passing the sauce through a fine-mesh sieve (which will strain out actual bits of egg) and diluting it with a touch more milk or cream. You can also smooth out a slightly curdled sauce by whizzing it in a blender or food processor and then straining it. But a really overcooked custard sauce will taste too eggy, so if you see "curds," start again.

Undercooking can be a problem, too, leaving you with a sauce that is more like wan eggnog. Fortunately, you can just put the sauce back on low heat and cook it a little longer, even if you cooked it the day before.

### HOW MUCH SAUCE PER SERVING?

This depends on how you are serving the sauce, of course, but 3 to 4 tablespoons per person would be average.

### SPECIAL EQUIPMENT

As with so many good things in cooking, custards require a heavy saucepan. Traditionally, you use a wooden spoon to stir custards and to test the thickness, but I prefer a heat-resistant rubber spatula, which scrapes the pan beautifully. An instant-read thermometer can help you find the sweet spot, but it is not obligatory. A fine-mesh sieve is good for straining.

### STORAGE

I like to eat my custard sauces cool, not warm, so I make them at least several hours or up to a day ahead of when I plan to serve them. I find that the flavors mature with time, too, so making these kinds of sauces ahead is definitely recommended. But don't make them too far ahead. Custards get funky after about 5 days, and they don't freeze well, unless you actually churn them into an ice cream.

---

#### DON'T LET THE SUGAR "COOK" THE YOLKS

Before you cook a custard sauce, you whisk together the egg yolks and sugar. But you have to combine them immediately— no dumping the sugar and yolks into a bowl and leaving them to sit for a few minutes while you do something else. That's because the sugar is hygroscopic, meaning it pulls moisture from nearby ingredients, in this case the yolks. It's like cooking the yolks without heat, and it leaves behind little dry bits of yolk that will make your sauce lumpy.

# CLASSIC VANILLA BEAN CRÈME ANGLAISE

So simple but so wonderful when it's well executed: satin smooth, lightly sweet, and perfumed with rich vanilla. You can use a high-quality pure vanilla extract instead of the bean, if it's more convenient. I think extract is fine for most dishes, but in this case, splitting and scraping the seeds from the fragrant, leathery bean is a reminder that "plain" vanilla comes from an exotic plant grown halfway around the world. If you do use extract in this recipe, add ½ teaspoon just when you've finished cooking the custard.

2 cups/480 ml whole milk

½ vanilla bean, split lengthwise

4 egg yolks

¼ cup/50 g granulated sugar

Tiny pinch of kosher salt

Heat the milk in a small saucepan over medium heat until it is just starting to steam; do not let it boil. Using the tip of a paring knife, scrape the vanilla seeds from the pod into the milk and stir to mix. Add the scraped pod, remove the pan from the heat, and let steep for about 30 minutes.

Gently reheat the vanilla-infused milk over medium-low heat until just beginning to simmer.

Meanwhile, in a medium bowl, whisk together the egg yolks, sugar, and salt until well blended. Do not whisk so much that the mixture gets foamy, however.

When the vanilla-infused milk is hot, slowly pour about half of it into the yolk-sugar mixture, whisking constantly until combined. Return the pan to medium-low heat, then whisk in the yolk mixture. Gently cook the sauce, frequently scraping the bottom and sides of the pan with a heat-resistant rubber spatula or a wooden spoon, until it thickens, 3 to 5 minutes. It should register 180°F/82°C on an instant-read thermometer.

Remove from the heat and remove and discard the vanilla pod. For a very smooth texture (or if you're worried that you've gotten some bits of overcooked egg in the sauce), strain the sauce through a fine-mesh sieve. Let cool, cover, and refrigerate until chilled, at least 1 hour.

**MAKES ABOUT 2½ CUPS/600 ML**

**STORAGE** Refrigerate in an airtight container for up to 5 days. The sauce does not freeze well.

**QUICK CHANGE**

*Creamy* Use half-and-half or heavy cream instead of milk for a richer sauce.

*Spirited* Add 1 tbsp dark rum, brandy, Calvados, Grand Marnier, Frangelico, or other liqueur or spirit to the sauce as soon as it has finished cooking.

*Espresso* Add 2 tsp instant espresso powder to the milk or cream as it heats.

*Cocoa* Add 2 tbsp unsweetened cocoa powder to the milk or cream before heating it. (To avoid lumps, stir a small amount of the milk or cream into the cocoa powder to make a paste first, then whisk in the rest of the milk.)

*Cardamom-vanilla* Add 3 green or white cardamom pods, lightly crushed, with the vanilla. Strain the finished sauce.

# CREAMY LIME CRÈME ANGLAISE

I make this sauce a little richer (thanks to cream) than the classic version because I like the way the sweet cream flavor plays off the perfume of the lime. This sauce is beautiful served with a blueberry cobbler or pie, a rhubarb crisp, a simple almond cake, and, of course, the rice pudding and meringue cookies on page 190.

2 cups/480 ml heavy cream

4 egg yolks

⅓ cup/65 g granulated sugar

⅛ tsp kosher salt

¼ cup/60 ml fresh lime juice, plus more if needed

1 tsp lightly packed finely grated lime zest

**MAKES ABOUT 2½ CUPS/600 ML**

**STORAGE** Refrigerate in an air-tight container for up to 5 days. The sauce does not freeze well.

**QUICK CHANGE** Use fresh Meyer lemon or orange juice and zest in place of the lime juice and zest.

Heat the cream in a small saucepan over medium heat until it is just starting to steam; do not let it boil.

Meanwhile, in a medium bowl, whisk together the egg yolks, sugar, and salt until well blended. Do not whisk so much that the mixture gets foamy, however.

When the cream is hot, slowly pour about half of it into the yolk-sugar mixture, whisking constantly until combined. Return the pan to medium-low heat, then whisk in the yolk mixture. Gently cook the sauce, frequently scraping the bottom and sides of the pan with a heat-resistant rubber spatula or a wooden spoon, until it thickens, 3 to 5 minutes. It should register 180°F/82°C on an instant-read thermometer.

Remove from the heat and stir in the lime juice and zest. Taste and add a bit more juice if needed. For a very smooth texture (or if you're worried that you've gotten some bits of overcooked egg in the sauce), strain the sauce through a fine-mesh sieve. Let cool, cover, and refrigerate until chilled, at least 1 hour.

# COCOA-COCONUT CRÈME ANGLAISE

I'm not sure my instructors at cooking school would have approved of this version of the classic crème anglaise, but I adore coconut milk and thought why not? The coconut milk behaves beautifully in this egg-thickened sauce and delivers a rich coconut flavor. A standard can of coconut milk holds 1¾ cups/400 milliliters, so with a full can you can make a double batch of sauce, or save the rest of the coconut milk for something else. Coconut milk freezes well, too, or you might look for a smaller can at the store.

The cocoa powder is quite dominant in this sauce, so if you would like a lighter chocolate flavor, cut the cocoa to 2 teaspoons. This would be a lovely sauce to go with a slice of flourless chocolate cake, a scoop of chocolate-chunk bread pudding, or a wedge of coconut Bundt cake like the one on page 248.

1 tbsp Dutch-processed unsweetened cocoa powder

¾ cup plus 2 tbsp/220 ml canned coconut milk
(stir together the thick cream and thinner milk before measuring)

2 egg yolks

3 tbsp granulated sugar

**MAKES ABOUT 1 CUP/240 ML**

**STORAGE** Refrigerate in an airtight container for up to 5 days. The sauce does not freeze well.

**QUICK CHANGE** Add 1 tbsp dark rum to the coconut milk before you heat it.

Put the cocoa powder in a small bowl and add a few spoonfuls of the coconut milk; stir to make a smooth paste (it's okay if a few lumps remain). Heat the remaining coconut milk in a small saucepan over medium heat. When hot, whisk in the cocoa-coconut milk paste and bring the mixture to just below a simmer.

Meanwhile, in a small bowl, whisk together the eggs yolks and sugar until well blended. Do not whisk so much that the mixture gets foamy, however.

When the cocoa-infused coconut milk is hot, slowly pour about half of it into the yolk-sugar mixture, whisking constantly until combined. Return the pan to medium-low heat, then whisk in the yolk mixture. Cook gently, frequently scraping the bottom and sides of the pan with a heat-resistant rubber spatula or a wooden spoon, until it thickens, 3 to 5 minutes. It should register 180°F/82°C on an instant-read thermometer.

Remove from the heat. For a very smooth texture (or if you're worried that you've gotten some bits of overcooked egg in the sauce), strain the sauce through a fine-mesh sieve. Let cool, cover, and refrigerate until chilled, at least 1 hour.

# MAPLE-NUTMEG CUSTARD SAUCE

The flavors in this creamy sauce are fairly subtle, so aim for balance. Using grade B maple syrup will give you a more pronounced maple flavor, and take care that the nutmeg doesn't overwhelm the maple. I use a rasp-style grater (mine is made by Microplane) to grate my fresh nutmeg. This sauce has a close-your-eyes-and-you're-in-a-Vermont-farmhouse kind of character, which is why I especially like it with apple desserts. Maple also likes walnut, so a walnut tart or walnut-studded spice cake would be a lovely partner, too.

1 cup/240 ml half-and-half, or ½ cup/120 ml each whole milk and heavy cream

2 egg yolks

¼ cup/60 ml pure maple syrup, preferably grade B

1 tbsp lightly packed dark or light brown sugar

Tiny pinch of kosher salt

Pinch of freshly grated nutmeg, plus more if needed

**MAKES ABOUT 1¼ CUPS/300 ML**

**STORAGE** Refrigerate in an airtight container for up to 5 days. The sauce does not freeze well.

**QUICK CHANGE** Add ¼ tsp ground ginger and 1 tbsp unsulfured dark or light molasses along with the maple syrup.

Heat the half-and-half in a small saucepan over medium heat until it is just starting to steam; do not let it boil.

Meanwhile, in a small bowl, whisk together the egg yolks, maple syrup, brown sugar, and salt until well blended. Do not whisk so much that the mixture gets foamy, however.

When the half-and-half is hot, slowly pour about half of it into the yolk-sugar mixture, whisking constantly until combined. Return the pan to medium-low heat, then whisk in the yolk mixture. Gently cook the sauce, frequently scraping the bottom and sides of the pan with a heat-resistant rubber spatula or a wooden spoon, until it thickens, 3 to 5 minutes. It should register 180°F/82°C on an instant-read thermometer.

Remove from the heat and stir in the nutmeg, then taste and add a bit more if you like. For a very smooth texture (or if you're worried that you've gotten some bits of overcooked egg in the sauce), strain the sauce through a fine-mesh sieve. Let cool, cover, and refrigerate until chilled, at least 1 hour.

# FLOURLESS "BROWNIE" CAKE with
# CLASSIC VANILLA BEAN CRÈME ANGLAISE

Everyone needs a dessert like this in his or her repertoire. This cake is about as easy to make as a batch of brownies, but the results are more delicate and refined—a lovely ending to a dinner party. Use the best-quality chocolate you can find because the cake is all about chocolate. I use Valrhona or Michel Cluizel when I feel like splurging. The sauce is simultaneously rich and light, a subtle supporting player to the drama of the chocolate. I like the fudgy texture the cake develops after a day in the fridge (it will need at least an hour to come to room temperature before serving, so plan accordingly), but it is also delicious still warm from the oven and a little fragile.

8 oz/225 g unsalted butter, plus more for the pan

1 lb/455 g dark chocolate (semisweet or bittersweet), coarsely chopped

¾ cup/150 g granulated sugar

5 large eggs

⅛ tsp kosher salt

2½ cups/600 ml Classic Vanilla Bean Crème Anglaise (page 185)

**MAKES ONE 10-IN/25-CM CAKE; SERVES 8 TO 12**

Heat the oven to 350°F/180°C/gas 4. Butter the bottom and sides of a 10-in/25-cm round springform pan.

Pour water to a depth of 1 to 2 in/2.5 to 5 cm into a medium saucepan and place over medium heat. Put the butter and chocolate into a medium stainless-steel bowl and rest the bowl in the pan over (not touching) the water. Heat, stirring occasionally, until the butter and chocolate have melted and the mixture is smooth. Remove the bowl from the heat and set aside to cool briefly.

In a stand mixer fitted with the whisk attachment, or in a large bowl with a handheld electric mixer, beat together the sugar, eggs, and salt on medium-high speed until thick and pale yellow, about 3 minutes. Using a rubber spatula, scrape the egg mixture into the chocolate mixture and gently fold together. Scrape the batter into the prepared pan and smooth the top.

Bake the cake until it is puffed and is starting to pull away from the sides of the pan, 30 to 35 minutes.

Let the cake cool on a rack for 30 minutes, then carefully run a thin knife blade around the inside edge of the pan to loosen the cake from the pan sides. Unclasp and lift off the pan sides. The cake may collapse a bit in the center and crack around the edges, which is fine.

To serve the cake while it's still warm, slice it into wedges and transfer the slices to dessert plates. Pour a generous ribbon of crème anglaise around each slice and serve right away. To serve the cake chilled and fudgy, let it cool completely, wrap it in plastic wrap, and refrigerate for up to 3 days. Take from the refrigerator an hour before serving, then slice and serve with the crème anglaise.

# RICE PUDDING with CARDAMOM MERINGUES, LIME CRÈME ANGLAISE, and CHUNKY MIXED-BERRY COULIS

This dessert has several components, but they all can be made ahead. In fact, the pudding and cookies must be made ahead. The cookies are the perfect mate to the crème anglaise, providing a delicious use for most of the unused egg whites, and I like the dry, crunchy contrast they bring to the creamy pudding and sauce. The berry coulis adds its wonderful fruity flavor, of course, but also brings dramatic color to the dish.

### MERINGUES

4 egg whites

¾ cup/75 g confectioners' sugar

½ cup/100 g granulated sugar

½ tsp kosher salt

¼ tsp ground cardamom

⅛ tsp pure vanilla extract

⅓ cup/30 g ground blanched almonds

### PUDDING

4 cups/960 ml whole milk

½ cup/105 g medium-grain white rice

Pinch of kosher salt

2 egg yolks

⅓ cup/65 g granulated sugar

About 1 cup/240 ml Creamy Lime Crème Anglaise (page 186)

About 1 cup/240 ml Chunky Mixed-Berry Coulis (page 198)

**SERVES 4 TO 6, WITH EXTRA COOKIES**

**TO MAKE THE MERINGUES,** heat the oven to 175°F/80°C, or to as low a temperature as possible. Line two large rimmed baking sheets with parchment paper or silicone baking mats.

In a stand mixer fitted with the whisk attachment, or in a large bowl with a handheld electric mixer, beat the egg whites on medium-high speed until foamy and thick, about 2 minutes. On low speed, slowly add both sugars and the salt and continue beating until the whites are dense, glossy, and hold soft but definite peaks, another 1 to 2 minutes. Using a rubber spatula, gently fold in the cardamom, vanilla, and almonds just until combined.

Using two small spoons, drop little mounds of the meringue onto the baking sheets, spacing them at least 1 in/2.5 cm apart. You can make the meringues any size you like, but smaller meringues bake faster—and they're prettier.

Bake the meringues until they are dry and crunchy on the outside and just a touch chewy on the inside, about 3 hours. Let them cool completely on their pans on racks. (The cooled meringues can be stored in an airtight container at room temperature for up to 1 week. They will soften slightly but will still taste good.)

**TO MAKE THE PUDDING,** in a medium saucepan, combine the milk, rice, and salt and bring to a boil over medium-high heat. Quickly reduce the heat to maintain a steady simmer, then cook the rice, stirring occasionally, until tender, about 20 minutes. The rice will not have absorbed all of the milk. Remove from the heat.

In a large bowl, whisk together the egg yolks and sugar until smooth. Slowly pour the hot rice-milk mixture into the yolk-sugar mixture while stirring constantly to blend. Pour everything back into the saucepan, return to very low heat, and cook, stirring constantly with a wooden spoon or heat-resistant rubber spatula, until the pudding thickens a bit, 2 to 3 minutes.

Remove from the heat and pour the pudding into a clean bowl. Let cool to room temperature, about 1 hour. Cover with plastic wrap and refrigerate until well chilled, at least 3 hours or up to 3 days.

Put a scoop of the rice pudding on each dessert plate or in each small, shallow bowl. Spoon crème anglaise around the base of each pudding, spoon coulis over the top, and tuck a few meringues at the edge of each plate or bowl. Serve right away.

# FRUIT SAUCES

PART OF ME THINKS IT'S A SHAME TO DO ANYTHING TO A PIECE OF RIPE FRUIT OTHER THAN BITE INTO IT. Why mess with perfection? But the other part of me (maybe the French-trained part) thinks that a ripe, juicy peach, a silky mango, or a handful of perfumed blackberries begs to be transformed into a sauce. The natural brightness of flavor, the yielding luscious textures, and the vivid colors of fruit are all indispensable qualities of a successful sauce.

Fruit sauces are perfect with fruit desserts because they amplify the flavors already in the dish. But even more, I like fruit sauces as a contrast to creamy ingredients, such as ricotta cheese, ice cream, or puddings, where the bright acidity of the fruit cuts through the richness of the creamy dessert. Fruit sauces are also excellent partners for all types of cake; the crumb of the cake soaks up the fruit sauce in a wonderful way. Just think of a delicious juice-soaked biscuit in a strawberry shortcake and you'll know what I mean.

Most of my fruit sauces are sweet and intended to pair with desserts, but with a few nudges toward the savory side, fruit can also become an exciting partner for meat, poultry, or fish.

## WHAT'S GOING ON IN THIS SAUCE?

Fruit sauces don't require mastering tricky techniques. You just need to make some decisions: raw or cooked, chunky or smooth, sweet or tart.

On the raw side, the simplest fruit sauce is a coulis (pronounced koo-LEE), which is a purée of raw fruit, most often berries. Depending on the flavor of the fruit, adjust the balance of sweet and tart with sugar and citrus of some kind. If the fruit is quite seedy, such as blackberries, you can strain the seeds out. With a moderately seedy fruit, such as raspberries, the choice is yours. The sauce will be a touch rustic with the seeds, refined and elegant without.

On the cooked side, heat transforms the flavor, texture, and color of fruit into something deeper. What you lose in freshness, you gain in complexity and intensity. Blueberries and plums are my favorite fruits for cooked sauces because they undergo a personality makeover, becoming almost spicy with shiny, viscous juices.

For a cooked sauce, the choice is the same: leave it chunky or purée it so that it's smooth. As with a coulis, if the fruit is seedy, I always purée and then strain it. But with something like a plum, which breaks down into lush and tender chunks, I sometimes leave the sauce as is—hovering between sauce and compote.

To turn fruit into a savory sauce, I generally keep most of the sweet ingredients intact, but incorporate onion or shallot, some type of spicy heat (fresh or dried chiles), and more tang and salt.

## WHAT CAN GO WRONG AND HOW CAN I FIX IT?

Even perfect fruit needs a flavor boost to be made into a sauce, and most fruit is far from perfect, especially the fruit you find in an average grocery store. If the fruit is underripe, the sauce may be too tart and also just lack flavor. If the fruit is a touch overripe, the sauce may be flat and need sharpening up.

The only way to create a perfectly balanced fruit sauce is by doing a lot of tasting as you make it. Taste the fruit before you add any other ingredients so you have a sense of its natural levels. Then get out your "tool kit": citrus juice (usually lemon or lime), sugar or honey, balsamic vinegar, salt, and something with spicy heat, such as cayenne or Espelette pepper (see ingredient note, page 103).

In most cases, a few drops of fresh lemon juice and some sugar will do the trick. A squeeze of orange juice or a drizzle of apple cider can also heighten the general fruitiness. Balsamic vinegar is a secret weapon that, if used judiciously, can easily dial up the sweet-tart balance. Spice and salt should always be subtle, below-the-radar flavors that act as catalysts to make the other flavors shine brighter. The recipes in this chapter include these ingredients, but feel free to add more of anything listed to accommodate the personality of your fruit.

## HOW MUCH SAUCE PER SERVING?

Portion sizes for fruit sauces vary quite a bit. For a colorful flourish to a slice of tart, you'll need 2 tablespoons per person, but for a dessert where the fruit sauce is a key element, such as the blintzes on page 208, aim for closer to ¼ to ⅓ cup/60 to 80 ml per person.

## SPECIAL EQUIPMENT

Depending on the sauce you're making, a blender or food processor comes in handy. Also, a heavy saucepan, a fine-mesh sieve, and a flexible but strong rubber spatula to push the sauce through the sieve are all good to have on hand.

## STORAGE

Most fruit sauces can be stored in airtight containers in the refrigerator for up to 5 days, though the brightness of any sauce will fade after a day or two. They can also be frozen for up to 2 months, again with some diminished brightness.

# MANGO-MINT COULIS

It doesn't take much to turn a ripe mango into a glorious sauce, but here I'm infusing the sauce with fresh mint to add an herbal note that makes mango even more delicious. A touch of lime balances out the brightness of the fruit.

The only mangoes I eat are the small, golden Ataulfo mangoes, also called Manila or Champagne mangoes. They're virtually fiber free, so each chunk of flesh is juicy, dense, and smooth, and the flavor is sprightly and perfumed. If you can't find fresh Ataulfo mangoes, frozen mango chunks will work in a pinch. This sauce is beautiful spooned around a slice of fresh fruit tart or grilled pineapple slices, and it's stunning on a creamy meringue Pavlova (see page 206).

½ cup/100 g granulated sugar

½ cup/120 ml water

½ cup/15 g lightly packed fresh mint leaves

2 cups/340 g fresh ripe or thawed frozen mango chunks (1-in/2.5-cm chunks, from about 2 medium Ataulfo mangoes, or 12 oz/340 g frozen mango chunks)

4 tsp fresh lime juice, plus more if needed

Tiny pinch of kosher salt

MAKES 1 CUP/240 ML

**STORAGE** Refrigerate in an airtight container for up to 5 days or freeze for up to 2 months.

**QUICK CHANGE** Use fresh basil leaves instead of mint.

In a small saucepan, combine the sugar and water and bring to a boil over medium-high heat, stirring until the sugar is dissolved. Cook for about 1 minute more, then remove from the heat. Add the mint, pushing the leaves into the syrup until they are submerged, and let steep for about 30 minutes. Taste the syrup, and if it's nicely minty, remove and discard the mint; otherwise, let it steep longer, up to 1 hour. After that, the syrup will taste too vegetal.

In a food processor or blender, whiz the mango until smooth. Add about 3 tbsp of the mint syrup and process until very smooth. Add the lime juice and salt and then taste and tinker with the balance of flavors by adding more lime juice or syrup as needed. If the sauce seems fibrous, push it through a fine-mesh sieve.

# RASPBERRY COULIS

There is no simpler fruit sauce than raspberry coulis, yet it's completely compelling thanks to its fuchsia color and perfumed, sweet-tart flavor. If you're lucky enough to go raspberry picking this summer, make a triple batch of the sauce and freeze what you don't use right away.

Drizzle this iconic coulis over ice cream, pour a ribbon around a slice of lemon tart, swirl it with whipped cream and lemon curd to make an instant parfait, or use it to dress up a slice of flourless chocolate cake.

8 oz/225 g fresh or thawed frozen raspberries

Confectioners' sugar

Fresh lemon juice

In a food processor or blender, whiz the berries until just shy of smooth (aside from the raspberry seeds). Add 2 tsp sugar and pulse to mix. Taste the sauce and add more sugar, if necessary. Add a few drops of lemon juice and taste again. You want the sauce to be sweet but not cloying, so tinker with the sugar and lemon until you have a nice balance. Serve the sauce as is or strain out the seeds using a fine-mesh sieve.

**MAKES ABOUT 1 CUP/240 ML**

**STORAGE** Refrigerate in an airtight container for up to 5 days or freeze for up to 2 months.

**QUICK CHANGE** Add 1 tbsp raspberry liqueur with the sugar.

# PEACH-RASPBERRY COULIS WITH A HINT OF ROSEMARY

I love the luscious character and aroma of fresh, ripe peaches, but they can be one-dimensional in a sauce. To offset this, I like to add fresh herbs and raspberries for their flavor. The raspberries also contribute color, which is pretty pooled around a slice of lemon tart or drizzled over ginger or lemon ice cream.

½ cup/100 g granulated sugar

½ cup/120 ml water

2 fresh rosemary sprigs, 4 in/10 cm long

1 lb/455 g very ripe peaches, peeled, pitted, and cut into chunks

½ cup/60 g fresh or mostly thawed frozen raspberries

Fresh lemon juice

Tiny pinch of kosher salt

**MAKES ABOUT 2 CUPS/480 ML**

**STORAGE** Refrigerate in an airtight container for up to 5 days or freeze for up to 2 months. The color may darken a bit.

**QUICK CHANGE** Use half peaches (or nectarines) and half apriums (a cross between an apricot and a plum).

In a small saucepan, combine the sugar and water and bring to a boil over medium-high heat, stirring until the sugar is dissolved. Cook for about 1 minute more, then remove from the heat. Add the rosemary, pushing the sprigs into the syrup until they are submerged, and let steep for about 15 minutes. Taste the syrup, and if the rosemary flavor isn't strong enough, let steep for another 5 to 10 minutes. Taste the syrup often so you can remove the rosemary when its flavor is nice and strong but not overwhelming. Rosemary can impart a sort of turpentine taste if you leave it for too long. Discard the sprigs.

In a food processor or blender, combine the peaches and raspberries and whiz until just shy of smooth (aside from the raspberry seeds). Add about ⅓ cup/ 75 ml of the rosemary syrup, process to combine, and then taste, adding more syrup until you like the balance of fruit and herb. Add 1 tsp lemon juice and the salt and then taste and tinker with the balance of flavors by adding more lemon juice or syrup as needed. Cover and refrigerate until chilled—this sauce tastes best cold—before serving.

# CHUNKY MIXED-BERRY COULIS

Straining half of the sauce preserves its nice compote character but helps remove many of the seeds. If you're using blackberries, the seeds can be a bit annoying. The sauce is best made primarily with cane berries—those in the raspberry and blackberry families— and blueberries. Too many strawberries can make the sauce wan. Serve the sauce over a scoop or two of lemon ice cream, swirled with some fromage blanc, folded into soft whipped cream, or with creamy rice pudding (see page 190).

1 lb/455 g mixed fresh or frozen berries such as blackberry, raspberry, boysenberry, blueberry, and strawberry, in any combination

¼ cup/50 g granulated sugar, plus more if needed

2 tbsp water

1 tbsp fresh lime juice, plus more if needed

Tiny pinch of kosher salt

**MAKES ABOUT 2 CUPS/480 ML**

**STORAGE** Refrigerate in an airtight container for up to 5 days or freeze for up to 2 months.

**QUICK CHANGE** Add ½ tsp peeled and finely chopped fresh ginger to the berries with the sugar and water.

In a medium, heavy saucepan, combine the berries, sugar, and water and bring to a simmer over medium-high heat. Simmer until the berries begin to break down and the juices are running, about 10 minutes for fresh berries and 25 minutes for frozen.

Transfer about half of the cooked fruit to a fine-mesh sieve set over a medium bowl. Using a rubber spatula, push the fruit through the sieve to purée it and remove the seeds (you can do this in a food processor, if you like, but the fruit should be soft enough to force through the sieve).

Stir the purée back into the rest of the sauce in the pan, then add the lime juice and salt. For a thicker sauce, cook for a few more minutes (but not so much that it gets "jammy"; the sauce will thicken as it cools). Taste and adjust with more sugar or lime juice if needed.

# BLACKBERRY-ALMOND SAUCE

Blackberries were exotic to me until I moved to the Pacific Northwest, where late-summer hikes in the woods yield handfuls of the wild berries and farmers' market stalls offer big, dusky berries engorged with deep purple juice. And although plentiful for a few weeks during late summer when they're in season, blackberries are nonetheless temperamental. Even ripe ones can be tart, and all blackberries are extremely seedy, which is why I always strain my blackberry sauces.

This sauce is a treat on pancakes, crepes, or waffles or on a fat slice of angel food cake, topped with whipped cream.

12 oz/340 g ripe blackberries

¼ cup/20 g confectioners' sugar, plus more if needed

1 tsp fresh lemon juice, plus more if needed

1 tbsp water

Tiny pinch of kosher salt

⅛ tsp pure almond extract

¼ tsp balsamic vinegar (optional)

**MAKES ABOUT 1 CUP/240 ML**

**STORAGE** Refrigerate in an airtight container for up to 5 days or freeze for up to 2 months.

**QUICK CHANGE** Use Demerara or turbinado sugar in place of the confectioners' sugar.

In a small, heavy saucepan, combine the berries, sugar, lemon juice, water, and salt and bring to a simmer over medium-high heat. Cover and cook just until the juices are running and the berries have slightly collapsed, 3 to 4 minutes. Do not let the juices caramelize.

Scrape everything into a food processor and whiz until smooth (aside from the blackberry seeds). Strain through a fine-mesh sieve into a small bowl, using a wooden spoon or rubber spatula to push as many solids through as you can. You will end up with 2 to 3 tbsp seeds, which you can toss out.

Stir the almond extract into the berry purée. Taste and adjust with more sugar or lemon juice if needed. Add the vinegar if the sauce needs extra punch. Serve slightly warm, at room temperature, or cool.

# SPICED BLUEBERRY SAUCE

Blueberries are wonderful eaten fresh, but they undergo a remarkable transformation when cooked—sort of like the pretty librarian who whips off her glasses and is suddenly sexy. As the blueberries cook, they'll burst and release lots of indigo juice, their flavor will develop a distinct spiciness (which I'm echoing here with additional spices), and the final sauce will be glossy and thick. Serve this sauce over pound cake with a scoop of ice cream alongside, or pour it over barely warm lemon pudding cake (see page 207).

12 oz/340 g fresh or frozen blueberries

¼ cup/50 g granulated sugar, plus more if needed

2 tbsp water

¼ tsp ground cinnamon

¼ tsp ground cardamom

⅛ tsp ground cloves

Tiny pinch of kosher salt

1 tsp fresh lemon juice, plus more if needed

**MAKES ABOUT 1 CUP/240 ML**

**STORAGE** Refrigerate in an airtight container for up to 5 days or freeze for up to 2 months.

**QUICK CHANGE** Omit the spices and lemon juice and add 1 tbsp fresh lime juice and 1 tsp lightly packed finely grated lime zest when the sauce is removed from the heat.

In a medium, heavy saucepan, combine the berries, sugar, water, cinnamon, cardamom, cloves, and salt over medium heat. Cover and cook until the juices are running, about 5 minutes. Uncover and simmer until the berries collapse a bit more and the juices reduce and thicken a bit, another couple minutes. The sauce won't actually look thick, but it will seem slightly syrupy.

Add the lemon juice, then taste and adjust with more sugar, lemon, or spices. You can serve the sauce chunky, or you can whiz it in a food processor and pass it through a fine-mesh sieve, which will make it very glossy and smooth. Serve slightly warm, at room temperature, or cool.

# HONEY-PLUM SAUCE

Plums are one of my favorite fruits to cook because they seem to love the heat. Their texture relaxes into a lush softness, their color intensifies, and their flavor becomes slightly spicy yet still retains its nice acidity. The color of this sauce will vary depending on the variety of plum you use. The sauce is delicious on pancakes or waffles, perfect with almond cake, and lovely with a moist square of warm gingerbread topped with a spoonful of crème fraîche.

2 lb/910 g ripe plums, halved, pitted, and cut into ¾-in/2-cm wedges

¼ cup/50 g granulated sugar, plus more if needed

¼ cup/60 ml honey

¼ cup/60 ml water

½ tsp fresh lemon juice, plus more if needed

¼ tsp ground cardamom

¼ tsp ground ginger

¼ tsp pure vanilla extract

**MAKES ABOUT 2½ CUPS/600 ML**

**STORAGE** Refrigerate in an air-tight container for up to 5 days or freeze for up to 2 months.

**QUICK CHANGE** Omit the cardamom and increase the ginger to ½ tsp.

In a medium, heavy saucepan, combine the plums, sugar, honey, water, lemon juice, cardamom, ginger, and vanilla and bring to a gentle boil over medium-high heat, stirring slowly to dissolve the sugar. Reduce the heat to maintain a simmer and cook, uncovered, until the plums are starting to fall apart and the juices have thickened quite a bit, 15 to 20 minutes.

If the fruit is getting mushy but the juices are still thin, using a slotted spoon, transfer most of the fruit to a bowl. Increase the heat to high and boil the juices until they are nicely thickened, then return the fruit to the pan. Taste the sauce and adjust with more sugar, lemon juice, or spices. You can serve the sauce chunky, or you can whiz it in a food processor to make it smooth. To make it perfectly smooth, push the sauce through a fine-mesh sieve. Serve slightly warm, at room temperature, or cool.

# STRAWBERRY-BALSAMIC SAUCE

I am making it my personal mission to get everyone to taste the incredible flavor of strawberries, brown sugar, and balsamic vinegar mixed together—preferably with some sour cream or vanilla ice cream close by—because I think it's one of the dessert world's perfect combinations. Each element echoes the others and the sweet-sour-savory dynamic is irresistible. Your balsamic vinegar should be decent, but not artisanal, quality. I like Lucini brand, which is sold in many grocery stores.

Garnish a classic strawberry shortcake with some of this sauce, serve it with a slice of vanilla sponge cake, or transform it into a luscious fool with whipped cream and fresh goat cheese (see page 210).

¼ cup/60 ml balsamic vinegar

¼ cup/50 g lightly packed light or dark brown sugar

12 oz/340 g strawberries, hulled and halved or quartered lengthwise if large

⅛ tsp pure vanilla extract

Tiny pinch of kosher salt

**MAKES 1¼ CUPS/300 ML**

**STORAGE** Refrigerate in an air-tight container for up to 5 days or freeze for up to 2 months.

**QUICK CHANGE** Replace half of the strawberries with raspberries.

In a large frying pan, combine the vinegar and sugar over medium heat, bring to a simmer, and cook, stirring, until syrupy, about 1 minute or so once it's come to a simmer. Watch out for the vinegar fumes, which can be startlingly potent! Add the berries and simmer, stirring gently, until they start to collapse and the juices are running but the berries have not turned to mush, 6 to 8 minutes.

Remove the pan from the heat and gently stir in the vanilla and salt. Taste and adjust the seasoning. You want a balance that is fruity and sweet, with just an intriguing edge of vinegar. Serve slightly cool or at room temperature.

# CHUNKY CHERRY MOSTARDA SAUCE

Mostarda is a wonderful, spicy Italian condiment that's not quite a chutney, not quite a pickle, but rather a sweet-hot chunky preserve of fruits with mustard. It's often served with cold boiled or roasted meats. In this simplified version, I'm playing the deep sweetness of Bing cherries against sinus-clearing dry mustard and brown mustard seeds.

The result is a perfect companion for pâté, ham, or even meat loaf. Or, use it in a riff on the old appetizer classic of pepper jelly poured over cream cheese by spooning some of the sauce over cream cheese or *fromage blanc*. Serve it with good crackers and a well-made Negroni for an enjoyable cocktail hour.

1 tbsp extra-virgin olive oil

½ cup/70 g finely chopped yellow onion

Kosher salt

1 lb/455 g Bing or other sweet cherries, pitted and coarsely chopped

¼ cup/50 g lightly packed light brown sugar, plus more if needed

¼ cup/60 ml rice vinegar, plus more if needed

½ tsp brown mustard seeds

½ tsp chopped fresh thyme

¼ tsp dry mustard

**MAKES 1½ CUPS/360 ML**

**STORAGE** Refrigerate in an air-tight container for up to 5 days. The sauce does not freeze well because the cherries get too mushy.

**QUICK CHANGE** Use chopped, pitted Italian prune plums instead of cherries.

In a medium, heavy saucepan, heat the oil over medium heat. Add the onion and ¼ tsp salt and cook, stirring often, until the onion is soft and fragrant, about 5 minutes. Add the cherries, sugar, vinegar, mustard seeds, thyme, and dry mustard, stir together, and bring to a simmer. Cover and cook, stirring occasionally, until the cherries partially collapse but have not turned to mush, 10 to 14 minutes.

Remove the pan from the heat, let cool slightly, and then taste and adjust the seasoning with salt, sugar, and vinegar if needed. Serve warm, at room temperature, or cold.

# SAVORY SPICED RHUBARB SAUCE

If you haven't yet made friends with rhubarb, now's the time. It's such a surprising ingredient: bite into a stalk raw and you can't believe humans actually eat it, but take a bite of rhubarb after it's simmered with some sugar, and you won't want to stop eating it. This sauce is sweet, sour, savory, and a perfect partner for sweet meats, such as pork loin, lamb chops, sausages, or ham.

2 tsp olive oil

2 tsp chopped shallot

1 tsp finely chopped fresh chile such as jalapeño

1 tsp peeled and finely chopped fresh ginger

1 tbsp balsamic vinegar

1 lb/455 g rhubarb stalks, fibrous ends peeled and cut into 1-in/2.5-cm chunks

⅓ cup plus 2 tsp/85 g lightly packed light or dark brown sugar

1 whole star anise

1 bay leaf

2 tbsp water

Kosher salt

⅛ tsp cayenne pepper, plus more if needed

1 tbsp unsalted butter, plus more if needed (optional)

**MAKES ABOUT 1½ CUPS/360 ML**

**STORAGE** Refrigerate in an airtight container for up to 5 days or freeze for up to 2 months.

**QUICK CHANGE** Omit the star anise and add ⅛ tsp ground cinnamon and a tiny pinch of ground cloves with the salt and cayenne.

In a medium, heavy saucepan, heat the oil over medium-high heat. Add the shallot, chile, and ginger and cook, stirring constantly, until soft and fragrant, about 2 minutes. Add the vinegar and simmer until reduced to a glaze, just a few seconds. Add the rhubarb, brown sugar, star anise, bay leaf, and water and bring to a boil over medium-high heat. Reduce the heat to a simmer and cook, stirring occasionally, until the rhubarb is very soft and starting to fall apart, 6 to 8 minutes.

Remove from the heat and remove and discard the star anise and bay leaf. Whisk in ½ tsp salt, the cayenne, and butter (if using). Taste and adjust the seasoning with salt or cayenne or more butter if the sauce tastes sharp. Serve warm.

# SAVORY BLACKBERRY-BASIL SAUCE

Ripe blackberries have a heavenly perfume, and in this sauce, I enhance that lovely fragrance with fresh basil. Blackberries also tend to be tart, so I keep the tart flavor balanced by using a *gastrique*, or caramel dissolved with vinegar. Depending on your berries, you may need to add more sugar to taste, too. Even though Aleppo chile isn't always easy to find, I'm calling for it here because it's my new favorite ground chile—fruity and almost winey, but not superhot. If you don't have Aleppo chile or another mild chile powder on hand, you can use cayenne pepper, but reduce the amount to a pinch. I love this sauce on grilled chicken thighs, grilled pork chops, or sautéed turkey cutlets.

2 tbsp granulated sugar, plus more if needed

2 tbsp balsamic vinegar, plus more if needed

12 oz/340 g ripe blackberries

1 tbsp finely chopped shallot or yellow onion

2 tbsp water

⅛ tsp coarsely ground Aleppo chile (see ingredient note, page 44) or other mild chile powder

Kosher salt and freshly ground black pepper

1 tbsp thinly sliced fresh basil

**MAKES ABOUT 1 CUP/240 ML**

**STORAGE** Refrigerate in an air-tight container for up to 5 days or freeze for up to 2 months.

**QUICK CHANGE** Add 1 tsp chopped fresh tarragon with the basil.

In a small, heavy saucepan, cook the sugar over low heat, stirring frequently so the sugar doesn't burn around the edges, until the sugar turns a deep copper color, about 10 minutes from when you turn on the burner.

Remove the pan from the heat, add the vinegar, and stir to dissolve the caramel (this is the *gastrique*). Stir in the berries, shallot, water, chile powder, ¼ tsp salt, and a few grinds of pepper. Return to low heat, cover, and simmer until the berries have softened and released their juices, 4 to 5 minutes.

Scrape everything into a food processor and whiz until smooth (aside from the blackberry seeds). Strain through a fine-mesh sieve into a small bowl, using a wooden spoon or rubber spatula to push as many solids through as you can. You will end up with 2 to 3 tbsp seeds, which you can toss out.

Stir the basil into the blackberry purée. Taste and adjust with more salt, pepper, vinegar, and sugar if needed. Serve warm or at room temperature.

# PAVLOVA with MANGO-MINT COULIS

A Pavlova should be in every cook's repertoire. It's simple to make and one of those desserts that you just can't stop eating because the textures are irresistible: the cloudlike meringue base is crunchy on the outside but like the best marshmallow on the inside, and the layer of luscious whipped cream contrasts with the juicy fruit on top—it's dynamic.

5 egg whites, at room temperature

1 tsp kosher salt

1 cup/200 g granulated sugar

1 tsp cornstarch

1 tsp distilled white or white wine vinegar

½ tsp pure vanilla extract

¾ cup/180 ml heavy cream

½ cup/120 ml crème fraîche

1 to 2 tbsp honey

4 cups/455 g mixed fresh fruit chunks such as peach, nectarine, plum, apricot, mango, kiwifruit, and berries, in any combination

1 cup/240 ml Mango-Mint Coulis (page 195)

**SERVES 6 TO 8**

Heat the oven to 350°F/180°C/gas 4. Line a large rimmed baking sheet with parchment paper or a silicone baking mat.

In a stand mixer fitted with the whisk attachment, or with a handheld electric mixer and a large bowl, beat the egg whites on medium-high speed until very foamy and white and beginning to grow in volume, about 2 minutes. Continue to beat as you sprinkle in the salt and then the sugar, a spoonful at a time. Then beat until you have a fluffy, glossy meringue that holds firm, swirly peaks, about 4 minutes more. On low speed, gently beat in the cornstarch, vinegar, and vanilla just until combined.

Pile the meringue onto the center of the prepared baking sheet. Using a large spoon or rubber spatula, spread the meringue in a 9-in/23-cm circle with a slight depression in the center, like a kiddie pool. Place the meringue in the oven, reduce the oven temperature to 300°F/150°C/gas 2, and bake until very dry on the top but still soft in the center when you press it, 1 to 1¼ hours. Don't let the meringue brown past a nice shade of ivory.

Turn off the oven but leave the meringue inside until the oven is completely cool.

In the stand mixer fitted with the whisk attachment, or with the handheld electric mixer and a clean medium bowl, beat the cream on high speed until it holds soft peaks, 1 to 2 minutes. Add the crème fraîche and 1 tbsp of the honey and beat for a few more seconds to blend. The cream should hold its shape but not be "curdly." Taste and fold in a bit more honey if you want the cream mixture to be sweeter.

Transfer the cooled meringue to a serving plate. Mound the cream in the center of the meringue and spread it with an offset spatula or the back of a spoon to make a pretty, cloudlike layer. Arrange the fresh fruit artfully over the cream. Let stand for at least 15 minutes or up to 2 hours (if it's not too hot in your kitchen) to allow the cream to meld with the meringue a bit and the fruit juices to run into the cream.

Cut into wedges, transfer the slices to dessert plates, and serve with the coulis spooned around each wedge.

# HOMEY LEMON PUDDING CAKE
## with SPICED BLUEBERRY SAUCE

If your mother didn't make this cake, your grandmother probably did. It's one of those easy, comforting desserts that feel appropriate for a family supper, a dinner party, or anything in between. The batter separates into three layers as it bakes: a light, spongy cake on top, a moist pudding in the middle, and a saucy layer on the bottom.

Even though this dessert makes its own sauce, I like to add a contrasting blueberry sauce as much for its deep purple color as for its flavor. Most recipes call for baking this kind of cake in a water bath, but I think that's too fussy. I just bake it at a lower temperature, which protects its delicate texture.

1 tbsp unsalted butter, for the baking dish

1½ cups/360 ml whole milk

4 large eggs, separated

⅓ cup/75 ml fresh lemon juice

1 tbsp lightly packed finely grated lemon zest

½ cup/65 g all-purpose flour

1¼ cups/250 g granulated sugar

½ tsp kosher salt

1 cup/240 ml Spiced Blueberry Sauce (page 200)

Position a rack in the lower third of the oven and heat to 350°F/180°C/gas 4. Butter an 8-in/20-cm square baking dish.

In a medium bowl, whisk together the milk, egg yolks, lemon juice, and lemon zest until blended. In another medium bowl, whisk together the flour, 1 cup/200 g of the sugar, and the salt. Whisk the dry ingredients into the wet ingredients until blended.

In a stand mixer fitted with the whisk attachment, or with a large bowl and a handheld electric mixer, beat the egg whites on medium-high speed until foamy and white, about 1 minute. With the mixer running, slowly add the remaining ¼ cup/50 g sugar, a little at a time, beating until fully incorporated, and then continue to beat until the whites are glossy and hold medium-firm peaks, about 4 minutes more.

Whisk about one-fourth of the egg whites into the cake batter to lighten it. Then, using a rubber spatula, gently fold the remaining egg whites into the batter just until no white streaks are visible. Pour the batter into the prepared baking dish.

Place the cake in the oven and immediately reduce the oven temperature to 300°F/150°C/gas 2. Bake until puffed and slightly dry on the top but still soft inside (the cake will wiggle when you shake the dish), 35 to 40 minutes. Let cool on a rack until barely warm, then scoop into dessert bowls and serve with the blueberry sauce.

**MAKES ONE 8-IN/20-CM CAKE;
SERVES 6 TO 8**

# RICOTTA BLINZTES with HONEY-PLUM SAUCE

The filling for these gently fried stuffed crepes is not too sweet, which makes them a wonderful breakfast or brunch dish. You can make the sauce and the crepes (stack them, wrap in plastic wrap, and refrigerate) a couple of days ahead, so you won't have to get out of bed too early to pull the dish together.

## CREPES

1 cup/240 ml whole milk, plus more if needed

2 large eggs

½ tsp kosher salt

¾ cups/90 g all-purpose flour

3 tbsp unsalted butter, melted, plus more for cooking the crepes

## FILLING

1 cup/225 g fresh whole-milk ricotta cheese

1 tbsp confectioners' sugar

2 tsp all-purpose flour

1 tsp lightly packed finely grated orange zest (optional)

¼ tsp pure vanilla extract

Pinch of kosher salt

1 large egg, beaten

1 tbsp plus 4 tsp unsalted butter

About 1 cup/240 ml Honey-Plum Sauce (page 201)

Confectioners' sugar for dusting

**MAKES 8 BLINTZES; SERVES 4**

**TO MAKE THE CREPES,** in a blender, combine the milk, eggs, and salt and whiz for a few seconds to blend everything together. Remove the lid and add the flour. Re-cover and process until very smooth, about 20 seconds. Remove the lid, pour in the butter, cover, and process until combined, about 10 seconds more.

Transfer the batter to a large glass measuring cup with a spout (or to a bowl into which you can easily dip a ¼-cup/60-ml ladle or measuring cup). Let the batter rest for at least 30 minutes at room temperature or refrigerate for up to 24 hours. When you are ready to make the crepes, test the consistency of the batter. It should be as thick as heavy cream, but not as thick as pancake batter. If it is too thick, whisk in more milk.

Heat a crepe pan with an 8-in/20-cm base, nonstick frying pan, or well-seasoned frying pan over medium-high heat until a drop of water flicked onto the surface sizzles on contact. Using a folded paper towel, spread about ½ tsp butter around the interior of the pan. The butter should sizzle on contact, but you don't want the pan so hot that the butter burns.

Pour about ¼ cup/60 ml of the batter into the center of the pan. As you pour, lift the pan from the heat and tilt and turn it in all directions so the batter spreads evenly across the bottom of the pan in a thin circle. If the crepe has any holes in it, quickly add a few drops of batter to fill them in. Or, if you have too much batter and the crepe looks too thick, immediately pour the excess back into the measuring cup or bowl. You can always trim off the "tail" that's left behind.

Cook the crepe until the edges begin to dry and lift from the edge of the pan and the bottom is nicely browned, about 1 minute. To check for color, use a table knife, thin offset spatula, or your fingers to lift up an edge of the crepe and look underneath. When the first side is ready, use the knife, spatula, or your fingers to lift the crepe and quickly flip it over. Smooth out any folded edges or pleats, and then cook until the center is firm and the second side is browned, too, about 20 seconds more.

Slide the crepe from the pan onto a large plate or cooling rack. Repeat with the remaining batter, adjusting the heat and spreading the pan with more butter as you cook. As each crepe is finished, stack it on top of the previous one. You should end up with eight crepes. The crepes will soften as they cool.

**TO MAKE THE FILLING,** in a small bowl, combine the ricotta, confectioners' sugar, flour, orange zest, vanilla, and salt and stir with a fork just until blended. Do not overmix or you will lose the fluffiness of the ricotta. Stir in the egg.

Heat the oven to 400°F/200°C/gas 6. Use 1 tbsp of the butter to grease the bottom of a 9-by-13-in/23-by-33-cm baking dish.

Lay the crepes, prettiest-side down, on a clean work surface. Spoon about 2 tbsp of the filling onto the center of each crepe, then spread the filling into a 3-by-1-in/7.5-by-2.5-cm oval. Fold the bottom and top edges of each crepe up to enclose the filling, and then fold in both sides to create neat, flattish rectangular blintzes about 3½ in/9 cm long.

In a large frying pan, melt about 2 tsp of the remaining butter over medium heat. When the butter is hot, arrange as many blintzes, seam-side up, in the pan as will fit in a single layer. Cook until the underside of each blintze is golden, about 2 minutes. Flip and cook until golden on the second side, another 2 minutes. Transfer the blintzes to the prepared baking dish. Repeat with any remaining blintzes and butter.

Put the baking dish in the oven and bake until the blintzes are slightly puffed, the filling is heated through, and the bottoms are slightly crisp, 7 to 10 minutes.

Arrange two blintzes, overlapping them slightly, on each of four plates. Spoon a generous ribbon of the plum sauce around each pair of blintzes. Dust the blintzes with confectioners' sugar. Serve warm.

# CRUSHED STRAWBERRY-BALSAMIC FOOL PARFAIT

Pastry chef and cookbook author Abby Dodge taught me about fools when we worked together at *Fine Cooking* magazine. She's a master at this kind of simple but sophisticated dessert, so I asked her to create one to pair with the Strawberry-Balsamic Sauce. You can try the same recipe with the blackberry, blueberry, or mixed-berry sauce.

1½ cups/360 ml Strawberry-Balsamic Sauce (page 202), chilled

1 cup/240 ml heavy cream

4 oz/115 g mild fresh goat cheese or *fromage blanc*, at room temperature

⅓ cup/65 g lightly packed light brown sugar

¼ tsp kosher salt

2¼ cups/240 g coarsely crushed amaretti or gingersnaps

6 strawberries, hulled and halved lengthwise

Have ready six parfait glasses or wineglasses.

Set aside about ½ cup/120 ml of the sauce. Scrape the remaining sauce into a food processor and pulse until the berries are crushed. (I like to leave some texture to the berries, but you can pulse until smooth, too.)

In a large bowl, using a handheld electric mixer, beat together the cream, goat cheese, sugar, and salt on medium-low speed until smooth, about 1 minute. Increase the speed to high and beat until firm peaks form when the beaters are lifted (don't forget to stop the mixer before lifting), about 2 minutes. Add the reserved sauce and the processed sauce and, using a rubber spatula, fold just until blended. (The mixture can be covered and refrigerated for up to 1 day before continuing.)

Spoon about 3½ tbsp of the cream mixture into each glass. Top with about 3 tbsp of the cookie crumbs. Spread about 3½ tbsp of the cream mixture over the cookie crumbs in each glass. Top with the remaining crumbs and then with the remaining cream mixture.

Serve immediately or cover and refrigerate up to 3 hours (the cookie crumbs will soften a bit). Top with the strawberry halves just before serving.

SERVES 6

# LAMB MEATBALLS in CHUNKY CHERRY MOSTARDA SAUCE with COUSCOUS

Something about this cherry sauce makes me crave lamb, and meatballs are one of my favorite ways to enjoy lamb. Both sauce and meat are slightly sweet, so be sure to dial the spice heat level high enough to provide contrast. The simply steamed greens also deliver a welcome earthiness. You can make the meatballs and the sauce up to a day ahead, so you don't need to juggle too many last-minute cooking chores.

¾ cup/40 g fresh bread crumbs

2 tbsp water plus 1½ cups/360 ml

1 lb/455 g ground lamb

⅓ cup/40 g finely crumbled feta cheese

¼ cup/10 g finely chopped fresh cilantro

1 clove garlic, minced

Kosher salt and freshly ground black pepper

1 large egg, lightly beaten

4 tbsp/60 ml extra-virgin olive oil, plus more if needed

1½ cups/360 ml Chunky Cherry Mostarda Sauce (page 203)

About 6 cups/170 g lightly packed roughly chopped mixed greens such as Swiss chard, kale, beet greens, and spinach, in any combination, rinsed well but not dried

1½ cups/255 g couscous

¼ cup/60 ml plain yogurt, stirred with a fork to loosen

¼ cup/10 g chopped fresh flat-leaf parsley or mint (optional)

**SERVES 4**

In a small bowl, sprinkle the bread crumbs with the 2 tbsp water and toss to moisten evenly.

In a large bowl, combine the lamb, moistened bread crumbs, feta, cilantro, garlic, 1 tsp salt, and ⅛ tsp pepper and mix gently with your hands to distribute the ingredients evenly. Add the egg and mix again. Do not squeeze or over-work the mixture. Shape the mixture into 24 uniform meatballs, shaping them between your palms.

In a large frying pan, heat 2 tbsp of the oil over medium heat. Working in batches if necessary, add the meatballs in a single layer, leaving enough room between them so you can turn them easily. Brown the meatballs, turning them as needed, until nicely colored on all sides, 7 to 9 minutes total per batch. They may not be fully cooked through, which is okay. Because of the cheese, the meatballs may stick a little, so use a thin metal spatula to dislodge them gently when you turn them. Transfer the meatballs to a large plate.

Pour off any excess fat from the pan. If there are any burned bits in the pan, wipe them out, but don't wipe out the good brown bits. Return the meatballs to the pan over low heat, pour in the sauce, and gently simmer the meatballs in the sauce, shaking the pan occasionally to coat them well, until cooked through, 5 to 6 minutes. Remove from the heat and keep warm.

Heat a large saucepan or frying pan over high heat and drop in about half of the greens. (You do not need to add any water; the rinsing water clinging to greens is sufficient moisture.) Toss the greens with tongs to encourage them to wilt, and keep adding more greens as each batch collapses and creates space in the pan. When all of the greens are in the pan, season them with ½ tsp salt, reduce the heat to medium, and cover the pan to steam the greens, uncovering the pan and tossing the greens frequently as they cook. If they seem to be drying out, add a few spoonfuls of water. Cook just until tender, 3 to 10 minutes, depending on the kind of greens you are using. Taste and adjust the seasoning with salt; keep warm.

In a small saucepan, bring the remaining 1½ cups/360 ml water to a boil over high heat. Stir in the couscous, ½ tsp salt, and remaining 2 tbsp oil, then remove from the heat. Cover and let sit undisturbed until the couscous has absorbed the water and is tender, about 5 minutes. Fluff the couscous with a fork. Taste and adjust the seasoning with salt and olive oil until the couscous is tasty, then fluff again.

Divide the couscous evenly among four warmed shallow serving bowls. Arrange a pile of greens on the couscous and top each serving with six meatballs and some sauce. Drizzle an equal amount of the yogurt over each serving, then sprinkle with the parsley (if using). Serve right away.

# CARAMEL SAUCES

I GET A THRILL FROM MAKING CARAMEL. TRANSFORMING CLOYING WHITE SUGAR INTO NUANCED TEETERING-ON-THE-EDGE-OF-BITTER CARAMEL is an example of what I love most about cooking: you start with one thing and you turn it into another, much better thing.

In the case of caramel sauce, "much better" means divine—sweet but with a nutty hint of bitterness for sophistication, and with layers of flavor that continue to unfold as you savor it. If the world is divided into chocolate people and caramel-ginger-lemon people (and I believe it is), I am the captain of the caramel team.

A caramel sauce is an impressive sauce to make. Many cooks find it a bit mysterious, but with a little technique work under your belt, you'll be making caramel sauces that are so incredibly delicious (and superior to commercial caramel sauces), you'll earn impressive cooking cred from everyone you share them with.

## WHAT'S GOING ON IN THIS SAUCE?

True caramel is sugar cooked to a temperature of around 350°F/180°C, which is the candy-making temperature at which thousands of flavor compounds develop. When a caramel cooked to this temperature cools, it will be hard and brittle, so to make it into a sauce you need to add liquid. For most of my sauces, I add heavy cream or crème fraîche (the latter for a tangy note) and often finish the sauce with butter. You can use other liquids such as coconut milk or fruit juice or even a little water would work for a simple sauce.

There are two ways to make your base caramel: cook dry sugar for a dry caramel or cook sugar with a little water for a wet caramel. The latter method gives you a time buffer; the sugar and water form a syrup, and then the water has to evaporate before the sugar can caramelize, so you have a bit more time before the sugar begins to brown. When you make a dry caramel, the sugar around the edges of the pan will melt and caramelize faster than the sugar at the center, which means you will need to swirl the pan to blend what is caramelized and what is not to avoid burning. It's a bit tricky, but it's also faster—and more dramatic! Give it a try once you are comfortable with making wet caramel.

A good caramel sauce depends on how dark the caramel is. If you stop cooking the sugar too soon, you will end up with a light caramel that offers sweetness without depth. It won't be much tastier than corn syrup. But cook the sugar too long and it will go from perfect to dark, burnt, and bitter in seconds, even fractions of seconds.

I like a hint of bitterness in my caramel, so I try to take it right up to the edge. Gauging doneness uses both your eyes and your nose. You will begin to smell "caramel" and then you will see a tiny suggestion of smoke. For me, that's the exact moment to add the cream or other liquid, so always have it measured and ready at the stove.

Fortunately, sugar is relatively inexpensive, so if you overcook it, you can just dump that batch and start over. You won't feel the same freedom once you have added the pricier cream and butter, of course.

## WHAT CAN GO WRONG AND HOW CAN I FIX IT?

The one thing that can go wrong—but I won't allow it to—is that you can seriously burn yourself with caramel. When the caramel is at its peak temperature, it is more than 350°F/180°C. Plus, the stuff is sticky, so if it splashes onto your hand, you can't just flick it off. Caramel will also burn if it splashes onto the burner of your stove.

But don't worry! I don't want to scare anyone away from making caramel sauce, and it's easy to make sure that you won't hurt yourself. In fact, I've never, ever burned myself on caramel. Here are three rules to ensure that you don't either:

1. Use a saucepan that has at least three times the volume of the amount of sauce you are making. When you add your cream or other liquid to the hot caramel, it will bubble up furiously, so you need a pan with enough room to accommodate the bubbling without overflowing. For instance, if your recipe calls for 1 cup/200 grams sugar and 1 cup/240 milliliters heavy cream, a 2-quart/2-liter saucepan is the minimum size you should use.

2. Keep little kids, dogs, and cats away from the stove when you make caramel.

3. Pay attention.

As I mentioned earlier, knowing when to stop cooking your caramel and add the liquid is key. You'll only be able to judge this stage properly if you can easily see the color of the caramel, so don't use a dark saucepan (such as anodized aluminum or cast iron). A plain stainless-steel saucepan is best. And never use a pan with a nonstick surface. Caramel temperatures are too hot for it, plus it is too dark to gauge color. To judge the color accurately, scoop out a tiny bit with a metal spoon and drip it onto a heatproof white plate.

Many cookbooks warn against the problem of crystallization when making caramel. They suggest that if you incorrectly handle the sugar as it heats, it will crystallize and become lumpy and blocky rather than melt into a smooth syrup. This comes about when stray undissolved sugar crystals "infect" your syrup and cause the whole batch to crystallize. The various methods to avoid this include brushing down the inside of the saucepan with cold water as you heat the sugar, putting a lid on the saucepan as the caramel cooks so the trapped condensation wets the sides of the pan, and never stirring the sugar as it melts.

I'm sure that it is technically possible for unwanted crystallization to occur, but in all my years of making caramel, it has never happened to me. I even tried to provoke it into occurring once at a former job in a test kitchen and I failed. So, here I will be a contrarian and say that I don't think it's a risk that is worth putting effort into avoiding. If your sugar crystallizes, just keep cooking and stirring it until it melts into submission. Or dump it out and start again.

## HOW MUCH SAUCE PER SERVING?

This depends on how you are serving the sauce, of course, but you probably don't need much more than 2 tablespoons per person.

## SPECIAL EQUIPMENT

You'll need a saucepan with a heavy base. Thin pans tend to have hot spots, which would cause the sugar to caramelize unevenly. You'll need a whisk, too.

## STORAGE

Caramel sauces are quick and can be prepared right before serving, if you like. Personally, I find that their flavor improves with a little time, so I like to make them a day ahead. These sauces will thicken as they cool, so to get the right pouring or drizzling consistency, you'll need to reheat a caramel sauce that you've made ahead. A gentle nudge in the microwave or a few minutes in a saucepan over very low heat should do the trick. Basic caramel sauces last a long time—at least 3 weeks in the fridge—and they freeze exceptionally well for up to 2 months.

### OTHER ROUTES TO CARAMEL

There's a whole class of caramel sauces that don't start by cooking granulated sugar (sucrose). There are milk caramels, like the Latin American dulce de leche and cajeta and the French confiture de lait. For these sauces, you slowly cook sweetened milk, either sugar mixed with whole milk or canned sweetened condensed cow's milk or goat's milk, the latter for cajeta. The slow cooking accomplishes the same thing that happens with the caramel sauces in this chapter: simple sugars are transformed into complex caramel. But in the case of milk caramels, the natural milk sugars add their flavors as well. These sauces have a soft, dairy deliciousness all their own, but they are time-consuming and I don't find myself making them often.

The other way to get a sauce with deep caramel tones is to fake it: simmer together brown sugar, butter, and cream and you've got a caramel-like sauce closer to toffee than caramel. I like the toffee flavors you get in these sauces, so I'm including two recipes in this chapter. Don't try to caramelize brown sugar on its own, however. It contains molasses, which will burn before the sugar toasts.

# SALTED CARAMEL SAUCE

Not so long ago, salted caramel was a novelty. But now that people have had a chance to taste how a pinch of salt elevates and adds complexity to caramel, it's become the new standard. If you're skeptical, start with a bit less salt than the recipe calls for and add more to taste.

1 cup/200 g granulated sugar

3 tbsp water

¾ cup/180 ml heavy cream or crème fraîche

1 tbsp unsalted butter

½ tsp kosher salt

¼ tsp pure vanilla extract

**MAKES ABOUT 1½ CUPS/360 ML**

**STORAGE** Refrigerate in an airtight container for up to 3 weeks or freeze in a ziplock freezer bag for up to 2 months.

**QUICK CHANGE** Add 1 tbsp dark rum (such as Myers's) with the butter and salt and use pure almond extract instead of vanilla.

In a medium, heavy saucepan, combine the sugar and water and bring to a boil over medium-high heat, stirring just until the sugar is moistened. Let the mixture boil, without stirring but with an occasional swirl of the pan, until it is a deep amber, smells like caramel, and you can see just the tiniest wisps of smoke, 9 to 12 minutes. The caramel will be very hot at this point. Remove the saucepan from the heat and carefully add a little bit of the cream; the caramel will bubble up furiously.

Return the pan to low heat and whisk in the remaining cream a little at a time (to avoid bubbling over), then whisk in the butter, salt, and vanilla. Continue to whisk until the sauce is very smooth, another minute or so. Remove the pan from the heat and let the sauce cool in the pan; it will thicken as it cools. Serve warm or at room temperature.

# GINGER CARAMEL SAUCE

I prefer to use fresh ginger (rather than ground) in this sauce because its flavor is more complex: you get spicy heat, as you would with ground ginger, but you get also bright, citrus notes. This sauce is delicious paired with anything with apples.

1 cup/240 ml heavy cream

1½ tbsp peeled and finely grated fresh ginger

1 cup/200 g granulated sugar

¼ cup/60 ml water

2 tbsp unsalted butter

⅛ tsp kosher salt

**MAKES 1½ CUPS/360 ML**

**STORAGE** Refrigerate in an air-tight container for up to 3 weeks or freeze in a ziplock freezer bag for up to 2 months.

**QUICK CHANGE** Add ½ tsp lightly packed finely grated orange zest with the butter and salt.

In a small, heavy saucepan, combine the cream and ginger and bring just to a simmer over medium-high heat. Remove from the heat and let the cream infuse for 20 to 30 minutes. Taste the cream, and if it isn't gingery enough, let it sit for another few minutes. Strain through a fine-mesh sieve into a bowl, pressing gently on the solids to extract the ginger flavor (press too hard and the cream will have a vegetal taste).

In a medium, heavy saucepan, combine the sugar and water and bring to a boil over medium-high heat, stirring just until the sugar is moistened. Let the mixture boil, without stirring but with an occasional swirl of the pan, until it is a deep amber, smells like caramel, and you can see just the tiniest wisps of smoke, 9 to 12 minutes. The caramel will be very hot at this point. Remove the saucepan from the heat and carefully add a little bit of the ginger-infused cream; the caramel will bubble up furiously.

Return the pan to low heat and whisk in the remaining cream a little at a time (to avoid bubbling over), then whisk in the butter and salt. Continue to whisk until the sauce is very smooth, another minute or so. Remove the pan from the heat and let the sauce cool in the pan; it will thicken as it cools. Serve warm or at room temperature.

# COCONUT-RUM CARAMEL SAUCE

Here, you can use the thick layer of coconut cream that settles on top of the thinner milk in a can of coconut milk or you can buy a can of coconut cream. If you opt for the former, be sure you don't shake the can before you open it, so the cream remains on top. If you decide to use the latter, don't reach for cream of coconut (such as the popular Coco Lopez brand) by mistake. It's a totally different product, full of stuff that you might be okay with if you're making a piña colada on vacation but not if you're making this sauce.

½ cup/100 g lightly packed dark brown sugar

½ cup/100 g granulated sugar

1 tbsp light or dark corn syrup

3 tbsp water

¾ cup/180 ml coconut cream

1 tbsp unsalted butter

1 tbsp dark rum such as Myers's

¼ tsp kosher salt

**MAKES ABOUT 1½ CUPS/360 ML**

**STORAGE** Refrigerate in an air-tight container for up to 2 weeks or freeze in a ziplock freezer bag for up to 2 months.

**QUICK CHANGE** Fold ½ cup/110 g crushed canned or finely chopped fresh pineapple into the sauce.

In a medium, heavy saucepan, combine both sugars, the corn syrup, and water and bring to a boil over medium-high heat, stirring just until the sugars are moistened. Let the mixture boil, without stirring but with an occasional swirl of the pan, until it is a deep amber, smells like caramel, and you can see just the tiniest wisps of smoke, 9 to 12 minutes. The caramel will be very hot at this point. Remove the saucepan from the heat and carefully add a little bit of the coconut cream; the caramel will bubble up furiously.

Return the pan to low heat and whisk in the remaining coconut cream a little at a time (to avoid bubbling over), then whisk in the butter, rum, and salt. Continue to whisk until the sauce is very smooth and slightly thickened, about 2 minutes more. Remove the pan from the heat and let the sauce cool in the pan; it will thicken as it cools. Serve warm or at room temperature.

# CHOCOLATE-CARAMEL SAUCE

Is this a caramel sauce or a chocolate sauce? That's an answer you'll only discover with repeated tastings of this luscious topping, so get your spoon ready. Pour this sauce over vanilla ice cream and garnish with lightly toasted nuts like a turtle sundae.

2 oz/55 g dark chocolate (about 60 percent cacao is best), chopped

½ cup/100 g granulated sugar

2 tbsp water

1 cup/240 ml heavy cream

4 tbsp/55 g unsalted butter

Kosher salt

¼ tsp pure vanilla extract

**MAKES 1½ CUPS/360 ML**

**STORAGE** Refrigerate in an air-tight container for up to 3 weeks or freeze in a ziplock freezer bag for up to 2 months.

**QUICK CHANGE** Use milk chocolate instead of dark chocolate and add 1 tbsp hazelnut liqueur such as Frangelico after blending the caramel and chocolate.

Put the chocolate in a medium heatproof bowl or saucepan; set aside.

In a medium, heavy saucepan, combine the sugar and water and bring to a boil over medium-high heat, stirring just until the sugar is moistened. Let the mixture boil, without stirring but with an occasional swirl of the pan, until it is a deep amber, smells like caramel, and you can see just the tiniest wisps of smoke, 9 to 12 minutes. The caramel will be very hot at this point. Remove the saucepan from the heat and carefully add a little bit of the cream; the caramel will bubble up furiously.

Return the pan to low heat and whisk in the remaining cream a little at a time (to avoid bubbling over), then whisk in the butter, ½ tsp salt, and the vanilla. Pour the hot caramel sauce over the chocolate, let it sit for a couple of minutes, and then whisk until the chocolate is melted and the sauce is smooth. Taste the sauce (don't burn your tongue!) and add more salt, if you like. Let the sauce cool; it will thicken as it cools. Serve warm or at room temperature.

# HONEY-ORANGE CARAMEL SAUCE

The key to this sauce is to make sure that the flavors of the caramel and the orange remain in balance. Unlike the other sauces in this chapter, I cook the sugar and honey only until amber, and not long enough to develop any bitter notes. The orange zest has enough delicious bitterness on its own. Use a rasp-style grater, such as a Microplane, to finely grate the zest. You can leave the zest in the sauce, but if you want the sauce very smooth, or if the orange flavor is too strong, strain it out.

½ cup/100 g granulated sugar

½ cup/120 ml honey

½ cup/120 ml heavy cream

¼ cup/60 ml fresh orange juice (from about 1 orange)

½ tsp lightly packed finely grated orange zest

⅛ tsp pure vanilla extract, plus more if needed

1 tbsp unsalted butter

Kosher salt

**MAKES 1½ CUPS/360 ML**

**STORAGE** Refrigerate in an airtight container for up to 3 weeks or freeze in a ziplock freezer bag for up to 2 months.

**QUICK CHANGE** Use tangerine or Meyer lemon zest and juice instead of orange.

In a medium, heavy saucepan, combine the sugar and honey (you need a lot of extra volume in the pan because the honey makes the mixture foam up during cooking) over medium-high heat. Cook, using a small whisk or metal spoon to stir frequently, until the sugar and honey are blended and the sugar melts. Continue to boil, stirring as needed to keep the foam from overflowing, until the mixture is rich amber and smells like caramel, 6 to 8 minutes. At this point, you can test the color of the caramel by spooning a few drops of it onto a heatproof white plate. Do not let the caramel get so dark that it starts to smell burnt or bitter.

Add the cream and orange juice and boil, stirring frequently, until the sauce has thickened a bit and is very smooth, 6 to 8 minutes. Remove from the heat, stir in the orange zest, vanilla, butter, and a pinch of salt. Taste and add more vanilla or salt if needed, but don't let those flavors overwhelm the delicate orange and honey notes. Strain the sauce, if you like. Serve warm or at room temperature.

# MARY JANE'S MOLASSES SAUCE

Molasses isn't everyone's cup of tea, but for those of us who love it, there's nothing better than a chewy molasses–peanut butter Mary Jane candy. That was my inspiration for this sauce, which is wonderful with apple cake or gingerbread, or over a big scoop of vanilla or coffee ice cream.

1 cup/200 g lightly packed light or dark brown sugar

¾ cup/180 ml heavy cream

¼ cup/60 ml unsulfured light or dark molasses, plus more if needed

¼ cup/70 g creamy peanut butter, plus more if needed

Kosher salt

1 tbsp honey, plus more if needed

MAKES 1¾ CUPS/420 ML

**STORAGE** Refrigerate in an air-tight container for up to 1 month or freeze in a ziplock freezer bag for up to 2 months.

**QUICK CHANGE** Add 1 tbsp pure maple syrup, preferably grade B, with the honey.

In a medium, heavy saucepan, combine the sugar, cream, molasses, peanut butter, and a pinch of salt and bring to a boil (you need a lot of extra volume in the pan because the mixture will foam up during cooking) over medium-high heat, stirring until blended. Once the mixture is at a boil, reduce the heat to a gentle simmer and cook, stirring occasionally, until slightly reduced and very syrupy, 4 to 6 minutes.

Remove the pan from the heat and stir in the honey until smooth. Let the sauce cool in the pan briefly, then taste and adjust with more molasses, honey, peanut butter, or salt if needed. The sauce will thicken as it cools. Serve warm or at room temperature.

# BUTTER-RUM TOFFEE SAUCE

Boiling brown sugar with butter and heavy cream makes a sauce that isn't technically caramel, but it shares the same deep and delicious tawny flavor. The rum you use here is key to the flavor of the sauce, so aim for a good dark Jamaican variety.

4 tbsp/55 g unsalted butter

⅔ cup/130 g lightly packed light or dark brown sugar

½ cup/120 ml heavy cream

¼ cup/60 ml light corn syrup

Kosher salt

3 tbsp dark rum such as Myers's

**MAKES ABOUT 1½ CUPS/360 ML**

**STORAGE** Refrigerate in an air-tight container for up to 3 weeks or freeze in a ziplock freezer bag for up to 2 months.

**QUICK CHANGE** Use bourbon instead of rum and add ½ tsp pure vanilla extract with the bourbon.

In a small, heavy saucepan, combine the butter, brown sugar, cream, corn syrup, and ½ tsp salt and bring to a boil over medium-high heat. Boil, stirring occasionally, until the sauce is smooth, glossy, and slightly thickened, about 4 minutes.

Remove from the heat and stir in the rum. Let the sauce cool slightly and then taste it and add a little more salt if needed. The sauce will thicken as it cools. Serve warm or at room temperature.

# BUTTERY APPLE BREAD PUDDING
## with GINGER CARAMEL SAUCE and CRÈME FRAÎCHE

Whenever I make bread pudding, I indulge in a fantasy about a life in which I'm cooking for farmhands or a big family or some other situation in which I need to make delicious food with extreme economy, not letting even a crust of bread go to waste. But I don't live on a farm, and you can make a great bread pudding from almost any kind of leftover bread, with the exception of "everything" bagels, perhaps, or a dark pumpernickel. I rarely have any leftover bread on hand, so if I want to make this pudding, I buy bread expressly for it. Challah or brioche makes a rich and tender pudding, and white artisanal loaves make a denser but still delicious pudding. You can serve this dessert warm from the oven or cold the next day, and it microwaves beautifully if you want to warm it up for breakfast.

1 lb/455 g bread such as challah, brioche, or a rustic white artisanal loaf, crusts left on unless tough, cut into 1-in/2.5-cm cubes

2½ cups/600 ml half-and-half or whole milk

1 cup/200 g plus 2 tsp granulated sugar

3 large eggs

1 tsp pure vanilla extract

½ tsp ground cinnamon

Large pinch of freshly grated nutmeg

Pinch of kosher salt

5 tbsp/70 g unsalted butter, plus more for the soufflé dish

1¾ lb/800 g apples such as Braeburn, Pink Lady, or Fuji, halved, cored, peeled, and cut into ⅛-in/3-mm slices

1 cup/240 ml crème fraîche

1 cup/240 ml Ginger Caramel Sauce (page 219)

Arrange the bread in a single layer on a large baking sheet and leave it on the counter overnight to dry out. (Or dry the bread in a 200°F/95°C oven for about 30 minutes.)

Heat the oven to 325°F/165°C/gas 3.

In a large bowl, whisk together the half-and-half, 1 cup/100 g sugar, eggs, vanilla, cinnamon, nutmeg, and salt until the sugar is dissolved. Add the bread to the bowl and gently fold it into the custard. It will take some time for the bread to absorb all of the custard, so keep folding.

In a large frying pan, melt 4 tbsp/55 g of the butter over medium-high heat. When it is hot, add the apples and cook, shaking the pan frequently and flipping the apples once or twice, for about 2 minutes. Reduce the heat to medium and continue cooking, stirring frequently, until the apples are soft and beginning to brown, 5 to 6 minutes more. Stir in the remaining 2 tsp sugar and continue to cook, stirring often, until the apples look golden and yummy, another 2 to 3 minutes.

Transfer the apples to a large plate to cool. When they are barely warm, fold them into the bread and custard.

Lightly butter the bottom and sides of a 2-qt/2-L soufflé dish or baking dish with high sides (you can use a shallower, wider dish, but you will need to shorten the cooking time). Transfer the bread-and-apple mixture to the dish, spreading it evenly. Cut the remaining 1 tbsp butter into small pieces and dot the top of the pudding.

*continued . . .*

SERVES 6

Bake the pudding until it is firm and no longer jiggly in the center and slightly puffed, 45 to 60 minutes. It can be hard to tell when the pudding is completely done, so if you have an instant-read thermometer, use it. The pudding should register 160°F/72°C in the center.

Let the pudding cool briefly. Meanwhile, in a small bowl, whisk the crème fraîche to loosen it. Scoop portions of the warm pudding onto small plates or into little bowls. Garnish each serving with a generous drizzle of caramel sauce and a nice dollop of crème fraîche. Serve right away.

# ROASTED PEARS with BUTTER-RUM TOFFEE SAUCE, VANILLA ICE CREAM, and TINY PECAN COOKIES

Roasting pears enhances their already soft and sweet personality, and here I up the ante by roasting them in a buttery toffee sauce. Look for firm pears so they won't become mushy in the heat of the oven. If you don't feel like roasting the pears, you can simply serve sliced pears with the sauce and cookies.

3 large or 6 small (such as Forelle) ripe yet firm pears

2 tbsp unsalted butter

¾ cup/180 ml Butter-Rum Toffee Sauce (page 224)

1 pt/480 ml premium vanilla ice cream

Tiny Pecan Cookies (page 230)

Heat the oven to 375°F/190°C/gas 5.

Peel the pears, halve lengthwise, and scoop out the core and any tough fibers (a melon baller does this beautifully).

In a large, ovenproof frying pan, melt the butter over medium-high heat (use two pans if all of the pears won't fit in a single layer). Arrange the pears, cut-side down, in the pan, nestling them so they fit together without crowding. Sauté until the cut sides are golden brown, 5 to 7 minutes, then carefully flip the pears over.

Pour the toffee sauce over the pears, put the pan in the oven, and roast until the pears are very tender, 15 to 20 minutes. You don't want the pears to get mushy, so begin checking them often after about 10 minutes.

Carefully transfer the pears to shallow bowls or dessert plates. If the sauce looks thin because of accumulated juices, put the pan on the stove top and simmer the sauce for a couple of minutes to reduce and thicken. When the pears have cooled just a touch, add a scoop of ice cream to each serving, drizzle the sauce from the pan over the pears and ice cream, and tuck a few cookies into the ice cream to serve. Pass the remaining cookies on a plate.

SERVES 6

## TINY PECAN COOKIES

This recipe makes a lot of cookies, but the dough freezes beautifully, so I suggest baking as many cookies as you like and then freezing the rest of the dough for next time. It will keep for up to 2 months. The cookies are meltingly delicious, so be sure to bake some extras for the cook.

¾ cup/85 g pecans

1 cup/225 g unsalted butter, at room temperature

⅓ cup/35 g confectioners' sugar

⅓ cup/65 g lightly packed light or dark brown sugar

½ tsp kosher salt

2 cups/255 g unbleached all-purpose flour, plus more for rolling

Position one rack in the upper third and a second rack in the lower third of the oven and heat to 375°F/190°C/gas 5. Spread the pecans in a single layer on a large rimmed baking sheet and toast in the oven on either rack until fragrant and a shade or two darker—but not burnt!—about 8 minutes. Transfer to a plate to cool, and then transfer to a food processor and pulse until finely chopped. Reduce the oven temperature to 325°F/165°C/gas 3.

In a stand mixer fitted with the paddle attachment, or in a large bowl with a handheld electric mixer, beat together the butter, both sugars, and salt on medium-high speed until well blended but not fluffy (you don't want to beat a lot of air into the dough), about 1 minute. On low speed, add the flour and beat just until the flour is incorporated. Add the pecans and mix just until combined. Do not overbeat the dough or you won't get the meltingly tender texture you want.

If the cookie dough is too soft to roll out, chill it for a few minutes until it is firm. Divide the dough in half. On a lightly floured work surface, roll out half of the dough into a round ¼ in/6 mm thick. Using a 1½-in/4-cm round cookie cutter, cut out as many cookies as possible. Arrange the cookies on a large ungreased baking sheet, spacing them at least 1 in/2.5 cm apart. Gently press the dough scraps together, reroll, and cut out more cookies. Repeat with the remaining half of the dough.

Bake the cookies until just slightly browned around the edges and on the bottom, dry on top, and not doughy in the center when you break one open, 12 to 15 minutes. Transfer the cookies to racks and let cool completely.

**MAKES ABOUT 7 DOZEN 1½-IN/4-CM COOKIES**

**STORAGE** The cookies will keep in an airtight container at room temperature for up to 1 week.

# SPICED APRICOT and PISTACHIO PARFAIT
## with HONEY-ORANGE CARAMEL SAUCE

Here is yet another recipe by my friend and fellow food writer Matthew Card. It's a great example of what you can do with simple ingredients from the pantry. Chances are you won't use a full batch of the caramel sauce for this dessert, but leftovers are great stirred into a smoothie, drizzled over oatmeal, or used as a sweetener in quick breads.

The apricots and caramel sauce will be easiest to divide evenly if at room temperature or even slightly warm. The ice cream may need to be softened with a spoon to make filling the glasses easier. If you don't have parfait glasses, feel free to use rocks glasses, juice glasses, or even small Mason jars.

16 green cardamom pods, crushed

4 whole cloves

1 cinnamon stick

½ cup/100 g granulated sugar

1¼ cups/300 ml water

Large pinch of kosher salt

6 oz/170 g dried apricots, preferably Turkish, chopped

1 to 2 tsp fresh lemon juice

2 to 3 cups/480 to 720 ml vanilla ice cream

½ to ¾ cup/60 to 90 g pistachio nuts, coarsely chopped

1 to 1½ cups/240 to 360 ml Honey-Orange Caramel Sauce (page 222)

4 to 6 fresh mint sprigs (optional)

In a medium saucepan, combine the cardamom, cloves, cinnamon stick, sugar, water, and salt and bring to a simmer over medium-high heat. Reduce the heat to medium-low and simmer for 10 minutes. Remove from the heat, strain through a fine-mesh sieve, and return the syrup to the pan. Add the apricots and simmer over medium heat until they are soft and the liquid is largely absorbed, 10 to 15 minutes. Transfer to a bowl, let cool, and add the lemon juice to taste.

Fill the bottom of each parfait glass with ¼ cup/60 ml ice cream. Divide half of the apricot mixture equally among the glasses, top with half of the pistachios, and drizzle with half of the caramel sauce. Repeat with the remaining ice cream and apricots; drizzle the tops with the remaining caramel sauce and sprinkle with the remaining pistachios. Tuck a mint sprig into each glass, if you like, and serve right away.

**SERVES 4 TO 6**

# CHOCOLATE SAUCES

PUT THE WORDS *CHOCOLATE* AND *SAUCE* TOGETHER AND YOU INSTANTLY HAVE A PARTY. There's something innately festive about liquid chocolate. Even better, making homemade chocolate sauce offers huge rewards for very little effort. Indeed, once you see how easy it is, you won't ever buy the low-quality mass-produced stuff or the high-priced artisanal products again. You are the artisan now.

And whatever your chocolate mood, you can make a multidimensional sauce to suit it. As you vary the type of chocolate you use and the other ingredients you add, you can create sauces that range from a lush and creamy ganache to a deep, dark cocoa sauce to an almost-chewy hot fudge sauce.

For many people, the best way to serve chocolate sauce is on a spoon, delivered directly from bowl to mouth. I do like to sneak a spoonful now and then, but I think chocolate sauce is in its full glory when it's involved with other dessert components. The most obvious is ice cream: a few chopped nuts and a dollop of whipped cream turn chocolate sauce and ice cream into a full-fledged sundae. Drizzle chocolate sauce over fat, ripe strawberries, or use it as fondue for dipping banana chunks, shortbread cookies, macadamia nuts, cubes of pound cake, or anything else that can be dipped. Simple cakes are prime candidates for chocolate sauces because their thirsty crumb soaks up the deliciousness. Or, drizzle dark, slightly bitter chocolate sauce over lightly grilled bread that has been brushed with extra-virgin olive oil and sprinkled with coarse salt, a riff on a Spanish snack.

## WHAT'S GOING ON IN THIS SAUCE?

For these sauces, you are essentially melting chocolate and adding a liquid to thin it out and create a saucy consistency. The liquid you add (water, cream, milk, spirits) and the flavorings you use (vanilla, citrus zest) will enhance the chocolate flavor, so you need to think about how your ingredients play together. Here are the key players:

**CHOCOLATE** Your final sauce is only as good as the chocolate you use, and a huge array of high-quality chocolates is available these days. My low-end chocolate choices are Ghirardelli's bittersweet 60 percent cacao and Lindt Excellence Smooth Dark 70 percent cacao, two brands that you can find in most grocery stores for a decent price. When I have the opportunity and the money, I will go for Scharffen Berger. If I am making a sauce for a special meal, I will use Valrhona or Michel Cluizel, two French brands that offer a range of single-origin chocolates, each with a slightly different character, from smoky to fruity to sharply acidic and citrusy. The best way to know which brand you want to use is to taste the chocolates and compare them—a tough assignment, I know.

**LIQUID** When choosing which liquid to use in a sauce, I first decide which aspect of the chocolate I want to emphasize. The deep, dark almost coffeelike side? In that case, I will use water, and I may even make my sauce with cocoa powder (see below), not chocolate. Or am I looking for the creamy, suave, nuttier side of chocolate? That calls for cream because its flavor will temper some of the acidic bite of chocolate and it will add its own luxurious texture.

**COCOA** For the most chocolaty flavor of all, skip the solid chocolate and go straight for cocoa powder, which consists of cocoa solids with around 80 percent of the cocoa butter removed. You may be surprised at how rich and glossy a sauce made from cocoa powder can be. I like the bolder flavor of a natural cocoa, but Dutch-processed cocoa is fine in a sauce, too. My favorite cocoa powder is a high-fat one (with about 25 percent cocoa butter) from Penzeys (penzeys.com).

**SUGAR** Whether or not I add sugar to my sauces depends on which chocolate I am using. But in general, I tend to add a little sugar to heighten the intensity of the sauce.

**SALT** I always add a healthy pinch of kosher salt to my chocolate sauces. It doesn't make the sauce taste salty, but rather it adds dimension to the overall flavor profile of the sauce.

## WHAT CAN GO WRONG AND HOW CAN I FIX IT?

There are two things to worry about when working with chocolate: scorching it and having it seize up (that is, turn into a grainy mass). But I've developed all of the recipes here so that these common chocolate pitfalls are not an issue. I don't heat or melt the chocolate on its own (the easiest way to accidentally scorch it), and I always add enough liquid to the chocolate to eliminate the risk of seizing. (To learn more about seizing, see facing page.)

One tip to keep in mind: be sure you've chopped your chocolate uniformly and finely enough so that it melts evenly. The typical thin 3- to 4-ounce/85- to 115-gram bar of chocolate is easy to chop with a chef's knife; just start at a corner and chop your way into the bar. As that corner becomes a flat edge, turn the bar and start chopping from another point. Thicker slabs of chocolate can be tricky, and you will definitely need a sturdy chef's knife or a heavy serrated knife for them. You can use an oyster knife or other short, stiff-bladed knife to cut off a chunk from the larger slab: insert it into the chocolate about 2 inches/ 5 centimeters from the edge and then pull to crack off a chunk. Then chop that chunk and repeat.

You can use your food processor, too, but if you have already cut your chocolate into pieces small enough to fit into the processor, you might as well finish the job by hand. For the recipes in this book, you don't need the chocolate to be chopped more finely than, say, the size of an almond.

## HOW MUCH SAUCE PER SERVING?

This depends on how you're serving the sauce, of course, but 2 to 3 tablespoons per person is average.

## SPECIAL EQUIPMENT

A sharp, sturdy chef's knife or serrated knife for chopping and an oyster knife if you will be breaking apart a large, thick slab. You will also need a heavy saucepan for heating cream and cooking the sauces and a whisk for blending.

## STORAGE

Chocolate sauces are better after a day or so of "mellowing," which allows the ingredients to marry (except for the Whipped Cream Chocolate Sauce on page 243, whose fluffy texture must be appreciated right away). That means they are an excellent addition to any host's repertoire of do-ahead desserts. They will keep in an airtight jar or other container in the refrigerator for several weeks and in the freezer for a couple of months or more.

Chocolate sauces do set up fairly firmly in the fridge, however, so you must reheat them gently. I use a double boiler to avoid any threat of scorching, but you can reheat directly in a saucepan if you use very low heat and stir a lot. Or, use your microwave on the lowest setting.

### WHAT IS "SEIZING" AND HOW DO I AVOID IT?

*Seizing* is one of my favorite cooking terms. It sounds so dramatic, almost dangerous! But if it happens to you, there will be some drama, so it's an apt term. Chocolate seizes if a small amount of water (or watery liquid such as brandy) finds its way into the chocolate while it is melting. That little bit of liquid messes up the balance among cocoa particles, sugar, and cocoa butter, causing the nonfat ingredients to clump together. If chocolate seizes, it will look grainy and matte rather than glossy and smooth. But if you add enough water at the outset, you won't have this problem.

The rule of thumb is any added liquid must be at least 25 percent of the weight of the chocolate. Another way to express the rule is for every four parts chocolate, you must have one part water.

### WHAT IS THE DIFFERENCE BETWEEN BITTERSWEET AND SEMISWEET CHOCOLATE?

The chocolate industry has not standardized these terms, which makes deciding which chocolate to buy confusing. According to the U.S. Food and Drug Administration (FDA), any chocolate that contains at least 35 percent chocolate liquor (another name for the ground cacao beans, which are made up of cocoa solids and cocoa butter, that become chocolate) can be called semisweet or bittersweet chocolate.

To confuse us even further, many chocolates now list the percentage of cocoa solids, usually expressed as cacao, they contain. The more cocoa solids in the chocolate, the fewer other ingredients it contains, so the chocolate flavor is more intense and possibly more bitter. For instance, it is safe to presume that a chocolate with 72 percent cacao will taste more bitter than one with 60 percent cacao.

But it's not always as simple as high percentage equals more bitter. That's because cacao percentage includes the cocoa butter content as well, and extra cocoa butter can be added to chocolate to give it a smoother flavor. In the end, it usually comes down to a matter of taste. Each type of chocolate will have a different flavor profile, depending on the source of the cacao beans, how long the beans were roasted, the amount of sugar or extra cocoa butter, and the addition of vanilla or other flavorings. The term *dark chocolate* is not regulated, so it can mean anything. But it is a good umbrella term for the range of semisweet and bittersweet, and it tells you that the chocolate isn't milk or white. I use the term *dark* in this book, and I specify a cacao percentage only when it is important for the recipe.

Chocolates with super-high cocoa percentages can behave differently in baking than those with lower ones, thanks to their correspondingly lower sugar contents. Fortunately, we don't have to worry much about that when making sauces. For sauces, it is easy to adapt to various chocolates by simply tasting the sauce as you go: Too bitter? Add another ½ teaspoon sugar. Too acidic or sharp? Add more cream or butter.

Be sure to distinguish between bittersweet and unsweetened chocolate, however. Unsweetened chocolate contains no sugar at all and is used only in baking. The exception is the remarkable 99 percent cacao chocolate from Michel Cluizel. Nibbling on a bar of his unsweetened chocolate is like enjoying a shot of perfectly pulled espresso: strong and bitter but complex and enjoyable nonetheless.

And please don't forget milk chocolate! Although it has recently been overshadowed by all of the interest in intensely dark chocolates, a good milk chocolate can be sublime. FDA standards are minimal—just 10 percent chocolate liquor and 12 percent milk solids—but the better brands have higher chocolate-liquor contents, making them a valid chocolate experience. Scharffen Berger milk chocolate at 41 percent is yummy, though my favorite is Bonnat, a French producer who makes three varieties of milk chocolate with 65 percent cacao. The texture of Bonnat makes me swoon.

# RICH DARK CHOCOLATE SAUCE

This is an excellent all-purpose sauce, and I firmly believe that it belongs in your fridge at all times. I use a basic ganache method to make it: I pour hot cream over chopped chocolate and then whisk until smooth. But I enhance the sauce with some corn syrup to punch up the sweetness and make it slightly thicker. I also finish it with some butter because it makes the texture lush and balances the acidity of the chocolate.

1 cup/240 ml heavy cream

1 tbsp light corn syrup

4 oz/115 g dark chocolate, chopped

2 tbsp unsalted butter

Pinch of kosher salt

In a small, heavy saucepan, combine the cream and corn syrup and bring to a simmer over medium-low heat. Do not allow the mixture to boil, which will give the cream a "cooked" taste. Remove from the heat and whisk in the chocolate, a few pieces at a time, until blended and smooth. If the cream cools off too much to melt the chocolate, return the sauce to low heat for a few seconds. Whisk in the butter and salt until the sauce is glossy. Serve warm or slightly cooled.

**MAKES ABOUT 1 CUP/240 ML**

**STORAGE** Refrigerate in an air-tight container for up to 1 month or freeze for up to 3 months. If making the sauce ahead, very gently reheat it in a saucepan to loosen it up, adding 2 to 3 tsp very hot water if needed to thin it out.

**QUICK CHANGE**

*Crème fraîche* Use 1 cup/240 ml crème fraîche instead of heavy cream for a slightly tangier, nuttier sauce.

*Mint* Add ¼ tsp pure peppermint extract with the butter and salt.

*Crunchy-peppermint* Add ¼ tsp pure peppermint extract and ¼ cup/30 g crushed peppermint candies or candy canes with the butter and salt. (To crush the candies, put them in a ziplock freezer bag and crush with a rolling pin, or crush them in a mortar with a pestle.)

*Mocha* Add 1 tsp instant espresso powder to the cream as it heats. If the sauce is too bitter, whisk in 1 tsp or so granulated sugar.

*Orange* Stir in 1 tsp lightly packed finely grated orange zest and 1 tbsp Grand Marnier with the butter and salt; taste and add a touch more corn syrup or some granulated sugar to balance the alcohol if necessary.

# RASPBERRY TRUFFLE SAUCE

Raspberry and chocolate are a clichéd combo, but there is a reason for this duo's popularity—it's delicious! I call it a truffle sauce because the center of most truffles is solid ganache—cream and chocolate—and this sauce is simply a loose, pourable ganache. Cooking the raspberry purée concentrates it so that more of the perfume of the berries and less of their acid come through. The addition of framboise, or raspberry eau-de-vie, intensifies the raspberry component.

6 oz/170 g fresh or thawed frozen raspberries

1 tbsp granulated sugar, plus more if needed

1 tbsp framboise (optional)

½ cup/120 ml heavy cream

4 oz/115 g dark chocolate (about 60 percent cacao), chopped

**MAKES ABOUT 1 CUP/240 ML**

**STORAGE** Refrigerate in an air-tight container for up to 2 weeks or freeze for up to 3 months. If making the sauce ahead, very gently reheat it in a saucepan to loosen it up, adding 2 to 3 tsp very hot water if needed to thin it out.

**QUICK CHANGE** Substitute ½ cup/120 ml passion fruit purée for the raspberries; you can skip the straining step.

In a food processor, purée the raspberries until smooth (except for any seeds). Transfer the berry purée to a small, heavy saucepan over medium-high heat and cook, stirring and scraping so the fruit doesn't stick and burn, until cooked down by about half, 4 to 6 minutes. You should have about ⅓ cup/75 ml purée. Stir in the sugar and liqueur (if using). Add the cream and bring just to a simmer; do not let it boil. Remove from the heat.

Put the chocolate in a stainless-steel or other heatproof bowl and set a fine-mesh sieve over it. Strain the raspberry cream through the sieve into the chocolate. Leave undisturbed for about 1 minute to melt the chocolate, then start whisking in small circles in the center of the bowl, widening your whisking toward the outer edges of the bowl as the sauce becomes glossy and smooth. Taste and add a touch more sugar if needed. Serve warm or at room temperature.

# CHOCOLATE-CHERRY PORT SAUCE

There's something old-fashioned about the flavors in this sauce, making it perfect for topping a dessert following a traditional holiday roast beef . . . maybe in a dining room with a glowing fire in the fireplace. No fireplace? Just serve this sauce and you'll get the same warm glow.

¼ cup/30 g finely chopped dried sweet cherries

⅓ cup/75 ml tawny or ruby port

1 cup/240 ml heavy cream

1 tbsp light corn syrup

4 oz/115 g dark chocolate, chopped

2 tbsp unsalted butter

¼ tsp pure almond extract

Pinch of kosher salt

**MAKES ABOUT 1½ CUPS/360 ML**

**STORAGE** Refrigerate in an air-tight container for up to 1 month or freeze for up to 3 months. If making the sauce ahead, very gently reheat it in a saucepan to loosen it up, adding 2 to 3 tsp very hot water if needed to thin it out.

**QUICK CHANGE** Add 1 tbsp kirsch (cherry liqueur) instead of the almond extract.

In a small, heavy saucepan, combine the cherries and port and bring to a simmer over medium heat. Remove from the heat and let sit until the cherries are soft and have cooled completely.

In a small, heavy saucepan, combine the cream and corn syrup and bring to a simmer over medium-low heat. Do not allow the mixture to boil, which will give the cream a "cooked" taste.

Put the chocolate in a stainless-steel or other heatproof medium bowl, and pour the cream mixture over the chocolate. Leave undisturbed for about 1 minute to melt the chocolate, then start whisking in small circles in the center of the bowl, widening your whisking toward the outer edges of the bowl as the sauce becomes glossy and smooth. Whisk in the butter and then stir in the cherry-port mixture, almond extract, and salt. Serve warm or slightly cooled.

# DOUBLE-CHOCOLATE PEANUT BUTTER SAUCE

These two flavors like each other very much, a fact proven by the enduring popularity of Reese's peanut butter cups. Using both milk chocolate and dark chocolate in this sauce adds complexity and balances the mellow nature of the peanut butter. I know I'm supposed to prefer natural peanut butter, but really, Jif is my choice here. Its smooth texture blends beautifully, and the small amount of salt and sugar in commercial peanut butter is more than welcome in this sauce.

3 oz/85 g milk chocolate, chopped

2 oz/55 g dark chocolate (about 70 percent cacao), chopped

⅓ cup/85 g creamy peanut butter

¼ cup/60 ml heavy cream, plus more if needed

1 tbsp unsalted butter

Kosher salt

**MAKES JUST OVER 1 CUP/240 ML**

**STORAGE** Refrigerate in an airtight container for up to 1 month or freeze for up to 3 months. If making the sauce ahead, very gently reheat it in a saucepan to loosen it up, adding 2 to 3 tsp very hot water if needed to thin it out.

**QUICK CHANGE** Use almond or hazelnut butter instead of peanut butter.

Pour water to a depth of 1 to 2 in/2.5 to 5 cm into a medium saucepan and place over medium heat. Rest a medium stainless-steel bowl in the pan over (not touching) the water. Put both chocolates and the peanut butter in the bowl and heat, stirring frequently and taking care not to allow the water to boil hard, until the chocolate is melted and the mixture is smooth.

Remove the bowl from the heat and stir in the cream, butter, and a tiny pinch of salt until smooth and creamy. Taste the sauce and add a few more drops of cream if it is too thick, or a pinch more salt if you are a salt lover. The sauce will thicken as it cools. Serve warm.

# MEXICAN-STYLE CHOCOLATE SAUCE

Adding flavors traditionally found in Mexican hot chocolate—cinnamon, almond, and chile, in particular—gives this sauce an intriguing complexity and spicy kick. If you're wary of chile heat, use less ground chipotle to start. Sometimes I stir this sauce into hot milk for a drink that combats drizzly winter mornings, but more often I pour it onto a simple cake topped with a scoop of ice cream.

4 oz/115 g dark chocolate, chopped

¾ cup/180 ml heavy cream

4 tsp granulated sugar

1 tsp instant espresso powder

½ tsp ground cinnamon

1 tsp pure vanilla extract

⅛ tsp pure almond extract

Pinch of ground chipotle or other good chile powder

Pinch of kosher salt

**MAKES ABOUT 1¼ CUPS/300 ML**

**STORAGE** Refrigerate in an airtight container for up to 1 month or freeze for up to 3 months. If making the sauce ahead, very gently reheat it in a saucepan to loosen it up, adding 2 to 3 tsp very hot water if needed to thin it out.

**QUICK CHANGE** Add 1 tbsp Kahlúa or other coffee liqueur to the cream as you heat it.

Put the chocolate in a medium stainless-steel or other heatproof bowl.

In a small, heavy saucepan, bring the cream just to a simmer over medium heat. Remove from the heat and stir in the sugar, espresso powder, cinnamon, vanilla, and almond extract, ground chipotle, and salt. Pour the cream mixture over the chocolate. Leave undisturbed for about 1 minute to melt the chocolate, then start whisking in small circles in the center of the bowl, widening your whisking toward the outer edges of the bowl as the sauce becomes glossy and smooth. If the sauce seems a little thick, whisk in a few spoonfuls of very hot water to loosen it up. Serve warm.

# SPICY CURRY-COCONUT CHOCOLATE SAUCE

My inspiration for this sauce is the delicious Naga chocolate bar made by Vosges Haut Chocolat, which pairs curry spices and coconut with milk chocolate. I have upped the ante here by adding fresh ginger and a slightly spicy glow from red pepper flakes. I like serving this sauce over rice pudding, coconut cream pie, or on crepes filled with sautéed bananas. Of course, it's also divine on Abby Dodge's delectable coconut Bundt cake on page 248.

3 tbsp granulated sugar, plus more if needed

2 tbsp water

1 tbsp peeled and minced fresh ginger

½ tsp mild curry powder

1/16 tsp red pepper flakes

¾ cup/180 ml coconut milk (stir together the thick cream and thinner milk before measuring)

Tiny pinch of kosher salt

3 oz/85 g milk chocolate, chopped

**MAKES ABOUT 1 CUP/240 ML**

**STORAGE** Refrigerate in an airtight container for up to 2 weeks or freeze for up to 2 months. If making the sauce ahead, very gently reheat it in a saucepan to loosen it up, adding 2 to 3 tsp very hot water if needed to thin it out.

**QUICK CHANGE** Add 1 green or white cardamom pod, crushed, to the sugar syrup with the other spices.

In a small, heavy saucepan, combine the sugar and water and bring to a boil over medium-high heat. Stir in the ginger, curry powder, and red pepper flakes. Remove from the heat and let sit for 30 minutes, gently pressing on the ginger with the back of a spoon a few times. Stir in the coconut milk and salt, return to medium heat, and bring to a gentle simmer, stirring often to dissolve the syrup on the sides of the pan.

Put the chocolate in a medium heatproof bowl and set a fine-mesh sieve over it. Strain the coconut milk mixture through the sieve into the chocolate. Leave undisturbed for about 1 minute to melt the chocolate, then start whisking in small circles in the center of the bowl, widening your whisking toward the outer edges of the bowl as the sauce becomes glossy and smooth. Taste and add a touch more sugar to balance the spices if needed. Serve warm or at room temperature.

# SOUR CREAM–HOT FUDGE SAUCE

Glossy, thick, and almost chewy, this fudge sauce differs from my other chocolate sauces because it is made with quite a bit of sugar and corn syrup as well as chocolate, which gives it that classic fudgy texture. I use both unsweetened chocolate and dark chocolate to keep the sugar level in check, and I finish with a big dollop of sour cream for a little bit of tang and a lush richness. If you don't have sour cream, you could use crème fraîche or heavy cream.

This is the sauce for the classic sundae, with whipped cream and a cherry on top, but it is also wonderful on less obvious desserts: a slice of banana pound cake, chocolate chip bread pudding, or a wedge of pecan tart.

½ cup/100 g granulated sugar

½ cup/100 g lightly packed light or dark brown sugar

¼ cup/60 ml light corn syrup

4 tbsp/55 g unsalted butter

4 oz/115 g dark chocolate (between 60 and 70 percent cacao), coarsely chopped or broken into small pieces

1 oz/30 g unsweetened chocolate, coarsely chopped

¼ cup/60 ml water

Tiny pinch of kosher salt

¼ cup/60 ml sour cream

**MAKES 2 CUPS/480 ML**

**STORAGE** Refrigerate in an airtight container for up to 1 month or freeze for up to 3 months. If making the sauce ahead, very gently reheat it in a saucepan to loosen it up, adding 2 to 3 tsp very hot water if needed to thin it out.

**QUICK CHANGE** Add ½ tsp pure peppermint extract with the sour cream.

In a medium, heavy saucepan, combine both sugars, the corn syrup, butter, both chocolates, water, and salt and bring to a boil over medium-high heat. As the mixture heats, stir occasionally to encourage everything to melt and blend together.

Reduce the heat until the sauce is at a simmer (if the heat is too high, you could scorch the chocolate along the sides of the pan) and simmer, stirring frequently, until very glossy and slightly thickened, about 5 minutes. Remove the pan from the heat and let the sauce cool down briefly, then stir or whisk in the sour cream. Serve hot, warm, or at room temperature.

# WHIPPED CREAM CHOCOLATE SAUCE

This is my version of a Hungarian chocolate sauce that my friend and fellow La Varenne alum Randall Price learned to make when he was chef for the American ambassador to Hungary. It's a sauce with an identity crisis: It's meant to be used as a sauce, but it's so thick and "dollopy" that it's almost like a chocolate mousse.

Randall served it over crepes filled with walnuts and dried fruit. I like to serve it with crepes smeared with a little mascarpone, or with a waffle topped with a scoop of ice cream. This sauce wants to be served right away, but you can make the base chocolate sauce well ahead of time and fold in the whipped cream just before serving.

6 tbsp/35 g unsweetened cocoa powder

½ cup/100 g granulated sugar, plus more if needed

¾ cup/180 ml whole milk

1 tbsp unsalted butter

Tiny pinch kosher salt

½ cup/120 ml heavy cream

**MAKES ABOUT 2 CUPS/480 ML**

**STORAGE** This sauce is best served right away, but it will be fine if refrigerated in an airtight container for up to 3 days. The sauce does not freeze well.

**QUICK CHANGE** Add 1 tbsp brandy or Cognac with the butter.

Using a rubber spatula or a wooden spoon, stir together the cocoa powder, sugar, and about ¼ cup/60 ml of the milk in a small, heavy saucepan to make a thick paste. As you stir, press out the lumps of cocoa powder with the back of the spoon or the spatula.

Put the pan over medium-high heat and slowly whisk in the remaining milk. Bring the sauce to a simmer and cook, stirring occasionally, until any foam on the top has disappeared and the sauce is very smooth and glossy, about 2 minutes. Whisk in the butter and salt, then taste and add a touch more sugar, if you like. Transfer to a medium bowl and let cool completely at room temperature, stirring often.

In a medium bowl with a handheld electric mixer, whip the cream on medium speed until it holds firm peaks. Pour about one-fourth of the chocolate sauce into the whipped cream and gently fold together with a rubber spatula until most of the sauce is blended; a few streaks are fine. Repeat with the rest of the sauce in three batches. When all of the sauce has been combined with the cream, fold until completely blended and smooth but still billowy. Serve right away.

# PROFITEROLES with CARDAMOM-COFFEE-CARAMEL CREAM and RICH DARK CHOCOLATE SAUCE

To my mind, profiteroles are the most Parisian of desserts, probably because I had my first taste of them when I went to the Sorbonne after graduating from college as a French major. I was with my newly acquired, older (and slightly dangerous) French boyfriend at the time, so the experience was as intense as the chocolate sauce! I've deviated from the classic filling here (it's usually vanilla pastry cream or vanilla ice cream) by flavoring my cream with cardamom, coffee, and caramel—bringing a bit of Scandinavia to Paris—and by folding in whipped cream for a lighter texture.

## PASTRY PUFFS

⅔ cup/165 ml water

6 tbsp/85 g unsalted butter

½ tsp kosher salt

⅔ cup/85 g all-purpose flour

3 large eggs

## FILLING

½ cup/100 g granulated sugar

1 tbsp water

1½ cups/360 ml heavy cream

1½ tsp instant espresso powder

⅛ tsp ground cardamom

3 egg yolks

2 tbsp all-purpose flour

Pinch of kosher salt

1 cup/240 ml Rich Dark Chocolate Sauce (page 236)

---

**MAKES 30 PUFFS; SERVES 6**

---

**TO MAKE THE PUFFS,** in a small saucepan, combine the water, butter, and salt and bring to a boil over high heat. Add the flour all at once, remove the pan from the heat, and immediately begin stirring with a wooden spoon. Stir until the flour mixture forms a ball, then return the pan to very low heat and continue stirring until the dough looks shiny and smooth, 1 to 2 minutes.

Remove the pan from the heat and stir in the eggs, one at a time, mixing in each egg fully before adding the next one. As each new egg is added, the dough will look slippery and curdled but will smooth out.

Position one rack in the upper third and a second rack in the lower third of the oven and heat to 400°F/200°C/gas 6. Line two large rimmed baking sheets with parchment paper (this is for easy cleanup; it is okay to bake the puffs directly on the baking sheets, if you like). Using two small spoons, spoon out 30 small mounds of dough, each one about the size of an unshelled walnut, spacing them at least 1 in/2.5 cm apart on the prepared pans. Dampen your fingertips and gently pat any wayward points of dough down so that the mounds are fairly smooth and domed.

Put the baking sheets in the oven, reduce the temperature to 375°F/190°C/gas 5, and bake the puffs until they have, well, puffed and are a deep golden brown, 18 to 25 minutes. If the puffs are baking unevenly, switch the pans between the racks and rotate them from back to front.

Transfer the puffs to a cooling rack. With the tip of a small knife, poke a tiny hole in the side of each puff to let steam escape. This keeps them from getting soggy.

**TO MAKE THE FILLING,** put ¼ cup/50 g of the sugar and the water in a small, heavy saucepan over medium-high heat and cook, swirling the pan occasionally as the sugar starts to melt, until the sugar is a deep amber, has a very fragrant caramel smell, and you see just the tiniest wisps of smoke, 4 to 6 minutes. Remove the pan from the heat and carefully pour in 1 cup/240 ml of the cream; it will steam and sputter, so stand back a bit. Return the pan to the heat and

*continued . . .*

stir to dissolve the caramel. Stir in the espresso powder and cardamom until combined and dissolved. Keep the caramel cream warm over very low heat; do not let it boil.

In a medium stainless-steel bowl, whisk together the egg yolks, the remaining ¼ cup/50 g sugar, the flour, and the salt until thoroughly blended. Pour in a bit of the hot caramel cream and whisk vigorously to blend into a paste. Add a little more caramel cream, whisk to blend, and then whisk the egg mixture back into the pan of caramel cream. Return the pan to medium-high heat and bring to a boil, whisking constantly. The pastry cream will thicken as it cooks; if it starts getting a little lumpy, just pull it from the heat and whisk away the lumps. Cook at a gentle boil for about 2 minutes to cook off the raw flour taste. Remove the pan from the heat and let the pastry cream cool completely, whisking occasionally to prevent a skin from forming on top.

In a medium bowl with a handheld electric mixer, whip the remaining ½ cup/ 120 ml cream on medium-high speed until it forms firm peaks. Whisk the cooled pastry cream to loosen it slightly, then carefully fold about one-fourth of the whipped cream into the pastry cream to lighten it. Fold in the remaining whipped cream just until blended. Chill for about 15 minutes, if you have the time.

Fit a pastry bag with a plain small tip, spoon the filling into the bag, and fill each puff by poking the tip into the puff and gently squeezing in the filling. If you don't have a pastry bag, slice each puff open along the equator, leaving a bit attached so you don't separate the top and bottom halves. Gently open up each puff, spoon some filling into the center, and pat the top back in place.

Pile five filled puffs onto each dessert plate or into each shallow bowl. Gently heat the chocolate sauce and either drizzle an equal portion over each serving, or bring the sauce to the table and let the diners pour the sauce themselves. Serve right away.

# CHOCOLATE-FLECK PANNA COTTA
## with RASPBERRY TRUFFLE SAUCE

One of my favorite gelato flavors is *stracciatella*, a pure cream base with fine shards of chocolate mixed in, like a sophisticated chocolate chip. I thought those simple, delicious flavors would translate well into a *panna cotta*, which is what we have here. It's important to shave the chocolate so the flecks are delicate. Also, don't wait too long before folding them into the cream base. If the gelatin in the cream has set up too much when you fold in the chocolate, you'll end up with a lumpy texture, rather than the desired smooth, just-set creamy consistency.

¼ cup/60 ml cold water

1½ cups/360 ml crème fraîche or heavy cream

1 envelope (2½ tsp) granulated unflavored gelatin

¾ cup/150 g granulated sugar

Pinch of kosher salt

2 cups/480 g plain whole-milk yogurt

Canola oil for the ramekins

2 oz/55 g dark chocolate, shaved with a vegetable peeler or cut into fine slivers with a chef's knife

1 cup/240 ml Raspberry Truffle Sauce (page 237), warmed just until fluid

Pour the water in a small bowl, sprinkle the gelatin over the top, and let sit for about 10 minutes so the gelatin "blooms" and softens.

Meanwhile, in a medium saucepan, combine ½ cup/120 ml of the crème fraîche; the sugar, and salt and bring to a simmer over medium heat, stirring to dissolve the sugar. Remove the pan from the heat and whisk in the gelatin mixture until completely dissolved and smooth. Stir in the remaining crème fraîche and the yogurt.

Strain the mixture through a fine-mesh sieve into a medium bowl that will fit in your fridge. Cover with plastic wrap and chill, stirring occasionally, until the mixture thickens to the consistency of pancake batter, about 45 minutes.

Meanwhile, lightly oil six ¾-cup/180-ml ramekins or little bowls; set aside.

When the cream mixture is like pancake batter (thick enough so the bits of chocolate won't sink to the bottom), carefully fold in the chocolate. Evenly divide the mixture among the prepared ramekins, cover, and chill until firm, about 8 hours or up to overnight.

Let the panna cottas sit at room temperature 10 to 15 minues, and then run a thin knife blade around the edge of each to loosen it from the mold. Quickly invert the mold onto a dessert plate and let the panna cotta slide out (give it a little shake if necessary). Pour a thick ribbon of the sauce around it and serve right away.

**SERVES 6**

# ABBY'S TOASTED COCONUT BUNDT CAKE
## with SPICY CURRY-COCONUT CHOCOLATE SAUCE

This flavor-packed cake comes from Abby Dodge, one of my original friends and teammates at *Fine Cooking* magazine and an awesome baker. I am not an awesome baker, so I asked Abby to share a recipe that could partner well with many of the sauces in this book, especially the exotic curry-coconut chocolate sauce. She outdid herself.

I like this cake because although it has the buttery, eggy richness of a traditional pound cake, it is also loaded with a triple coconut blast. Coconut milk and coconut extract give the cake richness and flavor, and toasted coconut brings the texture to a new level of creamy crunchiness. It is also delicious with any of the custard sauces (see pages 185–88) or the truffle sauce (see page 237) in this book.

8 oz/225 g unsalted butter, at room temperature, plus more for the pan

2¾ cups/350 g all-purpose flour, plus more for the pan

2 tsp baking powder

½ tsp salt

2 cups/400 g granulated sugar

4 large eggs, at room temperature

1 egg yolk, at room temperature

2 tsp pure vanilla extract

1½ tsp pure coconut extract

1 cup/240 ml coconut milk (stir together the thick cream and thinner milk before measuring)

1¾ cups/175 g sweetened shredded dried coconut, toasted

1 cup/240 ml Spicy Curry-Coconut Chocolate Sauce (page 241)

Heat the oven to 350°F/180°C/gas 4. Butter and flour a 10-cup/2.4-L Bundt pan or other fluted tube pan, tapping out the excess flour.

In a medium bowl, whisk together the flour, baking powder, and salt. In a stand mixer fitted with the paddle attachment, beat the butter on medium speed until smooth, about 2 minutes. On medium-high speed, add the sugar and beat until well blended and fluffy, about 2 minutes. Add the eggs and the egg yolk, one at a time, beating well after each addition. Stop to scrape down the sides of the bowl and the paddle as needed. Add the vanilla and coconut extract and beat until combined. On low speed, add the flour mixture in three batches alternately with the coconut milk in two batches, beginning and ending with flour mixture and mixing just until blended after each addition. Still on low speed, add the toasted coconut and mix just until blended.

Scrape the batter into the prepared pan and smooth the top. Bake the cake until the top is light brown and a toothpick inserted near the center comes out with just a few small crumbs clinging to it, about 55 minutes.

Let cool in the pan on a rack for about 15 minutes. Tap the edges of the pan on the counter to loosen the cake. Then rotate the pan, tapping as you turn it. Invert the cake onto the rack and lift off the pan. Let the cake cool completely, then transfer to a serving plate.

To serve, top with the chocolate sauce or cut into slices and transfer to dessert plates. Spoon a ribbon of the chocolate sauce around each slice.

**MAKES ONE 10-IN/25-CM BUNDT CAKE; SERVES 12 TO 14**

# INDEX

*Italic page numbers following sauce recipes indicate other recipes using that sauce.*